POLITICAL HANDBOOK
OF THE WORLD

1959

SELECTED PUBLICATIONS OF THE
COUNCIL ON FOREIGN RELATIONS

FOREIGN AFFAIRS (*quarterly*), edited by Hamilton Fish Armstrong.

THE UNITED STATES IN WORLD AFFAIRS (*annual*). Volumes for 1931, 1932 and 1933, by Walter Lippmann and William O. Scroggs; for 1934-1935, 1936, 1937, 1938, 1939 and 1940, by Whitney H. Shepardson and William O. Scroggs; for 1945-1947, 1947-1948, 1948-1949, by John C. Campbell; for 1949, 1950, 1951, 1952, 1953, and 1954, by Richard P. Stebbins; for 1955, by Hollis W. Barber; for 1956 and 1957, by Richard P. Stebbins.

DOCUMENTS ON AMERICAN FOREIGN RELATIONS (*annual*). Volume for 1952, edited by Clarence W. Baier and Richard P. Stebbins; for 1953 and 1954, edited by Peter V. Curl; for 1955, 1956 and 1957, edited by Paul E. Zinner.

POLITICAL HANDBOOK OF THE WORLD (*annual*), edited by Walter H. Mallory.

SOVIET ECONOMIC AID: The New Aid and Trade Policy in Underdeveloped Countries, by Joseph S. Berliner.

RAW MATERIALS: A Study of American Policy, by Percy W. Bidwell.

FOREIGN POLICY: THE NEXT PHASE, by Thomas K. Finletter.

NATO AND THE FUTURE OF EUROPE, by Ben T. Moore.

AFRICAN ECONOMIC DEVELOPMENT, by William A. Hance.

DEFENSE OF THE MIDDLE EAST: Problems of American Policy, by John C. Campbell.

INDIA AND AMERICA: A Study of Their Relations, by Phillips Talbot and S. L. Poplai.

NUCLEAR WEAPONS AND FOREIGN POLICY, by Henry Kissinger.

JAPAN BETWEEN EAST AND WEST, by Hugh Borton, Jerome B. Cohen, William J. Jorden, Donald Keene, Paul F. Langer and C. Martin Wilbur.

MOSCOW-PEKING AXIS: Strengths and Strains, by Howard L. Boorman, Alexander Eckstein, Philip E. Mosely and Benjamin Schwartz.

CLIMATE AND ECONOMIC DEVELOPMENT IN THE TROPICS, by Douglas H. K. Lee.

WHAT THE TARIFF MEANS TO AMERICAN INDUSTRIES, by Percy W. Bidwell.

UNITED STATES SHIPPING POLICY, by Wytze Gorter.

RUSSIA AND AMERICA: Dangers and Prospects, by Henry L. Roberts.

STERLING: Its Meaning in World Finance, by Judd Polk.

KOREA: A Study of U. S. Policy in the United Nations, by Leland M. Goodrich.

FOREIGN AFFAIRS BIBLIOGRAPHY, 1942-1952, by Henry L. Roberts.

JAPANESE AND AMERICANS: A Century of Cultural Relations, by Robert S. Schwantes.

THE FUTURE OF UNDERDEVELOPED COUNTRIES: Political Implications of Economic Development, by Eugene Staley.

AMERICAN AGENCIES INTERESTED IN INTERNATIONAL AFFAIRS, compiled by Ruth Savord and Donald Wasson. (*Revised edition*, 1955).

THE UNDECLARED WAR, 1940-1941, by William L. Langer and S. Everett Gleason.

THE CHALLENGE TO ISOLATION, 1937-1940, by William L. Langer and S. Everett Gleason.

MIDDLE EAST DILEMMAS, by J. C. Hurewitz.

BRITAIN AND THE UNITED STATES: Problems in Cooperation, a joint report prepared by Henry L. Roberts and Paul A. Wilson.

TRADE AND PAYMENTS IN WESTERN EUROPE: A Study in Economic Co-operation, 1947-1951, by William Diebold, Jr.

PUBLIC OPINION AND FOREIGN POLICY, by Lester Markel and others.

SURVEY OF AMERICAN FOREIGN RELATIONS (in four volumes, 1928-1931), prepared under the direction of Charles P. Howland.

POLITICAL HANDBOOK OF THE WORLD

Parliaments, Parties and Press

as of January 1, 1959

è

Edited by
WALTER H. MALLORY

PUBLISHED BY HARPER & BROTHERS, NEW YORK

For COUNCIL ON FOREIGN RELATIONS, INC.

58 EAST 68TH STREET, NEW YORK 21

The Council on Foreign Relations is a non-profit institution devoted to study of the international aspects of American political, economic and strategic problems. It takes no stand, expressed or implied, on American policy.

The authors of books published under the auspices of the Council are responsible for their statements of fact and expressions of opinion. The Council is responsible only for determining that they should be presented to the public.

Copyright, 1959, by Council on Foreign Relations, Inc.

Printed in the United States of America

Library of Congress catalog card number: 28-12165

Published in Great Britain and the British Commonwealth, excluding Canada, by London: Oxford University Press

FOREWORD

The POLITICAL HANDBOOK is designed to furnish the necessary factual background for understanding political events in all countries which have independent governments—colonies and trust territories are not included.

The sources from which information has been gathered for this volume are many and varied. Some of them are official and some private. It is impossible to quote or refer to these sources, but the editor considers them reliable.

With reference to the sections on the press, two points are to be observed. First, an effort has been made to select those papers which are most apt to be quoted abroad; many papers of large circulation and strong local influence are necessarily omitted. Second, in listing the proprietor of a paper, the term has been used to indicate the chief proprietor or controlling shareholder. Where circulation figures of newspapers are given, they have been quoted, in most cases, from the *Editor & Publisher, International Year Book, 1958*.

The editor wishes to take this occasion to express his sincere thanks to the many correspondents in all parts of the world who have supplied information for this volume, and especially to Frank D. Caruthers, Jr., Miss Margherita King, Joseph Barber, and the staff of the Council on Foreign Relations Library who have most ably assisted with the collection and checking of material, and the preparation of the manuscript.

Valuable suggestions have been offered by the readers of previous editions. They are hereby gratefully acknowledged. Many of these have been incorporated in this new issue. Since the POLITICAL HANDBOOK will be revised and republished at regular intervals, criticisms and suggestions will be welcomed.

WALTER H. MALLORY

New York, January 1, 1959

COUNCIL ON FOREIGN RELATIONS

OFFICERS AND DIRECTORS

JOHN J. MCCLOY
Chairman of the Board

HENRY M. WRISTON
President

FRANK ALTSCHUL
Vice-President & Secretary

DAVID ROCKEFELLER
Vice-President

ELLIOTT V. BELL
Treasurer

WALTER H. MALLORY
Executive Director

GEORGE S. FRANKLIN, JR.
Executive Director

FRANK D. CARUTHERS, JR.
Assistant Treasurer

HAMILTON FISH ARMSTRONG
WILLIAM A. M. BURDEN
ARTHUR H. DEAN
LEWIS W. DOUGLAS
ALLEN W. DULLES
THOMAS K. FINLETTER
JOSEPH E. JOHNSON

GRAYSON L. KIRK
R. C. LEFFINGWELL
PHILIP D. REED
WHITNEY H. SHEPARDSON
CHARLES M. SPOFFORD
ADLAI E. STEVENSON
MYRON C. TAYLOR

JOHN H. WILLIAMS

COMMITTEE ON STUDIES

HENRY M. WRISTON
Chairman

HAMILTON FISH ARMSTRONG
ARTHUR H. DEAN
BYRON DEXTER
CARYL P. HASKINS

JOSEPH E. JOHNSON
GRAYSON L. KIRK
AUGUST MAFFRY
WILLARD L. THORP

JOHN H. WILLIAMS

STUDIES PROGRAM

PHILIP E. MOSLEY
Director of Studies

WILLIAM DIEBOLD, JR.
Director of Economic Studies

JOHN C. CAMPBELL
Director of Political Studies

CONTENTS

Afghanistan	1	New Zealand	138
Argentina	2	Nicaragua	141
Australia	4	Norway	143
Austria	9	Pakistan	146
Belgium	12	Panama	148
Bolivia	15	Paraguay	150
Brazil	17	Peru	152
Bulgaria	20	Philippines	155
Burma	23	Poland	158
Canada	25	Portugal	162
Ceylon	32	Rumania	165
Chile	33	Salvador	168
China	37	South Africa	169
Colombia	44	Spain	173
Costa Rica	46	Sweden	176
Cuba	48	Switzerland	179
Czechoslovakia	51	Thailand (Siam)	183
Denmark	54	Turkey	186
Dominican Republic	58	Union of Soviet Socialist Republics	189
Ecuador	60	United Arab Republic	195
Finland	62	United Nations	199
France	65	United States	208
Germany	73	Uruguay	218
Great Britain	81	Vatican City	221
Northern Ireland	88	Venezuela	222
Greece	90	Yugoslavia	224
Guatemala	93		
Haiti	95		
Honduras	96	Other Countries	
Hungary	98	Albania	227
Iceland	101	Cambodia	227
India	103	Ethiopia	227
Indonesia	107	Ghana	227
International Court of Justice	205	Guinea	228
		Korea	228
Iran	110	Laos	228
Iraq	111	Liechtenstein	228
Ireland	113	Malaya	229
Israel	116	Monaco	229
Italy	118	Mongolia	229
Japan	122	Morocco	229
Jordan	127	Muscat (Oman)	230
Lebanon	128	Nepal	230
Liberia	129	Sa'udi Arabia	230
Libya	130	Sudan	230
Luxembourg	131	Tunisia	231
Mexico	133	Viet Nam	231
Netherlands	135	Yemen	231

AFGHANISTAN

Capital: Kabul
Area: 250,966 square miles (estimated)
Population: 13,000,000 (1952 estimate)

Ruler

ALA-HAZRAT AL-MUTAWAKIL AL-ALLAH
MOHAMMAD ZAHIR SHAH
Born October 15, 1914; ascended the throne
on November 8, 1933

Cabinet
Appointed September 3, 1953

PARLIAMENT

SENATE	THE NATIONAL ASSEMBLY
(Majlis-e-Ayan)	(Majlis-e-Shora-e-Melli)
Appointed by the King.	Elected April 21–June 16, 1955 (convened June 18, 1955), for a three-year term.
President: FAZL-E-AHMAD MUJADDEDI	President: MOHAMMAD NAUROZ
Number of Members 20	Number of Members 171

THE CABINET

The members of the Cabinet are: Sardar Mohammad Da'ud (Prime Minister, Minister of National Defense, and Minister of Planning); Ali Mohammad (First Deputy Prime Minister); Sardar Mohammad Na'im (Second Deputy Prime Minister and Minister of Foreign Affairs); Abdullah Malikyar (Finance); Dr. Mohammad Yusuf (Mines and Industries); G. A. Sherzad (Commerce); Mohammad Morid (Communications); Mir Mohammad Yusuf (Agriculture); Sayyid Abdullah (Acting Minister of Justice and of the Interior); Dr. Ali Ahmad Popol (Acting Minister of Education); Mohammad Kabir (Acting Minister of Public Works); Mir Shamsuddin Majruh (President of the Department of Tribal Affairs); Sayyid Mohammad Qasim Rishtiya (President of the Press Department). The Ministry of Public Health is vacant.

PRESS

The three leading daily newspapers are published at Kabul under the general supervision of the Royal Afghan Press Department.

Name of Paper	Circulation	Editor
Anis (in Persian)	10,000	Mohammad Qasim Wajid
Islah (in Pashto and Persian)	10,000	Mohammad Ibrahim Abbassy
Haiwad (in Pashto)	10,000	Mohammad Shah Irshad

ARGENTINA

Capital: Buenos Aires
Area: 1,079,965 square miles
Population: 19,857,700 (1957 estimate)

President
DR. ARTURO FRONDIZI (U.C.R.I. Party)
Assumed office on May 1, 1958, for six-year term

PARLIAMENT
(Congreso Nacional)

UPPER CHAMBER (Senado) *Elected February 23, 1958*	LOWER CHAMBER (Cámara de Diputados) *Elected February 23, 1958*
Number of members 46	Number of members 187

RECENT POLITICAL EVENTS

General Juan Domingo Perón was elected President of Argentina on February 24, 1946, and re-elected on November 11, 1951, for a second six-year term. But prior to his election he had for three years been the head of an army clique which actually ruled the country. On September 19, 1955, his government was overthrown, bringing to an end more than twelve years of his dictatorship. The military took over, and on September 21, 1955, Maj. Gen. Eduardo Lonardi assumed power as "Provisional President." He ruled for less than two months and was succeeded by General Aramburu.

Provisional President Aramburu called for a general election on February 23, 1958, which resulted in a victory for the "Unión Civica Radical Intransigente." It obtained an overwhelming majority in the Lower Chamber and all seats in the Senate as well as all the Provincial Governments.

THE CABINET

The Cabinet comprises 8 Ministers and 12 Secretaries as follows: Carlos R. Vítolo, Interior; Carlos A. Florit, Foreign Relations and Worship; Gabriel del Mazo, National Defense (War Secretary, General Hector Solanas Pacheco; Navy Secretary, Admiral Adolfo B. Estévez; and Air Force Secretary, Brigadier Ramón A. Abrahin); Luis R. Mackay, Education and Justice; Hector V. Noblía, Public Health and Social Assistance; Alfredo Allende, Labor and Social Welfare; Justo P. Villar, Public Works and Services (Communications Secretary, Adolfo T. Cosentino; Public Works Secretary, Justo P. Villar; and Transport Secretary, Alberto López Abuin); Emilio Donato del Carril, Economy (Agriculture and Livestock Secretary, Bernardino C. Horne; Treasury Secretary, Ricardo Lumi; Finance Secretary, Antonio López; Commerce Secretary, José C. Orfila; Industry and Mining Secretary, Alberto V. Tedín; and Energy and Fuels Secretary, Gregorio A. Meira).

ARGENTINA

PRESS

Unless otherwise noted, papers are published in the capital city.

Name of Paper	Circulation	Character	Proprietor, Editor, etc.
Argentinisches Tageblatt	10,000	German.	Dr. Ernesto F. Alemann (*Dir.*)
El Avisador Mercantil	6,500	Commercial daily.	Dr. A. Fernández del Casal (*Dir.*)
Buenos Aires Herald	25,000	Independent; long-established British daily.	Norman Ingrey (*Dir.*)
Clarín	297,000	Independent.	Roberto J. Noble (*Dir.*)
*Crítica (evening)	225,000	Independent.	Santiago Nudelman (*Dir.*)
El Cronista Comercial	14,000	Commercial daily.	Duilio Anzisi (*Dir.*)
*Democracia	200,000	Independent.	Alfonso M. Romanelli (*Dir.*)
*La Epoca (evening)	35,000	Independent.	Rubén Angel Corbacho (*Dir.*)
La Hora	42,000	Communist Party.	Rodolfo Ghioldi (*Dir.*)
Freie Presse	13,000	German.	Federico Mueller (*Dir.*)
*La Voz del Plata (ex-El Laborista)	40,000	Independent.	Luis E. Arana (*Dir.*)
*El Mundo	220,000	Independent.	Elbio Coelho (*Dir.*)
El Nacional	80,000	Pro-Government.	Marcos Merchensky (*Dir.*)
La Nación	261,000	Independent; long-established, influential journal.	Bartolomé Mitre (*Dir.*)
*Noticias Gráficas (evening)	141,000	Independent.	José Barcia (*Dir.*)
La Prensa	341,000	Independent; long-established, influential journal.	Alberto Gainza Paz (*Dir. & Pub.*)
El Pueblo	15,000	Catholic.	Oscar Font Guido (*Dir.*)
*La Razón (evening)	375,000	Independent.	Ricardo Peralta Ramos (*Dir.*)
The Standard	12,000	British weekly; oldest English newspaper in South America.	Alfredo C. Dougall (*Dir.*)
La Nueva Provincia (Bahia Blanca)	32,000	Independent.	Diana Julio de Massot (*Dir.*)
Los Principios (Córdoba)	34,000	Catholic.	Rogelio Nores Martínez (*Dir.*)
La Voz del Interior (Córdoba)	46,000	Radical Party.	Raúl Silvestre Remonda (*Dir.*)
Los Andes (Mendoza)	55,000	Independent.	Felipe Calle (*Dir.*)
*El Día (La Plata)	67,000	Independent.	Jerónimo Carol (*Dir.*)
La Capital (Rosario)	60,000	Independent.	Carlos Ovidio Lagos (*Dir.*)
El Litoral (Santa Fé)	46,000	Independent.	Salvador Riobó Caputo (*Dir.*)
La Gaceta (Tucumán)	80,000	Independent.	Enrique García Hamilton (*Prop. & Dir.*)

* Newspapers formerly owned by the Provisional Government, inherited from the Perón régime, but recently sold to private owners by public auction.

AUSTRALIA

Capital: Canberra
Area: 2,974,581 square miles (not including overseas Territories)
Population 9,801,235 (1958 estimate)

Sovereign
QUEEN ELIZABETH II

Governor-General
FIELD MARSHAL SIR WILLIAM SLIM

Cabinet
Coalition: Liberal and Country Parties
Appointed on December 19, 1949
Re-organized several times since

Prime Minister
Robert Gordon Menzies (Liberal)
Assumed office December 19, 1949
Re-appointed December 10, 1958

PARLIAMENT
(Federal Parliament)

UPPER CHAMBER (Senate)

Election November 22, 1958 (*six-year term; renewed by halves every three years*)

President: SIR ALISTER M. McMULLIN (Liberal)

Parties	Representation
Liberal and Country Parties	32
Labor Party	26
Democratic Labor Party	2
Total	60

LOWER CHAMBER (House of Representatives)

Election of November 22, 1958 (*three-year term*)

Speaker: JOHN McLEAY (Liberal)

Parties	Representation
Liberal and Country Parties	77*
Labor Party	47
Total	124

*Liberal—58, Country Party—19.

THE GOVERNMENT

Australia is a Federation, along much the same lines as the United States, but with the British system of responsibility of Executive to Parliament instead of the Presidential model. The Federal or Commonwealth Parliament is thus restricted to legislating along certain lines, subject to judicial review by the High Court. The State governments, of which there are six, like those of the USA, have unrestricted legislative power outside the fields allotted to the Commonwealth by the Federal Constitution. The Commonwealth has overriding defense, fiscal and financial powers.

AUSTRALIA

RECENT POLITICAL EVENTS

Labor was in office from October 7, 1941, until December 19, 1949, first under Mr. John Curtin, and, after his death on July 5, 1945, under Mr. Joseph Benedict Chifley.

In the general election on December 10, 1949, Labor was defeated by a Liberal and Country Party coalition which campaigned on the issue of greater encouragement of the free enterprise system and an end to economic controls. Mr. Menzies, leader of the Liberals, formed a coalition cabinet on December 19, 1949. The coalition government was returned to power April 28, 1951. In the Senate elections of May 9, 1953, the government retained a marginal majority, and in the House of Representatives contest of May 29, 1954, was returned but with a majority of 7 versus its former majority of 15. In the general election of December 10, 1955, the government greatly increased its majority in the House, but lost its majority in the Senate. In the November 22, 1958, election the government increased its majority in the House and also achieved a Senate majority.

PARTY PROGRAMS AND LEADERS

THE LABOR PARTY: With a continuous history since the 1890's, Labor is the oldest of the existing parties. After holding power in the Federal Parliament in the early years of World War I, it suffered a split over conscription for overseas military service and was in opposition during the 1920's. After a brief term of office between 1929-31 the party was again in opposition for another ten years. Its advent to power in October 1941, a few months before the Pacific War began, meant that it had to complete the mobilization of the nation for a war close to home. It instituted controls over money, manpower, materials and production generally, the Parliament's defense power being held sufficient to justify these. Assuming office as a minority government, it was given majorities at the 1943 and 1946 elections.

Labor is largely a trade union party, tightly organized and pledged to a policy of gradual socialization. It lays great emphasis upon social services, which it believes should be financed either out of revenue or upon the New Zealand principle of a universal tax. Although the powers of the Commonwealth to nationalize industries were much in doubt, Labor set up a government airline, planned a government shipping line, and a national health service. In 1947 it passed legislation aiming at nationalizing the private commercial banks, but this was subsequently ruled invalid.

Labor appeals for the vote of the small farmer as well as for that of the trade unionist and salaried worker.

In international affairs, Labor stands for Australian independence within the framework of the British Commonwealth, and lays great stress on international organizations such as the U.N. Traditionally it has been the party of Australian Nationalism, and in 1944 it joined with New Zealand in a South Pacific "Anzac Pact" which would increase the international bargaining power of the two Dominions. It initiated Australia's great postwar immigration program and strongly upholds the policy of excluding non-European races. This policy is supported by all parties except the Communist Party.

Leaders: H. V. Evatt, former Deputy Prime Minister and Minister for External Affairs (Leader of the Opposition); A. A. Calwell, former Minister for Immigration (Deputy Leader of the Opposition).

DEMOCRATIC LABOR PARTY: Established as anti-communist Labor Party on a Federal basis in 1957, with branches in all States except Queensland.

Leaders: Senator G. R. Cole, Leader (Tasmania); Senator F. P. McManus, Deputy Leader (Victoria).

THE LIBERAL PARTY: Organized in the immediate post-war period as successor to the United Australia Party (UAP), the Liberal Party has consolidated those non-Labor forces in Australia which do not adhere to the Country Party (see below). The 1946 elections increased its membership in the House of Representatives from 14 to 17, and the 1949 elections from 17 to 52, dropping to 51 in 1951, and to 47 in 1954, and rising to 57 in 1955, and to 58 in 1958. The (UAP), after a heavy defeat at the 1943 elections, was absorbed into the Liberal Party.

The Liberal Party, which espouses private enterprise and deprecates government ownership and commercial operations (other than railways, utilities, irrigation and power projects, broadcasting and communications) has a looser party organization than that of Labor. It attacks the Labor Party's program of socialization and its support of the use of the strike weapon by unions. Its successful campaigns in the last three elections have been mainly on its record of conservative financial policies, economic stability, counter-inflationary measures, and wholehearted cooperation within the British Commonwealth and with the United States in foreign affairs.

Leaders: R. G. Menzies (Prime Minister), H. E. Holt (Treasurer).

THE COUNTRY PARTY: A product of the post-World War I period, the Country Party claims to represent the interests of farmers and all who live in country districts. It now has 19 members in the House of Representatives.

The policy of the Country Party is largely concerned with rural issues. It advocates guaranteed prices for farmers under producer marketing control, irrigation and decentralization schemes, and extension of transport and communications in rural areas.

Although the Party has consistently rejected proposals for merging with the UAP or Liberals, it campaigned with the latter in 1949, 1951, 1954, 1955, and 1958 and is at present represented in the Coalition Cabinet.

Leaders: John McEwen (Deputy Prime Minister and Minister for Trade), C. W. Davidson (Postmaster General).

THE CABINET

R. G. Menzies, Prime Minister (Liberal); J. McEwen, Deputy Prime Minister and Minister for Trade (Country Party); Senator W. H. Spooner, Vice-President of the Executive Council and National Development (Liberal); W. McMahon, Labor and National Service (Liberal); H. E. Holt, Treasurer (Liberal); R. G. Casey, External Affairs (Liberal); A. G. Townley, Defense (Liberal); A. S. Hulme, Supply (Liberal); P. M. C. Hasluck, Territories (Liberal); Senator S. D. Paltridge, Shipping and Transport and Civil Aviation (Liberal); C. W. Davidson, Postmaster General (Country Party); A. R. Downer, Immigration (Liberal); Sir Garfield Barnick, Attorney General (Liberal). *Ministers not in the Cabinet:* Senator W. J. Cooper, Repatriation (Country Party); Dr. D. A. Cameron, Health (Liberal); J. O. Cramer, Army (Liberal); F. M. Osborne, Air (Liberal); G. Freeth, Interior and Works (Liberal); H. S. Roberton, Social Services (Country Party); Senator N. H. D. Henty, Customs and Excise (Liberal); C. F. Adermann, Primary Industry (Country Party); Senator J. G. Gorton, Navy (Liberal).

AUSTRALIA

PRESS

Name of Paper	Circulation	Political Affiliation	Proprietor, etc.
Advertiser (Adelaide)	178,266	Conservative; largest circulation of any paper in South Australia; politically influential.	Advertiser Newspapers, Ltd. (*Prop.*) Sir Lloyd Dumas (*Mg. Dir.*)
News (Adelaide)	118,823	Independent; evening paper.	Rohan Rivett (*Ed.*)
Courier-Mail (Brisbane)	220,740	Conservative; authority on political and commercial affairs in Queensland.	Queensland Newspapers Pty., Ltd. (*Prop.*) T. C. Bray (*Ed.*)
Telegraph (Brisbane)	154,030	Conservative; evening paper.	J. F. Wakefield (*Ed.*)
Mercury (Hobart)	43,909	Conservative; leading newspaper of Tasmania.	Davies Bros. Ltd. (*Prop.*) G. F. Davies (*Mg. Dir.*)
Examiner (Launceston)	22,979	Conservative; daily.	W. R. Rolph & Sons, Ltd. (*Prop.*) R. J. Williams (*Ed.*)
Age (Melbourne)	171,337	Independent; moderate labor leanings; authoritative daily.	David Syme & Co. (*Prop.*) Sir Harold Campbell (*Ed.*)
Herald (Melbourne)	439,212	Conservative evening daily.	Herald and Weekly Times Ltd. (*Prop.*) H. D. Giddy (*Ch.*) J. F. Williams (*Mg. Dir.*)
Sun News-Pictorial (Melbourne)	554,475	Conservative; pictorial daily.	Herald and Weekly Times (*Prop.*) F. Daly (*Ed.*)
Newcastle Morning Herald (Newcastle)	51,338	Independent; labor leanings.	E. M. Morriss (*Mgr.*) E. K. Lingard (*Ed.*)
Daily News (Perth)	95,692	Conservative; only evening daily in West Australia.	S. K. Joynt (*Ed.*)
West Australian (Perth)	146,296	Conservative; leading daily of Western Australia.	West Australian Newspaper Co., Ltd. (*Prop.*) J. E. Macartney (*Mg. Ed.*)
Daily Mirror (Sydney)	279,318	Independent; evening paper.	Truth and Sportsman, Ltd. (*Prop.*)
Daily Telegraph (Sydney)	290,000	Conservative; morning paper.	Consolidated Press, Ltd. (*Prop.*) Frank Packer (*Mg. Dir.*) D. R. McNicoll (*Ed.*)
Sun (Sydney)	284,121	Conservative; evening paper.	Associated Newspapers, Ltd. (*Prop.*) R. A. Henderson (*Mg. Dir.*) L. Clinch (*Ed.*)
Sydney Morning Herald (Sydney)	301,484	Conservative; Australia's oldest morning paper.	John Fairfax, Ltd. (*Prop.*) Warwick Fairfax (*Chairman*) Angus Maude (*Ed.*)

WEEKLY NEWSPAPERS AND MAGAZINES

Sun-Herald (Sydney)	615,808	Conservative Sunday paper, largest circulation.	John Fairfax & Sons, Ltd., and Associated Newspapers, Ltd. (*Props.*) R. A. Henderson (*Mg. Dir.*)
Sunday Telegraph (Sydney)	560,000	Conservative.	Consolidated Press, Ltd. (*Prop.*)
Sunday Mirror (Sydney)	350,000	Independent.	Truth and Sportsman, Ltd. (*Prop.*) Ezra Norton (*Mg. Dir.*)
Chronicle (Adelaide) (weekly)	23,906	Illustrated; Statewide circulation.	Advertiser Newspapers, Ltd. (*Prop.*) Sir Lloyd Dumas (*Mg. Dir.*)

AUSTRALIA

Name of Paper	Circulation	Political Affiliation	Proprietor, Editor, etc.
Sunday Mail (Adelaide)	285,320	Independent; Sunday paper.	News, Ltd. (*Prop.*) K. V. Parish (*Ed.*)
Weekly Times (Melbourne) (weekly)	108,534	Illustrated; wide circulation.	Herald and Weekly Times Ltd. (*Prop.*) F. W. Murphy (*Ed.*)
Bulletin (Sydney) (weekly)	31,227	Nationalistic; circulates throughout Australia.	Bulletin Newspaper Co. (*Prop.*) H. K. Prior (*Mg. Dir.*) D. Adams (*Ed.*)
Century (Sydney) (weekly)	21,000	Independent Labor. (Mr. Lang)	K. Schmidt (*Ed.*)
Financial Review (Sydney) (weekly)	10,000	Financial.	John Fairfax & Sons, Ltd. (*Prop.*)
Truth (Editions in all States except N. S. W. and W. A.) (weekly)	674,515	Public affairs.	Truth and Sportsman, Ltd. (*Prop.*)
Australian Worker (Sydney) (weekly)	53,176	Labor.	M. J. McCarthy (*Ed.*)
The Australian Outlook (Sydney)	2,000	National and international affairs.	Australian Institute of International Affairs (*Pub.*) H. D. Black (*Ed.*)
Australian Journal of Politics and History		Political, historical, cultural.	Prof. Gordon Greenwood (*Ed.*)
Australian Quarterly (Sydney)	1,800	Political, economic and cultural.	D. A. S. Campbell (*Ed.*)
The Economic Record (Semi-annual)	2,500	Economic.	Prof. R. Downing (*Ed.*)]

NEWS AGENCIES

Australian Associated Press	Independent; international news service; owned and controlled by principal metropolitan dailies of Australia, associated with Reuter's.	Angus McLachlan (*Ch.*)
Australian United Press	Independent; domestic news service, controlled by subscribing country papers.	

AUSTRIA

Capital: Vienna
Area: 32,369 square miles
Population: 6,983,000 (1956 estimate)

President
ADOLF SCHAERF (Socialist)
Elected May 5, 1957
Assumed office May 22, 1957

Cabinet
People's Party—Socialist Coalition
Assumed office July 4, 1956

Chancellor
JULIUS RAAB (People's Party)

PARLIAMENT

UPPER CHAMBER
(Bundesrat)

Members are nominated by Provincial Assemblies.
President: (Office passes every six months to each of the Provinces in alphabetical order)

Parties	Representation
People's Party	26
Socialist Party	24
Total	50

LOWER CHAMBER
(Nationalrat)

Election of May 13, 1956 (for four-year term)
President: FELIX HURDES
(People's Party)

Parties	Representation
People's Party	82
Socialist Party	74
Liberal Party	6
Communist Party	3
Total	165

THE GOVERNMENT

On April 27, 1945, after the liberation of Vienna by the Soviet Army, an Austrian Provisional Government was set up under the leadership of Dr. Karl Renner, a Socialist (who had also served as first Chancellor of the Austrian Republic after the collapse of the Austro-Hungarian Monarchy in 1918). This was the first independent authority in Austria since the country had been occupied by Hitler in 1938.

The *Anschluss* with Germany was declared null and void, and on May 1, 1945, the Austrian Constitution of 1920, as amended in 1929, was put into operation again. Under the supervision of the Allied Commission, composed of the four occupying powers, plans were perfected for elections for a National Assembly and for Provincial Assemblies.

On December 19, 1945, the second Republic of Austria was established with the convocation of the newly elected National Assembly. On December 20, 1945, the upper and lower chambers of Parliament, sitting in joint session, elected Dr. Karl Renner President, who appointed Ing. Leopold Figl Chancellor. The second national elections, held in October 1949, resulted in a victory for the two coalition parties and witnessed the emergence of a new party, the Union of Independents. The latter was reorganized in 1956 under the name of the Liberal Party. Elections in 1953 and 1956 also resulted in victory for the People's and the Socialist parties.

On May 15, 1955, the State Treaty, restoring an independent and democratic Austria, was signed in Vienna by the foreign ministers of the four occupying powers and Austria, and went into effect on July 27, 1955. All occupying troops were withdrawn by October 25, 1955.

PARTY PROGRAMS AND LEADERS

PEOPLE'S PARTY: Middle-class party, dominated by peasants and businessmen. Largely Catholic; but not directly affiliated with the Church. Places emphasis on Austrian patriotism, strongly opposes communism, advocates free enterprise and the abatement of class difference through its doctrine of Solidarismus, by which is understood a spirit of national unity transcending all "selfish interests." The People's Party constitutes a federation of three free associations: one composed of peasants, another of businessmen and the third of workers and white-collar employees. It is the largest party in seven of the nine Austrian provinces.

Leaders: Chancellor Julius Raab (Party Chairman), Alfred Maleta (Party Secretary), Felix Hurdes (First President of the Nationalrat), Leopold Figl, Fritz Bock, Ferdinand Graf, Franz Thoma, Heinrich Drimmel, Josef Kraus, Johann Wagner, Lois Weinberger, Eduard Hartman, Josef Krainer, Hermann Withalm and Reinhard Kamitz.

SOCIALIST PARTY: Represents overwhelming majority of workers and part of lower middle-class. Exercises predominant influence on the Trade Union Federation and on its constituent labor unions. Party favors, in general terms, economic planning and far-reaching social services. Advocates moderate reforms through democratic processes, plays down Marxist ideology. Vigorously opposes Communists, whose attempts to divide the party or to draw away its membership have so far been unsuccessful.

Leaders: Vice-Chancellor Bruno Pittermann (Party Chairman), Otto Probst and Alois Piperger (Party Secretaries), Franz Olah (Leader in Parliament), Johann Boehm (President of the Trade Union Federation), Oskar Helmer, Bruno Kreisky, Karl Waldbrunner, Anton Proksch, Oscar Pollak, Franz Jonas, Karl Maisel, Felix Slavik.

LIBERAL PARTY: An unstable new party formed in 1955, composed of dissident elements; important are re-enfranchised ex-Nazis, returning ex-soldiers, remnants of the Landbund (anti-clerical peasantry) and German national parties of the First Republic, and middle class elements and workers who have deserted coalition parties. Policy is as yet ill-defined but is highly critical of present Coalition Government and advocates fewer economic controls, anti-clericalism, reduced functions of government to cut expenses, and "social justice." Stresses cultural affinity of Austrian and German peoples.

Leaders: Friedrich Peter (Party Chairman), Willfried Gredler, Heinrich Zechmann, Hubert Knaus, Max Stendebach and Jörg Kandutsch.

COMMUNIST PARTY: Advocates establishment of a "people's democracy" without, however, clearly defining that concept. Opposes and attempts to

AUSTRIA

obstruct, practically without exception, all measures of the Coalition Government. Calls for nationalization, land reform (without state farming), and broader social welfare. Opposes Austrian military preparedness, attacks NATO, demands Austrian neutrality in East-West conflict. Received 4.4 per cent of popular vote in 1956 elections.

Leaders: Johann Koplenig (Chairman), Friedl Fuernberg, Heinrich Fritz, Franz Honner and Rudolf Richter (Secretaries), Ernst Fischer and Gottlieb Fiala.

THE CABINET

The Cabinet is composed as follows: Julius Raab (People's Party), Chancellor; Bruno Pittermann (Socialist Party), Vice-Chancellor; Leopold Figl (People's Party), Foreign Affairs; Oskar Helmer (Socialist Party), Interior; Reinhard Kamitz, (People's Party) Finance; Fritz Bock (People's Party), Trade; Karl Waldbrunner (Socialist Party), Communications and Electric Power; Franz Thoma (People's Party), Agriculture; Anton Proksch (Socialist Party), Social Administration; Heinrich Drimmel (People's Party), Education; Otto Tschadek (Socialist Party), Justice; Ferdinand Graf (People's Party), Defense; and the following State Secretaries: Bruno Kreisky (Socialist Party), Foreign Affairs; Franz Gschnitzer (People's Party), Foreign Affairs; Hermann Withalm (People's Party), Finance; Franz Grubhofer (People's Party), Interior; Eduard Weikart (Socialist Party), Trade; and Karl Stephani (Socialist Party), Defense.

PRESS

Most Austrian newspapers are owned by the political parties. Unless otherwise indicated, papers are published in the capital city.

Name of Paper	Circulation	Political Affiliation	Proprietor, Editor, etc.
Neue Tageszeitung	20,000	People's Party.	Dr. Heinz Schramm-Schiessl (*Ed.*)
Kleines Volksblatt	114,000	People's Party.	Dr. Franz Groessl (*Ed.*)
Arbeiter-Zeitung	129,000	Socialist Party.	Dr. Oscar Pollak (*Ed.*)
Volksstimme	43,000	Communist Party.	Erwin Scharf (*Ed.*)
Neues Oesterreich	72,000	Coalition.	Dr. Friedrich Lorenz (*Ed.*)
Neuer Kurier	122,000	Independent.	Dr. Hugo Portisch (*Act. Ed.*)
Die Presse	50,000	Independent.	Milan Dubrovic (*Ed.*)
Express	121,000	Independent.	Gerd Bacher (*Ed.*)
Wiener Zeitung	25,000	Official gazette.	Dr. Franz Stamprech (*Ed.*)
Salzburger Nachrichten (Salzburg)	37,000	Independent.	Dr. Gustav Canaval (*Ed.*)
Oberoesterreichische Nachrichten (Linz)	45,000	Independent.	Walter Pollak (*Ed.*)
Tiroler Tageszeitung (Innsbruck)	38,000	Independent.	Dr. Anton Klotz (*Ed.*)
Kleine Zeitung (Graz)	75,000	Independent.	Dr. Otto Schoenherr (*Ed.*)
Neue Zeit (Graz)	50,000	Socialist Party.	Dr. Hans Paller (*Ed.*)
Südost-Tagespost (Graz)	44,000	People's Party.	Dr. Wilhelm Antropp (*Ed.*)

BELGIUM

Capital: Brussels
Area: 11,775 square miles
Population: 8,951,443 (1957 estimate)

Ruler
KING BAUDOUIN
Son of King Leopold; born September 7, 1930
Created Prince Royal August 11, 1950
Acceded to throne July 17, 1951

Cabinet
Coalition of Social Christians and Liberals
Appointed November 6, 1958

Premier
GASTON EYSKENS (Social Christian)

PARLIAMENT

UPPER CHAMBER
(Sénat-Senaat)

Election of June 1, 1958 (for four years)*
President: PAUL STRUYE (Social Christian)

Parties	Representation
Social Christian	90
Socialist	65
Liberal	18
Communist	1
Independent (Catholic)	1
Total	175*

LOWER CHAMBER
(Chambre des Représentants-Kamer van Volksvertegen-woordigers)

Election of June 1, 1958 (for four years)
President: PAUL KRONACKER (Liberal)

Parties	Representation
Social Christian	104
Socialist	84
Liberal	21
Communist	2
Independent (Catholic)	1
Total	212

* In the general election 106 Senators are chosen. In addition 46 are elected by Provincial Councillors and 23 by their fellow Senators, making a total of 175.

PARTY PROGRAMS AND LEADERS

SOCIAL CHRISTIAN PARTY (former Catholic Party—now called PSC): A unitary Catholic party, including members whose views range from conservatism to leftism, but with a strong center group. The left wing favors social reforms like those of the Socialists and supports the interests of Catholic trade unions. The nobility, Flemish peasants, industrialists, and labor groups who are practicing Catholics, are generally supporters of the party. Its strength is greater in Flanders than in French speaking areas. The party gave its unqualified approval to the North Atlantic Treaty and Western European Union, the Common Market and Euratom.

Leaders: Auguste De Schrijver (first President of the Party after World

War II), Gaston Eyskens (Prime Minister), Theo Lefèvre (President of the Party), Pierre Wigny (Minister of Foreign Affairs), Paul Struye (President of the Senate), Frans Van Cauwelaert (Former President of the Chamber).

SOCIALIST PARTY: A moderate, constitutional, socialist party with an orthodox socialist program. Recently it has placed little stress on nationalization but has been chiefly interested in extension of social welfare programs. It favors the development of state schools as opposed to parochial schools, and supports the North Atlantic Treaty Organization, Western European Union, the Common Market and Euratom.

Leaders: Achille Van Acker (former Prime Minister), Victor Larock (former Foreign Minister), Max Buset (President of the Party), Henri Fayat (former Minister of Foreign Trade), Georges Bohy (Floor Leader in Chamber), Henri Rolin (Floor Leader in Senate), Fernand Dehousse (Senator, President of Assembly of Council of Europe), Camille Huysmans (former President of the Chamber).

LIBERAL PARTY: A party which favors relatively unhampered "free enterprise," and less government expense, but which also supports various social reforms. It supports Belgium's present policy of uniting with other democratic countries for defense and economic well-being. The party lost heavily in the elections of June 4, 1950, regained some strength in the 1954 elections and lost four seats in the 1958 elections.

Leaders: Maurice Destenay (President of Party), Roger Motz (former President of the Party), Charles Janssens (Floor Leader in Chamber), Albert Lilar (Deputy Premier), Charles Moureaux (Floor Leader in Senate), Robert Gillon (former President of the Senate).

COMMUNIST PARTY: A small and completely orthodox Communist Party. Following closely the policies of other Communist Parties in Western Europe, it has developed a violent anti-U.S. stand in foreign policy. In domestic policy it also follows unswervingly the current Communist Party line. It lost substantial Parliamentary strength in the elections of 1950, 1954 and 1958.

Leaders: René Beelen, Ernest Burnelle, Gerard Van Moerkerke (National 3-man Secretariat).

THE CABINET

The members of the Cabinet are: Gaston Eyskens (Social Christian) Premier; Albert Lilar (Liberal) Vice-Premier; Jean Van Houtte (Social Christian) Finance; Albert de Vleeschauwer (Social Christian) Agriculture; Pierre Wigny (Social Christian) Foreign Affairs; Oscar Behogne (Social Christian) Labor; Paul W. Segers (Social Christian) Communications; Pierre Harmel (Social Christian) Cultural Affairs; Omer Vanaudenhove (Liberal) Public Works; Arthur Gilson (Social Christian) National Defence; Maurice Van Hemelrijck (Social Christian) Congo & Ruanda-Urundi; Léon Servais (Social Christian) Social Security; Paul Meyers (Social Christian) Public Health; Paul van den Boeynants (Social Christian) Middle Classes; Laurent Merchiers (Liberal) Justice; Charles Moureaux (Liberal) Public Education; Jacques Van der Schueren (Liberal), Economic Affairs; Jacques Van Offelen (Liberal) Foreign Trade; René Lefebvre (Liberal) Interior.

BELGIUM

PRESS

Unless otherwise noted, papers are published in capital city.

Name of Paper	Circulation	Political Affiliation	Proprietor, Editor, etc.
Le Soir	300,000	Independent.	Marie-Thérèse Rossel (*Prop.*)
La Libre Belgique	225,000	Catholic conservative.	Victor Zeeghers (*Ed.*)
La Dernière Heure	190,000	Liberal.	Marcel Brebart (*Pub.*)
Le Drapeau Rouge	8,000	Communist.	Gérard van Moerkerke (*Ed.*)
La Cité	35,000	Catholic Labor.	José Desmarets (*Dir.*)
Le Peuple	90,000	Socialist.	Albert Housiaux (*Ed.*)
Het Laatste Nieuws	300,000	Liberal.	M. A. Maertens (*Dir.*)
De Nieuwe Gids	15,000	Catholic right.	J. Delaforteire (*Ed.*)
De Standaard	15,000	Catholic Flemish.	Albert De Smaele (*Ed.*)
La Lanterne	40,000	Liberal Independent.	Pol Fenat (*Ed.*)
Het Nieuws van den Dag	85,000	Catholic Independent.	Jean Duplat (*Prop.*)
Echo de la Bourse	25,000	Independent; financial.	Maurice Henriquet (*Ed.*)
Gazet van Antwerpen	120,000	Catholic labor.	Alfred Somville (*Ed.*)
Le Matin (Antwerp)	20,000	Liberal.	Georges Desguin (*Ed.*)
La Métropole (Antwerp)	35,000	Catholic.	M. van der Straten Waillet (*Ed.*)
De Nieuwe Gazet (Antwerp)	25,000	Liberal.	J. Burton (*Ed.*)
Volksgazet (Antwerp)	125,000	Socialist.	Ad. Molter (*Ed.*)
La Meuse (Liège)	200,000	Independent.	F. E. Petit (*Dir.*)
Het Volk (Ghent)	150,000	Catholic labor.	R. Reyntjens (*Ed.*)
Vooruit (Ghent)	55,000	Socialist.	A. de Block (*Pub.*)
Le Journal de Charleroi (Charleroi)	50,000	Socialist independent.	Marius Bufquin des Essarts (*Pub.*)
La Nouvelle Gazette (Charleroi)	85,000	Liberal.	Marcel Evrard (*Pub.*)
Le Rappel (Charleroi)	70,000	Catholic independent.	Jean Valschaerts (*Ed.*)

BOLIVIA

Capital: Sucre (La Paz actual Seat of Government)
Area: 419,470 square miles
Population: 3,235,000 (1956 estimate)

President
HERNÁN SILES ZUAZO (MNR)
Elected June 17, 1956
Assumed office August 6, 1956, for four-year term

PARLIAMENT

UPPER CHAMBER (Senado)	
Election of July 20, 1958 (Six-year term; renewed by thirds every two years)	
President: FEDERICO ALVAREZ PLATA (MNR)	
Parties	Representation
Nationalist Revolutionary Movement (MNR)	18
Total	18

LOWER CHAMBER (Cámara de Representantes)	
Election of July 20, 1958 (Four-year term; renewed by half every two years)	
President: GERMAN QUIROGA GALDO (MNR)	
Parties	Representation
Nationalist Revolutionary Movement (MNR)	65
Socialists (FSB)	3
Total	68

RECENT POLITICAL EVENTS

General elections were held on June 17, 1956, for the first time since May 1951. In these elections, held under a new, MNR-decreed Electoral Law, for the first time in Bolivian history all requirements of literacy and sex were removed. Congressional elections were held on July 20, 1958. Five political parties participated; 478,366 persons voted. The MNR received 391,437 votes; the FSB, 56,950 votes; the *Partido Comunista de Bolivia* (PCB), 6,913 votes; the *Partido Social Cristiano* (PSC), 2,937 votes; and the Trotskyite *Partido Obrero Revolucionario* (POR), 1,994 votes, with remaining ballots either blank or void.

PARTY PROGRAMS AND LEADERS

NATIONALIST REVOLUTIONARY MOVEMENT (MNR): This party, which has held power since it led the successful revolution of April 1952, was founded in 1941. It collaborated with the military régime of Colonel Gualberto Villarroel from 1943 until its overthrow in July 1946. Thereafter it was the principal opposition party to the succeeding coalition PUSR governments and the 1951–52 Military Junta. Its candidates received a plurality of votes in the May 1951 elections, which were subsequently annulled by the Military Junta. It sparked, in April 1952, a mass revolution of urban and rural workers which, with the aid of elements of the National Police Force, defeated the army, overthrew the Military Junta, and established an MNR government headed by Victor Paz Estenssoro. The Party's program consists of nationalization (1952) and government operation of the three principal tin mining companies (Patiño, Hochschild and Aramayo Groups), agrarian reform, educational reform, economic diversification, stimulation of agricultural production, and incorporation of the large Indian population into the political and economic life of the country.

Leaders: Victor Paz Estenssoro, Hernán Siles Zuazo, Federico Alvarez Plata, Walter Guevara Arze.

BOLIVIAN SOCIALIST FALANGE (FSB): Rightist, nationalistic party. In 1958 elections only party to win seats outside of government MNR.

Leaders: Oscar Unzaga de la Vega, General Bernardino Bilbao Rioja, Elías Belmonte Pabón, Jaime Ponce Caballero, Mario R. Gutierrez, Gonzalo Romero Alvarez Garcia.

REVOLUTIONARY WORKERS PARTY (POR): This is a Trotskyist-Communist Party with membership drawn principally from factory and mine workers; one faction affiliated with the Fourth International.

Leaders: Orthodox Group: Hugo Gonzalez Moscoso and Victor Villegas Basoaldo; *Dissident Group:* Guillermo Lora.

COMMUNIST PARTY OF BOLIVIA (PCB): Formally established in the latter part of 1952. Adheres strictly to the Stalinist-Soviet line.

Leaders: Orthodox Group: José Luis Cueto, Alfredo Arratia, Mario Monje. *Dissident Group:* Sergio Almaraz, Ricardo Bonell, José Pereyra.

THE CABINET

The members of the Cabinet are: Victor Andrade, Foreign Affairs and Worship; Walter Guevara Arze, Government, Justice and Immigration; Eufronio Hinojosa, Finance and Statistics; Mario Diez de Medina, National Defense; Germán Monroy Block, Education; Jorge Tamayo Ramos, National Economy, Mines and Petroleum (Acting); Jorge Antelo, Agriculture, Livestock and Colonization; Anibal Aguilar Peñarrieta, Labor and Social Security; Hernando Poppe Martinez, Public Works and Communications; Julio Manuel Aramayo, Public Health; Vicente Alvarez Plata, Rural Affairs; Remy Monroy, Sub-Secretary for Production. Guillermo Bedregal Gutierrez is Secretary General to the President.

PRESS

Unless otherwise noted, papers are all published in La Paz.

Name of Paper	Circulation	Political Affiliation	Proprietor, Editor, etc.
El Diario	18,000	Independent.	José Carrasco (*Prop.*)
La Nación	8,000	Government daily.	Herberto Añez (*Dir.*)
Presencia	10,000	Catholic.	Huáscar Cajias (*Dir.*)
Ultima Hora	12,000	Independent.	Alfredo Alexander (*Dir.*)
La Patria (Oruro)	10,000	Independent.	Enrique Miralles (*Prop.*)
El Pueblo (Cochabamba)	6,000	Government daily.	Saturnino Rodrigo (*Dir.*)
El Pueblo (weekly)	8,000	Communist.	Fernando Siñani (*Prop.* and *Dir.*)
Unidad (weekly)	2,000	Official Communist organ.	Ramiro Otero (*Dir.*)

BRAZIL

Capital: Rio de Janeiro
Area: 3,285,318 square miles
Population: 60,000,000 (1956 estimate)

President
JUSCELINO KUBITSCHEK DE OLIVEIRA
Elected on October 3, 1955; inaugurated on January 31, 1956

Cabinet
Coalition; appointed January 31, 1956

PARLIAMENT
(Congresso Nacional)

SENATE (Senado Federal)		CHAMBER OF DEPUTIES (Camara dos Deputados)	
Two-thirds elected in 1954, one-third on October 3, 1958		*Election of October 3, 1958 (four-year term)*	
Parties	Representation	Parties	Representation
Social Democratic	23	Social Democratic	114
Labor	16	National Democratic Union	74
National Democratic Union	13	Labor	60
Republican	4	Social Progressive	28
Social Progressive	3	Republican	18
Others (3 parties)	4	Others (6 parties)	32
Total	63	Total	326

RECENT POLITICAL EVENTS

In general elections held October 3, 1950, Getulio Vargas, backed chiefly by the Labor and Social Progressive Parties, was elected President over Brigadier Eduardo Gomes of the National Democratic Union and Christiano Machado of the Social Democratic Party. Vargas, who had formerly held the presidency for fifteen years, assumed office on January 31, 1951, for a period of five years. He committed suicide in 1954 and was succeeded by Vice-President Café Filho.

On November 8, 1955, President Café Filho took leave because of ill health and turned the office over to Carlos Luz, Speaker of the Chamber of Deputies, who in turn resigned on November 11 under pressure of the Army. The Vice-President of the Senate, Nereu Ramos, then became Acting President.

Elections were held on October 3, 1955, resulting in the victory of Juscelino Kubitschek who was sworn in as President on January 31, 1956, for a five-year term. João Goulart is the Vice-President.

POLITICAL PARTIES AND LEADERS

There are 11 parties represented in the National Congress. Two of the major parties joined forces to elect President Kubitschek in the 1955 presidential elections and continue to be the mainstay of his support in Congress.

They are the conservative Social Democratic Party, which is the party of the President, and the Brazilian Labor Party, headed up by Vice-President Goulart. The Republican Party also supported the Kubitschek-Goulart slate and is represented in the President's cabinet in the person of the Education Minister. Although the Social Progressive Party supported its leader, Adhemar de Barros, former Governor of São Paulo, for the Presidency, it subsequently joined Kubitschek's congressional majority. The principal opposition party is the National Democratic Union, of which Juracy Magalhães, the National Chairman, Carlos Lacerda (leader in the Chamber of Deputies), Afonso Arinos (leader of the opposition bloc in the Chamber), and Prado Kelly are outstanding leaders. When Ernani do Amaral Peixoto was appointed Ambassador to the U. S. in June 1956, Senator Benedito Valadares assumed chairmanship *ad interim* of the Social Democratic Party.

THE CABINET

The members of the Cabinet in order of precedence are: Carlos Cirilo, Jr. (Justice), Adm. Jorge do Paço Matoso Maia (Navy), Lt. Gen. Henrique Teixeira Lott (War), Francisco Negrão de Lima (Foreign Affairs), Lucas Lopes (Finance), Lucio Meira (Public Works and Communications), Mario Maneghetti (Agriculture), Clovis Salgado (Education and Culture), Fernando Nóbrega (Labor), Brig. Francisco de Assis Correa de Mello (Air), Mario Pinotti (Health).

PRESS

The press has no strict political affiliation.
Unless otherwise noted, papers are published in the capital city.

MORNING DAILIES

Name of Paper	Circulation	Character	Proprietor, Editor, etc.
Brazil Herald	10,000	English language paper.	Joseph S. Brown (*Dir.*)
Correio da Manhã	60,000	Outstanding newspaper; conservative; moderate opposition.	Paulo Bittencourt (*Dir.*)
Diario Carioca	60,000	Pro-Government.	Danton Jobim (*Dir.*)
Diario de Noticias	77,000	Independent; largest morning paper; liberal opposition.	S. A. Diario de Noticias (*Prop.*)
Jornal do Brasil	30,000	Opposition paper.	João Batista McDowell (*Dir.*)
Jornal do Comércio	6,000	Oldest paper in Rio; independent; conservative.	San Thiago Dantas (*Ed.*)
O Dia	100,000	Sensational, read by labor.	Othon Paulino (*Dir.*)
O Jornal	50,000	Leading paper of Chateaubriand chain; commercial news.	Theophilo de Andrade (*Dir.*)

AFTERNOON DAILIES

A Noticia	50,000	Sensational, read by masses.	Chagas Freitas (*Dir.*)
Diario da Noite	90,000	Chateaubriand paper; sensational.	Austregesilo Athayde (*Dir.*)
O Globo	125,000	Independent; progressive.	Roberto Marinho (*Dir.*)
Tribuna da Imprensa	30,000	Independent, crusading, aggressive, liberal; opposition.	Carlos Lacerda (*Dir.*)
Ultima Hora	115,000	Excessively nationalistic, pro-Government.	Paulo da Silveira (*Dir.*)

BRAZIL

PROVINCIAL PAPERS

Name of Paper	Circulation	Character	Proprietor, Editor, etc.
Diario de Noticias (Salvador) (morning)	16,000	Democratic.	Odorico Tavares (*Ed.*)
Estado da Bahia (Salvador)	16,000	Democratic.	Odorico Tavares (*Ed.*)
A Tarde (Salvador) (evening)	8,000	Democratic.	
Estado de Minas (Belo Horizonte)	30,000	Chateaubriand paper.	Oswaldo Chateaubriand (*Dir.*)
Folha de Minas (Belo Horizonte)	20,000	Chateaubriand paper.	Jair Rebelo Horta (*Dir.*)
O Dia (Curitiba)	8,000	Independent.	Dr. Marcial Maciel (*Dir.*)
O Estado (Florianópolis) (evening)	10,000	Long-established.	Rubens A. Ramos (*Dir.*)
Diario de Pernambuco (Recife)	30,000	Oldest paper in North Brazil, devoted to agricultural and commercial interests. Chateaubriand paper.	Fernando Chateaubriand (*Dir.*)
Folha da Manhã (Recife)	15,000	Semi-official.	Dr. P. Germano de Magalhães (*Dir.*) Nilo Pereira (*Ed.*)
Folha do Povo (Recife)	2,000	Communist.	Sindulfo Josué (*Dir.*)
Jornal do Commercio (Recife)	37,000	Conservative.	Francisco Pessôa de Queiroz (*Mg. Dir.*) Esmaragdo Marroquim (*Ed.*)
Correio do Povo (Pôrto Alegre)	60,000	Old paper.	Breno Alcaraz Caldas (*Ed.*)
Diario de Noticias (Pôrto Alegre)	40,000	Chateaubriand paper.	Ernesto Corrêa (*Ed.*)
A Tribuna (Santos)	40,000	Conservative.	M. Nascimento, Jr. (*Dir.*)
Correio Paulistano (São Paulo)	40,000	Republican Party organ.	João de Scantimburgo (*Dir.*)
Diario da Noite (São Paulo) (evening)	80,000	Chateaubriand paper.	Edmundo Monteiro (*Dir.*)
Diario de São Paulo (São Paulo)	85,000	Democratic.	Edmundo Monteiro and Armando de Oliveira (*Dirs.*)
Diario Popular (São Paulo) (evening)	20,000	Long-established.	Dr. Rodrigo Soares, Jr. (*Dir.*)
O Estado de São Paulo (São Paulo)	70,000	Excellent newspaper; conservative; critical of Government.	Julio de Mesquita Filho and Plinio Barreto (*Dirs.*)
Folha da Manhã and Folha da Noite (São Paulo) (morning and evening)	135,000	Independent.	Alcides Ribeiro Meireles (*Dir.*)
A Gazeta (São Paulo) (afternoon)	85,000	Conservative; critical of Government.	Miguel de Arco e Flexa (*Dir.*)

NEWS AGENCIES

Agência Nacional		Official.	Manuel Fernandes (*Dir.*)
Asapress		Independent.	João Baptista Machado (*Prop.*)
Meridional		Chateaubriand papers only.	Francisco Busto (*Dir.*)

BULGARIA

Capital: Sofia
Area: 42,796 sq. mi. (including So. Dobrudja)
Population: 7,629,254 (1956 estimate including So. Dobrudja)

Chief of State
DIMITUR GANEV (Communist), President of the Praesidium of the National Assembly; appointed November 30, 1958, after the death of Georgi Damyanov

Cabinet
Fatherland Front (Communists—16, Agrarians—3, Independent—1)
Appointed January 15, 1958

Premier
ANTON YUGOV (Communist)
Appointed April 17, 1956

NATIONAL ASSEMBLY
President: FERDINAND KOSOVSKY (Communist)
Election of December 22, 1957
Number of members (all of Fatherland Front) . . . 254

RECENT POLITICAL EVENTS

Elections for a constituent Grand National Assembly were held on October 27, 1946, with the opposition Agrarians and Social Democrats contesting the poll. Despite what the Governments of the United States and Great Britain termed intimidation, coercion and fraud in the election itself, the opposition won 101 seats in the Grand National Assembly. These elections were followed by the formation of the first Communist-led government of Bulgaria, backed up by an absolute Communist majority in the Assembly.

On February 10, 1947, Bulgaria was awarded a Peace Treaty in Paris. Pending the entry into force on September 15, 1947, of that treaty, the Sofia régime inaugurated a series of political trials of alleged conspirators among all strata of Bulgarian life, which reached its peak on August 16, 1947—a day on which the death penalty was pronounced over Nikola Petkov. All opposition press was suppressed, the opposition Agrarian Union dissolved, and its 89 representatives in the Assembly deprived of their parliamentary mandate. A week after the coming into force of the Peace Treaty, Nikola Petkov, a founder of the Fatherland Front, a signatory of the Armistice Agreement, and the leader of the Bulgarian opposition, was executed in Sofia. His death marked the end of virtually any effective opposition to the Communist-dominated régime.

On December 4, 1947, the new Constitution drafted on a Soviet model was adopted by the Assembly. In succession, the régime has enacted legislation for complete state ownership or control of industry, banking, foreign and internal trade, and collectivization of agriculture.

On February 2, 1948, the reorganization of the Fatherland Front was achieved. It advanced from the coalition stage of five independent political parties into a sole public-political organization, with program and by-laws compulsory for all participating parties, under secure Communist leadership. As first step to the reduction of the nominal independence of other political groups in the country, the merger was effected of the Social Democrats into the Communist ranks, and an ever-growing stress was laid on the acknowledged leadership and supremacy of the Communist Party. On February 11, 1949, the Zveno National Union and the Radical Party merged with the Fatherland Front. On May 30, 1952, the Communist Premier, Vulko Chervenkov, was elected President of the National Committee of the Fatherland Front and Ferdinand Kosovky was elected Secretary.

Elections for the second National Assembly were held December 20, 1953. The Government presented a single list of candidates. They were all, of course, elected.

Consolidation of Communist Party control has been accompanied by a steady trend toward direct Soviet control. Several high positions in the Bulgarian Government have been given to former Soviet officers of Bulgarian birth, most notably Peter Panchevski, former Minister of Defense; Ivan Kinov, Deputy Minister of Defense; and Ivan Mihailov, Vice-Premier and Minister of Defense. Soviet specialists have been introduced into all aspects of the Bulgarian economy and enjoy preferential treatment from the Bulgarian Government. On October 25, 1950, the special status of Soviet nationals in Bulgaria was publicly acknowledged when the National Assembly passed an act granting to Soviet citizens residing in Bulgaria equal rights in Bulgaria with Bulgarian citizens, including the right to hold any public office.

PARTY PROGRAMS AND LEADERS

COMMUNIST PARTY: Leading party in the Fatherland Front. Composed of a compact, well-organized group of workers, peasants and intellectuals with a high proportion of Soviet-trained specialists in its all-powerful Central Committee. It directs the Government, Praesidium, Assembly, Army, Militia (police), General Workers' Trade Union, Union of People's Youth, National Women's Association, and, in no less degree, every public organization in Bulgaria, political parties included. The Party has a Central Committee of 89 members and 48 candidate members, which holds quarterly meetings to define aims and policy of the Party and the State. Its decisions are unfailingly unanimous, discussion and deliberation being left to the Politburo of 10 members which is the apex of power in the State.

Leaders: The Politburo of the Central Committee of the Communist Party includes: Vulko Chervenkov, Anton Yugov, Raiko Damyanov, Todor Zhivkov, Georgi Tsankov, Encho Staikov, General Ivan Mihailov, Dimitur Ganev, Boris Taskov, Boyan Bulgaranov. There are three Candidate Members: Todor Prahov, Dimitur Dimov, Mladen Stoyanov.

AGRARIAN NATIONAL UNION: Remnants of the dissident Agrarian organization which had been given parity with the Communists in 1945.

Leaders: Georgi Traikov (First Deputy Premier); Stoyan Tonchev (Minister of Communal Economy, Public Works and Roads); Radi Naidenov (Minister of Justice).

No organized semblance remains of the former agrarian or bourgeois opposition. Leaders and party organizations have long since been eliminated from public life.

THE CABINET

Members of the Cabinet are: Anton Yugov, Premier (Communist); Raiko Damyanov, First Deputy Premier (Communist); Georgi Traikov, First Deputy Premier (Agrarian); Vulko Chervenkov, Deputy Premier (Communist); Zhivko Zhivkov, Minister of Education and Culture (Communist); Ivan Mihailov, Deputy Premier and Minister of Defense (Communist); Dancho Dimitrov, Minister of Transportation and Communications (Communist); Ivan Prumov, Minister of Agriculture and Forests (Communist); Stoyan Tonchev, Minister of Communal Economy, Public Works, and Roads (Agrarian); Radenko Videnski, Minister of Construction and Building Material (Communist); Kiril Lazarov, Minister of Finance and State Control (Communist); Karlo Lukanov, Minister of Foreign Affairs (Communist); Tano Tsolov, Minister of Heavy Industry (Communist); Atanas Dimitrov, Minister of Food Industry (Communist); Radi Naidenov, Minister of Justice (Agrarian); Petur Kolarov, Minister of Public Health and Social Welfare (Communist); Boris Taskov, Minister of Trade (Communist); Kimon Georgiev, Minister of Electrification and Water Economy (Independent); Georgi Tsankov, Minister of Interior (Communist); Stanka Tsenkova, Minister of Light Industry (Communist); Rusi Hristozov, Chairman of State Planning Commission (Communist).

PRESS

Unless otherwise noted, papers are published in the capital city.

Name of Paper	Political Affiliation	Proprietor, Editor, etc.
Otechestven Front	Official organ of Fatherland Front.	Ilia Kyulyovski (*Ed.*)
Rabotnichesko Delo	Organ of Communist Party.	Georgi Bokov (*Ed.*)
Zemedelsko Zname	Organ of Agrarian National Union.	Haralampi Traikov (*Ed.*)
Vecherni Novini	Organ of Communist Party, Fatherland Front and Sofia People's Council.	Angel Todorov (*Ed.*)
Narodna Armya	Official Army Organ.	Petur Stanchev (*Ed.*)
Otechestven Glas (Plovdiv)	Fatherland Front organ.	Mihail Mihailov (*Ed.*)
Chernomorsky Front (Burgas)	Fatherland Front organ.	Georgi Tomov (*Ed.*)
Narodno Delo (St. Dimitrov)	Fatherland Front organ.	G. N. Dimitrov (*Ed.*)
Septemvri (Stara Zagora)	Fatherland Front organ.	D. Barov (*Ed.*)
Narodno Delo (Varna)	Fatherland Front organ.	Editorial Committee.
Dunavska Pravda (Rousse)	Organ of Communist Party.	Tz. Tzviatkov (*Ed.*)
Narodna Mladezh	Organ of People's Union.	Editorial Committee.
Novo Vreme (monthly)	Organ of Central Committee of the Communist Party.	Editorial Committee.

NEWS AGENCIES AND PRESS ASSOCIATIONS

Bulgarian Telegraph Agency	Official, in service of Ministry of Foreign Affairs.	Ilia Kyulyovski (*Dir.*)
Administration for Radio and Information	Official, in service of Council of Ministers.	V. Ivanov (*Dir.*)
Association of Bulgarian Journalists	Controlled by Fatherland Front.	Slavcho Vassev (*Pres.*)

BURMA

Capital: Rangoon
Area: 261,789 square miles
Population: 19,856,000 (1957 estimate)

President
U WIN MAUNG
Took office March 13, 1957

Cabinet
Caretaker Government appointed to rule
until elections are held in 1959

Prime Minister
GENERAL NE WIN
Appointed by President on resignation
of U Nu on October 28, 1958

PARLIAMENT

CHAMBER OF NATIONALITIES	CHAMBER OF DEPUTIES
Speaker: SAO SHWE THAIKE	*Speaker:* U TIN
Number of Members 125	Number of Members 250

RECENT POLITICAL EVENTS

Burma's independence from Great Britain became effective on January 4, 1948. A Constituent Assembly was elected April 9, 1947, and the Constitution adopted on September 24, 1947. The orientation of the Government is toward moderate socialism which places emphasis on joint government-private enterprise, exploitation of natural resources, government ownership of transport and utilities, the extension of cooperative enterprises, and land nationalization. Recently greater stress has been put on restoring internal security, and on the role of private capital.

In the general elections of 1956, while the AFPFL retained a preponderant majority in both houses, the opposition National United Front, a coalition of leftist groups, made considerable headway, capturing 49 seats in the 250-member Chamber of Deputies. Thus, for the first time since Burma attained her independence, the AFPFL is faced with significant opposition. Following the general elections, U Nu withdrew from the Premiership and was succeeded by U Ba Swe, Secretary General of the Burma Socialist Party and Vice President of the AFPFL. He resumed office in 1957.

On October 28, 1958, following months of political unrest, General Ne Win, the Commander-in-Chief, was appointed Premier by the President and pledged his Government to uphold the Constitution and democracy, to restore law and order, and to try to hold free elections within six months.

BURMA

THE CABINET

The members of the present Caretaker Cabinet are: U Thein Maung (former Chief Justice of Supreme Court), U Chan Tun Aung (Chief Justice of High Court), U Kar (Lecturer at Rangoon University), U Kyaw Nyein (Chairman of Union Bank), U Khin Maung Phyu (Chief Secretary of Union Government), U San Nyunt (former Election Commissioner), U Chit Thoung (Government Chemical Engineer), U Ba Kyar (retired Session Judge). The portfolios of the Ministers will be announced later.

PRESS

Unless otherwise noted, papers are published in Rangoon.

Name of Paper	Circulation	Political Orientation	Proprietor, Editor, etc.
BURMESE LANGUAGE PAPERS			
Bamakhit	20,000	Strongly anti-Communist.	U On Kin (*Prop. and Ed.*)
Hanthawaddy	18,000	Pro-Western democracy but independent.	U Ba Pe (*Pub.*) U Sein (*Ed.*)
Htoon	5,000	Anti-Government, distrusts West.	U Tun Pe (*Ed.*)
Mandaing	10,000	Pro-AFPFL.	U Hla Kyi (*Ed.*)
Mirror	15,000	Left of Center.	U Thaung (*Ed.*)
Ludu (Mandalay)	7,000	Strongly pro-Communist.	U Hla (*Ed.*)
New Light of Burma	10,000	Conservative; pro-Government.	U Soe Maung (*Ed.*)
The Vanguard	5,000	Pro-Communist.	U Kyi Myint (*Ed.*)
Rangoon Daily	20,000	Nationalistic, critical of West.	U Yu Maung (*Ed.*)
ENGLISH LANGUAGE PAPERS			
Burman	3,000	Independent.	U Ba Chit Tin (*Prop. and Ed.*)
Nation	15,000	Independent; pro-Western democracy; vigorously anti-Communist.	U Law Yone (*Ed.*)
New Times of Burma	5,000	Generally pro-Government.	U Pe Tin (*Ed.*)
CHINESE LANGUAGE PAPERS			
China Commercial Times	4,000	Pro-Communist.	Yu Sou Kyi (*Ed.*)
Freedom Daily News	1,200	Anti-Communist, pro-KMT.	Wu Chi (*Ed.*)
New Rangoon Evening Post	3,000	Pro-Communist.	Lee Pit Sein (*Ed.*)
New China Pao	3,200	Pro-Communist.	Lim Hoe Chee (*Ed.*)
Zin Min Pao	4,000	Chinese Communist Party organ.	Too Pun Poon (*Ed.*)
INDIAN LANGUAGE PAPER			
Rasika Ranjani	3,000	Neutralist.	R. S. Pillay (*Ed.*)

CANADA

Capital: Ottawa
Area: 3,845,774 square miles
Population: 17,048,000 (1958 estimate)

Sovereign
QUEEN ELIZABETH II
Born in 1926; proclaimed Queen February 8, 1952

Governor-General
THE RT. HON. VINCENT MASSEY
Assumed office February 28, 1952

Cabinet
Progressive Conservative
Assumed office June 21, 1957

Prime Minister
JOHN GEORGE DIEFENBAKER (Progressive Conservative)
Assumed office June 21, 1957

PARLIAMENT

UPPER CHAMBER (Senate)
Appointed for life by Governor-General in Council.
Speaker: MARC ROBERT DROUIN (Progressive Conservative)

Parties	Representation
Liberal	74
Progressive Conservative	16
Independent Liberal	1
Independent	2
Vacancies	9
Total	102

LOWER CHAMBER (House of Commons)
Elected March 31, 1958*
Speaker: ROLAND MICHENER (Progressive Conservative)

Parties	Representation
Progressive Conservative	208
Liberal	49
Cooperative Commonwealth Federation	8
Total	265

* In the 1958 general election, the Progressive Conservatives polled 54% of the popular vote, the Liberals 33%, the C.C.F. 10%, Social Credit 2%, and others 1%.
The House of Commons has a maximum life of five years but it may be dissolved at any time on the advice of the Prime Minister.

PARTY PROGRAMS AND LEADERS

Though there are differences at any one time between the political programs of the parties in Canada, there have been few fundamental differences between the actual policies pursued by Liberal and Conservative administrations. Wide diversity of opinion exists within each of these parties, and the legislation sponsored by either of them has been the result of compromise.

The fundamental difference between the parties of Canada and those of Europe grows out of the federal character of the Canadian Constitution. While each party maintains, at least during general elections, a national organization, it depends basically upon organizations in each province which carry on provincial election campaigns, and also assist the national organization at federal elections. Each provincial organization is autonomous and is relatively free to adopt any platform of principles which it chooses, so that between the provincial organizations there is frequently a diversity of emphasis in the selection of paramount issues. The strength within the major parties of different classes and sections of the community differs, and this difference in party composition explains in large measure those differences in party policies which exist at any given moment. The appearance of the Cooperative Commonwealth Federation and the Social Credit parties subjected the traditional two-party system to heavy strains. However, the elimination of the Social Credit party from the Federal scene in the 1958 election, and the substantial reduction of the C.C.F. have greatly altered this situation.

PROGRESSIVE CONSERVATIVE PARTY: The former Conservative Party is now called the Progressive Conservative Party. After twenty-two years in opposition the party showed great strength in the 1957 general election, and consolidated its position in the 1958 landslide. It is the traditional high-tariff party. It negotiated the Ottawa Agreements in 1932 and advocates bargaining tariffs with other countries, notably the United States. In 1935 it approved increased state intervention in national economic life by enacting measures to provide for the cooperative marketing of some farm products, to safeguard investors, and to secure consumers from exploitation. The Party emphasizes to a greater degree than does the Liberal Party Canada's British connections and its membership in the Commonwealth, but in effect its foreign policy does not differ from that of the Liberals.

Leader: John G. Diefenbaker. *Other Leading Members:* Members of the Cabinet; Leslie Frost, Premier of Ontario; Robert Stanfield, Premier of Nova Scotia; Hugh J. Flemming, Premier of New Brunswick; Dufferin Roblin, Premier of Manitoba; Leon Balcer, M.P., President of the Progressive Conservative Association; Allister Grosart, Director of Party Organization.

LIBERAL PARTY: The Liberals were in power for 22 years, from 1935 to 1957. They now form the Liberal opposition. It is traditionally the low-tariff party, and the party which emphasizes Canada's equality of status with other self-governing states of the Commonwealth. It has, however, never made very drastic tariff reductions when in office. While supporting public ownership of railroads, radio broadcasting, etc., its general policy was formerly one of opposition to growing state intervention in the economic life of the country, and the increased powers of the executive which usually accompany such intervention. Since 1935, however, it introduced a fairly comprehensive scheme of social security. Extensive economic controls exercised during World War II were progressively reduced, and allowed to lapse after the end of the Korean War. Formerly the defender of Provincial rights, it has now left this function to the Progressive Conservative Party.

Leader: Lester B. Pearson (former External Affairs Minister). *Other Leading Members:* Paul Martin, M.P. (former Minister of National Health and Welfare), Joseph R. Smallwood (Premier of Newfoundland), Maj. Gen. A. Bruce Matthews (President, National Liberal Federation), H. Erskine Kidd (General Secretary), Paul C. Lafond (Associate General Secretary).

COOPERATIVE COMMONWEALTH FEDERATION: A democratic socialist party, originally organized in August 1932 as a federation of labor, farmer and socialist parties. It advocates the establishment of a planned economy; the public ownership of certain key industries; a broader social security program, including national health insurance and pensions for the incapacitated; a large-scale, subsidized, low-rental housing program; a system of guaranteed forward prices for agricultural production and national marketing legislation to permit orderly marketing of agricultural products in national and international markets; public investment and other measures to increase purchasing power and reduce unemployment; and a national labor code. In international policy the CCF, while supporting military preparedness as a defense against communism, advocates greater emphasis on economic aid and technical assistance to underdeveloped countries. The party reached its peak strength of 28 in 1945. It elected 8 members to the federal house in the 1958 elections.

Leaders: M. J. Coldwell (President of Party), Hazen Argue, M.P., (Leader in the House of Commons). *Other Leading Members:* T. C. Douglas (Premier of Saskatchewan), David Lewis (National Chairman), Stanley Knowles (Vice President of Party), and Mme Therese Casgrain (Vice-President of Party), Carl Hamilton (National Secretary) and Andrew Brewin (National Treasurer).

SOCIAL CREDIT PARTY: Established in Alberta in 1935 and returned to office continuously as the Provincial Government since that date. Has formed the Provincial Government of British Columbia since 1952. Advocates a national economy based on individual enterprise. Rejects idea of world government; emphasizes national sovereignty and cooperation with the United Nations.

The party won no seats in the 1958 general election.

Leader: Solon E. Low (National Leader, recently resigned). *Other Leading Members:* E. C. Manning (Premier of Alberta), W. A. C. Bennett (Premier of British Columbia).

THE CABINET

The members of the Cabinet are: John George Diefenbaker, Prime Minister; Howard Charles Green, Minister of Public Works; Donald Methuen Fleming, Minister of Finance and Receiver General; Alfred Johnson Brooks, Minister of Veterans Affairs; George Hees, Minister of Transport; Leon Balcer, Solicitor General of Canada; George Randolph Pearkes, Minister of National Defense; Gordon Minto Churchill, Minister of Trade and Commerce; Edmund Davie Fulton, Minister of Justice and Attorney General; George Clyde Nowlan, Minister of National Revenue; Douglas Scott Harkness, Minister of Agriculture; Ellen Louks Fairclough Minister of Citizenship and Immigration; J. Angus MacLean, Minister of Fisheries; Michael Starr, Minister of Labour; William McLean Hamilton, Postmaster General; James MacKerras Macdonnell, Minister without Portfolio; William J. Brown, Minister without Portfolio; Paul Comtois, Minister of Mines and Technical Surveys; Jay Waldo Monteith, Minister of National Health and Welfare; Francis Alvin G. Hamilton, Minister of Northern Affairs and National Resources; Sidney Earle Smith, Secretary of State for External Affairs; Raymond Joseph O'Hurley, Minister of Defense Production; Henri Courtemanche, Secretary of State.

CANADA

PRESS

PRINCIPAL DAILY NEWSPAPERS
(*m.* morning; *e.* evening)

Name of Paper	Circulation*	Political Affiliation	Proprietor, Editor, etc.
ALBERTA			
Albertan (*m.*) (Calgary)	35,298	Independent.	Albertan Publishing Co., Ltd. A. M. Raymond (*Ed.*)
Herald (*e.*) (Calgary)	63,889	Independent.	The Southam Co., Ltd. R. L. Sanburn (*Ed.*)
Journal (*e.*) (Edmonton)	99,916	Independent.	The Southam Co., Ltd. Fraser M. Gerrie (*Ed.*)
Herald (*e.*) (Lethbridge)	16,330	Independent-Liberal.	Lethbridge Herald Co., Ltd. (*Pub.*) Don H. Pelling (*Mg. Ed.*)
BRITISH COLUMBIA			
Province (*m.*) (Vancouver)	131,811	Independent.	The Southam Co., Ltd. Ross Munro (*Ed.*)
Sun (*e.*) (Vancouver)	191,031	Independent-Liberal.	Sun Publishing Co., Ltd. Jack Scott (*Ed. Dir.*)
Colonist (*m.*) (Victoria)	29,080	Independent.	Victoria Press Ltd. Stuart Keate (*Pub.*)
Times (*e.*) (Victoria)	23,213	Liberal.	Victoria Press Ltd. Seth R. Halton (*Pub.*)
MANITOBA			
Free Press (*e.*) (Winnipeg)	115,376	Independent-Liberal.	Winnipeg Free Press Co. Ltd. Thomas Kent (*Ed.*)
Tribune (*e.*) (Winnipeg)	71,714	Independent.	The Southam Co. Ltd. Eric Wells (*Mg. Ed.*)
NEW BRUNSWICK			
Telegraph-Journal (*m.*)	24,989	Independent.	{ New Brunswick Pub. Co. Ltd.
Times-Globe (*e.*) (Saint John)	20,045	Independent.	T. F. Drummie (*Pres.*) Stuart Trueman (*Ed.*)
NEWFOUNDLAND			
News (*m.*) (St. John's)	9,198	Independent-Liberal.	J. S. Currie (*Ed.*)
Telegram (*e.*) (St. John's)	19,264	Independent.	Evening Telegram Ltd. S. R. Herder (*Mg. Ed.*)
NOVA SCOTIA			
Chronicle-Herald (*m.*) (Halifax)	63,379	Independent.	{ The Halifax Herald Ltd. (*Pub.*)
Mail-Star (*e.*) (Halifax)	41,149	Independent.	Eric R. Dennis (*Ed.*)
Cape Breton Post (*e.*) (Sydney)	26,695	Independent.	Post Pub. Co. Ltd. (*Pub.*) Roy D. Duchemin (*Mg. Ed.*)
ONTARIO			
Expositor (*e.*) (Brantford)	20,963	Independent.	Preston & Sons Ltd. (*Pub.*) P. M. Preston (*Mg. Ed.*)
Spectator (*e.*) (Hamilton)	98,040	Independent.	The Southam Co., Ltd. J. G. O'Neil (*Ed.*)
Whig-Standard (*e.*) (Kingston)	20,524	Independent-Liberal.	The Kingston Whig-Standard Co. Ltd. Arnold Edinborough (*Ed.*)
Record (*e.*) (Kitchener-Waterloo)	33,099	Independent.	The News Record Ltd. John E. Motz (*Ed. and Pub.*)

CANADA

Name of Paper	Circulation*	Political Affiliation	Proprietor, Editor, etc.
Free Press (m. and e.) (London)	98,782	Independent.	London Free Press Ptg. Co. Ltd. (Pub.) A. R. Ford (Ed.)
Citizen (e.) (Ottawa)	60,029	Independent.	The Southam Co. Ltd. M. D. Yarrow (Mg. Ed.)
Journal (e.) (Ottawa)	61,741	Independent-Conservative.	Journal Pub. Co. Ltd. Grattan O'Leary (Pres.)
Le Droit (e.) (Ottawa)	28,726	Independent; in French.	Syndicat d'Oeuvres Sociales Ltée. Camille L'Heureux (Ed.)
Examiner (e.) (Peterboro)	19,622	Independent.	Peterborough Examiner Co. Ltd. Robertson Davies (Ed.)
Standard (e.) (St. Catharines)	25,261	Independent.	The St. Catharines Standard Ltd. F. H. Whitelock (Ed.)
Times-Journal (e.) (St. Thomas)	10,691	Independent.	Times-Journal of St. Thomas Ltd. T. Keith (Ed.)
Globe and Mail (m.) (Toronto)	251,105	Independent.	The Globe and Mail Ltd. Oakley Dalgliesh (Ed. and Pub.)
Star (e.) (Toronto)	378,524	Independent-Liberal.	Toronto Star Ltd. Beland Honderich (Ed.)
Telegram (e.) (Toronto)	250,157	Independent-Conservative.	Telegram Publishing Co. Ltd. B. T. Richardson (Ed.)
Star (e.) (Windsor)	76,652	Independent.	Hawthorne Publishing Co. Ltd. W. L. Clark (Ed.)

PRINCE EDWARD ISLAND

Name of Paper	Circulation*	Political Affiliation	Proprietor, Editor, etc.
Guardian (m.) (Charlottetown)	14,644	Independent.	Thomson Newspapers. Frank Walker (Ed.)
Patriot (e.) (Charlottetown)	5,190	Liberal.	Thomson Newspapers. J. E. Burnett (Mg. Ed.)

QUEBEC

Name of Paper	Circulation*	Political Affiliation	Proprietor, Editor, etc.
Gazette (m.) (Montreal)	104,178	Independent-Conservative.	Gazette Printing Co. Ltd. E. A. Collard (Ed.)
La Presse (e.) (Montreal)	219,354	Independent; in French.	La Cie. de Publication de la Presse, Ltée. Eugene Lamarche (Mg. Ed.)
Star (e.) (Montreal)	163,686	Independent.	Montreal Star Co. Ltd. George V. Ferguson (Ed.)
l'Action Catholique (e.) (Quebec)	61,498	Independent; in French.	L'Action Sociale, Ltée. L. P. Roy (Ed.)
L'Évènement-Journal (m.)	11,323	Liberal; in French.	Alfred Renaud (Mg. Ed.)
Le Soleil (e.) (Quebec)	112,889	Liberal; in French.	Le Soleil, Ltée. Raymond Dube (Ed.)
La Tribune (e.) (Sherbrooke)	28,894	Independent; in French.	La Tribune, Ltée. Pierre Paul Blais (Ed.)
Le Nouvelliste (e.) (Three Rivers)	30,468	Independent; in French.	Nouvelliste Pub. Co., Ltd. Hervé Biron (Ed.)

SASKATCHEWAN

Name of Paper	Circulation*	Political Affiliation	Proprietor, Editor, etc.
Leader-Post (e.) (Regina)	47,211	Independent-Liberal.	The Leader-Post Ltd. D. B. Rogers (Ed.)
Star-Phoenix (e.) (Saskatoon)	36,527	Liberal.	The Saskatoon Star-Phoenix Ltd. E. Knowles (Ed.)

* Circulation is taken from *Editor & Publisher, International Yearbook, 1958.*

CANADA

PRESS ASSOCIATIONS

Name of Paper	Political Affiliation	Proprietor, Editor, etc.
The Canadian Press (Toronto, Ontario)	Mutual and cooperative association of daily newspapers; exchange arrangements with Associated Press; also receives news direct from Reuter's.	Charles Peters (*Pres.*) Gillis Purcell (*Gen. Mgr.*)
British United Press International (Montreal, Quebec)	A subsidiary of United Press International.	Philip Curran (*Canadian Manager*)

PERIODICALS

(*w.* weekly; *m.* monthly; *q.* quarterly)

Name of Journal	Character	Proprietor, Editor, etc.
Canadian Banker (*q.*) (Toronto)	Journal of Canadian Bankers' Association.	C. S. Howard (*Mg. Ed.*)
Canadian Home Journal (*m.*) (Toronto)	Articles and short stories.	Mary-Etta Macpherson (*Ed.*)
Canadian Bar Review (*m.*) (Ottawa)	Journal of Canadian Bar Association.	G. V. V. Nicholls (*Ed.*)
Canadian Business (*m.*) (Montreal)	Magazine of Canadian Chamber of Commerce.	Howard Gamble (*Ed.*)
Canadian Forum (*m.*) (Toronto)	Political, literary, and economic.	P. S. Giffen and S. Stykilt (*Mg. Eds.*)
Canadian Geographical Journal (*m.*) (Ottawa)	Journal of the Canadian Geographical Society.	G. M. Dallyn (*Ed.*)
Canadian Historical Review (*q.*) (Toronto)	Historical.	University of Toronto Press (*Pub.*) John T. Saywell (*Ed.*)
Canadian Journal of Economics and Political Science (*q.*) (Toronto)	Journal of Canadian Economic and Political Science Association.	J. H. Dales (*Mg. Ed.*)
Country Guide (*m.*) (Winnipeg)	Farmer's journal.	Country Guide Ltd. (*Pub.*) H. S. Frey and P. M. Abel (*Eds.*)
Culture (Quebec)	Political, literary, economic, and religious, in French and English.	L'Association de Recherches sur les Sciences Religieuses et Profanes au Canada (*Pubs.*)
Dalhousie Review (*q.*) (Halifax) (Dalhousie University)	Political, literary, and economic.	W. Graham Allen (*Ed.*)
External Affairs (*m.*) (Ottawa)	Canada's external relations; in English and French.	Department of External Affairs (*Pub.*)
Family Herald and Weekly Star (*w.*)	Farm paper.	Montreal Star Co., Ltd. (*Pub.*)
Financial Post (*w.*) (Toronto)	Financial and economic.	R. A. McEachern (*Ed.*)
Financial Times (*w.*) (Montreal)	Financial and economic.	E. C. Ertl (*Pres.*) A. R. W. Young (*Ed.*)
Free Press Prairie Farmer (*w.*) (Winnipeg)	Liberal; farm journal.	Winnipeg Free Press Co. Ltd. (*Pub.*) J. A. M. Cook (*Ed.*)
Industrial Canada (*m.*) (Toronto)	Organ of Canadian Manufacturer's Association.	A. L. Abbott (*Ed.*)
International Journal (*q.*) (Toronto)	Journal of Canadian Institute of International Affairs.	H. I. Nelson (*Ed.*)
Actualité Economique (*q.*) (Montreal)	Organ of L'École des Hautes Études Commerciales; in French.	
Labour Gazette (*m.*) (Ottawa)	Labor.	Department of Labor (*Pub.*) H. J. Walker (*Ed.*)

CANADA

Name of Journal	Character	Proprietor, Editor, etc.
Le Canada Français (Quebec)	Political, literary and economic; in French.	L'Université Laval (*Prop.*) L'Abbé Aimé Labrie (*Dir.*)
Le Samedi (*w.*) (Montreal)	Stories and articles; in French.	Jean Chauvin (*Ed.*)
Monetary Times (*m.*) (Toronto)	Financial and economic.	S. C. Wilson (*Ed.*)
Maclean's Magazine (*semi-m.*) (Toronto)	Articles and short stories.	Ralph Allen (*Ed.*)
New Liberty (*m.*) (Toronto)	Articles and stories.	Keith Knowlton (*Ed.*)
Northern Miner (*w.*) (Toronto)	Mining.	John W. Carrington (*Ed.*)
Queen's Quarterly (*q.*) (Kingston)	Political, literary and economic.	Queen's University (*Prop.*) J. E. Hodgetts (*Ed.*)
Relations (*m.*) (Montreal)	Organ of L'École Sociale Populaire; social and political; in French.	Albert Plante (*Dir.*)
Revue de l'Université d'Ottawa (*q.*) (Ottawa)	Literary, philosophical, historical and theological; in French.	Rodrigue Normandin (*Ed.*)
Revue Moderne (*m.*) (Montreal)	Articles and stories; in French.	Leo Cadieux (*Ed.*)
Revue Populaire (*m.*) (Montreal)	Articles and stories; in French.	Jean Chauvin (*Ed.*)
Revue Trimestrielle Canadienne (*q.*) (Montreal)	Political, literary, historical, scientific and economic; in French.	Association des Anciens Élèves, École Polytechnique (*Prop.*) Edouard Montpetit (*Ed.*)
Saturday Night (*w.*) (Toronto)	Political, literary and economic.	Consolidated Press (*Prop.*) Arnold Edinborough (*Ed.*)
University of Toronto Quarterly (*q.*)	Political, literary and economic.	Douglas Grant (*Ed.*)
University of Toronto Law Journal (*annual*)	Legal.	W. P. M. Kennedy (*Ed.*)
Western Producer (*w.*) (Saskatoon)	Farmer's Cooperative.	A. P. Waldron (*Ed.*)

CEYLON

Capital: Colombo
Area: 25,332 square miles
Population: 9,300,000 (1957 estimate)

Sovereign
QUEEN ELIZABETH II

Governor General
SIR OLIVER GOONETILLEKE
Appointed in 1954

Prime Minister
S. W. R. D. BANDARANAIKE
Assumed office April 12, 1956

PARLIAMENT
(Legislature)

UPPER CHAMBER (Senate)	LOWER CHAMBER (House of Representatives)
President: SIR CYRIL DE ZOYSA	Speaker: H. S. ISMAIL
Number of members* 30	Number of members 100

* Five appointed by Governor General, five elected by the House every two years, for six-year terms.

THE CABINET

The members of the Cabinet are: S. W. R. D. Bandaranaike (Prime Minister, Defense and External Affairs), C. P. de Silva (Lands and Land Development), M. W. H. de Silva (Justice), P. H. W. de Silva (Industries and Fisheries), Stanley de Zoysa (Finance), Philip Gunawardena (Agriculture and Food), T. B. Ilangaratne (Labor, Housing and Social Services), A. P. Jayasuriya (Home Affairs), Jayaweera Kuruppu (Local Government and Cultural Affairs), C. A. S. Marikkar (Posts, Broadcasting and Information), Maithripala Senanayake (Transport and Works), Richard Senanayake (Commerce and Trade), Mrs. Wimala Wijewardene (Health), Sarath Wijesinghe (Nationalized Services and Road Transport).

PRESS
All papers are published in Colombo.

Name of Paper	Circulation	Political Affiliation	Editor
Times of Ceylon	21,000	Independent.	Tori de Souza
Lankadipa	56,000	Independent.	D. B. Dhanapala
Ceylon Observer	22,000	Independent.	Tarzie Vitachi
Ceylon Daily News	46,000	Independent.	Cecil D. Graham
Janata	33,889	Independent.	Denzil Pieris
Silumina (Sunday)	142,614	Independent.	Denzil Pieris
Dinamina	74,000	Independent.	P. Nissanka
Virakesari	20,000	Independent, in Tamil.	K. P. Haran

CHILE

Capital: Santiago
Area: 296,717 square miles
Population: 7,211,000 (1958 estimate)

President
JORGE ALESSANDRI RODRIGUEZ
Assumed office November 3, 1958, for six-year term

Cabinet
Non-Party
Appointed November 3, 1958

PARLIAMENT
(Congreso Nacional)

UPPER CHAMBER
(Senado)
Election of March 3, 1957 (Eight-year term; renewed by halves every four years)
President: HERNÁN VIDELA LIRA
(Liberal)

Parties	Representation
Liberal	9
Radical	9
Socialist	9
National Popular	7
United Conservative	6
Christian Democrat	2
Independent	1
Republican Movement	1
Vacant	1
Total	45

LOWER CHAMBER
(Cámara de Diputados)
Election of March 3, 1957 (Four-year term)
President: RAÚL JULIET GÓMEZ
(Radical)

Parties	Representation
Radical	37
Liberal	30
United Conservative	22
National Popular	15
Christian Democrat	14
Socialist	9
Democrat	5
Communist	5
Others	10
Total	147

RECENT POLITICAL EVENTS

In a five-way presidential race, rightist candidate, Jorge Alessandri (supported by the Liberal and the United Conservative parties along with certain independent elements) emerged as victor on September 4, 1958, having received approximately one-third of the total votes cast. Almost another third of the votes were cast for the left-wing candidate, Salvador Allende, who was supported by the Socialists, Communists and other leftist groups. Congress, following tradition in Chile, selected Alessandri for President since he received the largest number of popular votes. The 1958 presidential elections were the first held under the newly passed election law which requires the names of candidates to appear on a single ballot.

The new election law, which makes it more difficult for small political groups to win elections, had its effects during 1958 as the Agrarian Laborite and National Parties combined to form the National Popular Party.

The Center-Right coalition in Congress, which was effective during the early part of 1958, was replaced in April by a Center-Leftist combination of all parties other than the Liberal and the Conservatives. This coalition repealed the "Law for the Permanent Defense of Democracy," and as a result the Communist Party became legal, after ten years of illegality.

Alessandri formed his first Cabinet on a technical non-party basis even though his major support during the campaign came from the Liberal and Conservative Parties.

PARTY PROGRAMS AND LEADERS

RADICAL PARTY: Although the largest single party in Chile, its candidate, Luis Bossay, came in fourth in the 1958 presidential election. Following the election, the left-wing of the party was overthrown, and the party's right-wing took the ascendancy. Nevertheless, the Radicals can still be characterized as a left-of-center party with certain doctrinaire radicalism in respect to religion and social questions.

Leaders: Senator Humberto Aguirre Doolan, President; Carlos Martinez Sotomayor, Vice President; Deputy Raúl Morales Adriazola, Secretary General; Jaime Tormo Rodriguez, Treasurer. Senator Luis Bossay (1958 Presidential Candidate), Juan Mauras (former President of Chamber of Deputies), Senator Julio Duran, Alberto Baltra (former President of Party), Senator Angel Faivovich, Gabriel Gonzalez Videla (former President of Chile), Deputy Raúl Juliet, Deputy Humberto Enriquez, Pedro Enrique Alfonso.

LIBERAL PARTY: An element of the rightist segment of Chilean politics, the Liberal Party has traditionally included a number of experienced businessmen and landholders, although its general program has been somewhat more "progressive" than the United Conservative Party. Although a large element of the liberal membership had at one point favored the candidacy of Christian Democratic Senator Eduardo Frei, the Party determined to support Senator Jorge Alessandri in his successful bid for the Presidency in 1958.

Leaders: Senator Hugo Zepeda Barrios, President; Ruperto Murillo Gaete, Director General; Deputy Sergio Sepulveda, Vice President; Victor Braun, Vice President; Osvaldo Garcia Burr, Secretary General. Senator Fernando Alessandri, Senator Gregorio Amunategui, Deputy Jorge Errazuriz.

UNITED CONSERVATIVE PARTY: This party is composed primarily of strict adherents of the Catholic Church from all economic classes, although historically it has been led by men of social distinction and wealth and representatives of the old land-owning aristocracy.

Leaders: Jorge Prieto Letelier, President; Senator Francisco Bulnes Sanfuentes, First Vice President; Ismael Pereira, Second Vice President. Deputy Hector Correa, Deputy Luis Valdes, Senator Juan Antonio Coloma, Deputy Raúl Yrrarazaval.

NATIONAL POPULAR PARTY: This new political grouping, essentially a center party, was formed at the end of 1958 by the amalgamation of the former Agrarian Laborite and National Parties. The Agrarian Laborite Party, which originally was formed from various rightist groups including pro-German elements during World War II, has been closely identified with ex-President Ibañez, and was his major support when elected in 1952. The National Party originally stemmed from land-owning elements in the southern portion of Chile. This new party is now fourth largest in representation in Congress.

Leaders: Senator Julian Echavarri, President; Orlando Latorre, First Vice President; Sergio Onofre Jarpa, Second Vice President; Deputy Mario Hamuy, Secretary General. Deputy Julio von Muhlenbrock, Jaime Sanfuentes, Senator Guillermo Perez de Arce.

CHRISTIAN DEMOCRATIC PARTY: A new group constituted in 1957 by the union of the former National Falange and the Social Christian Conservatives. The Christian Democratic Party was created by adherents to the presidential aspirations of Senator Eduardo Frei. Members of the party are primarily from groups with a close affiliation with the Catholic Church, and the party has attempted to associate itself with the social reform programs commonly attributed to Christian Democratic Parties in Europe. In spite of its church connections, the party associated itself with the Communists in a majority bloc formed in 1958 in Congress.

Leaders: Patricio Aylwin, President; Pablo Larraín, First Vice President; Eugenio Ballesteros, Second Vice President; Sergio Jerez, Secretary General. Radomiro Tomic; Deputy José Musalem; Jorge Rogers, Senator Eduardo Frei, 1958 Presidential candidate; Deputy Rafael Agustin Gumucio, ex-President of Party; Bernardo Leighton.

UNITED SOCIALIST PARTY: Formed in 1957 through a union of the former Popular Socialist Party and the Socialist Party, this combined group is a member of the left-wing Popular Action Front (FRAP) coalition. Essentially a Marxist group, the United Socialists cooperated with the Communists to support the candidacy of FRAP Presidential candidate Salvador Allende. Since the election in 1958, the Socialists have shown indications of preferring to go it alone without alliances with other parties, including the Communists.

Leaders: Salomon Corbalan Gonzalez, Secretary General; Senator Salvador Allende, 1958 FRAP Presidential candidate; Aniceto Rodriguez, ex-head of Popular Socialists; Senator Raúl Ampuero; Federico Klein.

COMMUNIST PARTY: With the removal from the books of the Law for the Permanent Defense of Democracy, the Communists became a legal Party, and took an active part in the 1958 Presidential election. The Communists have a strong influence on the Popular Action Front (FRAP) and the principal labor federation in Chile (CUTCH). The Party supports traditional Communist objectives with particular emphasis on closer relationships between Chile and Communist China and Russia.

Leaders: Elias Lafferte Gaviño, President; Luis Corvalan, Secretary General.

DEMOCRATIC PARTY: Another member of the left-wing Popular Action Front (FRAP). Individual groups within the Party, however, announced support of each of the four major presidential candidates during the 1958 elections.

Leaders: Alejandro Serani Burgos, President; Deputy Humberto Martones Morales; Luis Minchel.

MINOR PARTIES: In addition to the ones listed above, Chile has a number of smaller parties, with marginal influence in the affairs of the country. These include the Republican Movement, the Labor Party, the People's Party, the Radical Doctrinaire Party, and the Democratic Doctrinaire Party. A total of seventeen parties officially took part in the 1957 Congressional election, of which twelve succeeded in electing one or more Congressmen.

THE CABINET

The members of the Cabinet are: Enrique Ortúzar (Interior and Secretary General of the Government), Germán Vergara (Foreign Affairs), Roberto Vergara (Finance, Economic Affairs and Mines), Francisco Cereceda (Education), Julio Philip (Justice and Lands), Carlos Vial Infante (Defense), Pablo Perez (Public Works), Jorge Saelzer (Agriculture), Eduardo Gomian (Labor and Health).

PRESS

Unless otherwise noted, papers are published in the capital city.

Name of Paper	Circulation	Character	Proprietor, Editor, etc.
El Diario Ilustrado	35,000	Conservative and Church.	Luis Silva (*Dir.*)
Tercera de la Hora	55,000	Radical.	Guillermo E. Feliu (*Ed.*)
El Mercurio (Santiago and Valparaiso)	70,000	Liberal; independent; large circulation; founded at Valparaiso in 1827.	Estate of Agustín Edwards (*Prop.*) Rafael Maluenda (*Ed.*)
La Nación	45,000	Government organ.	Raúl Ferrada (*Ed.*)
El Debate (evening)	10,000	Rightist views.	Anibal Correa (*Ed.*)
El Siglo	10,000	Communist daily.	Roberto Landaeta (*Ed.*)
Clarín	40,000	Non-partisan.	Daniel del Solar (*Ed.*)
La Segunda (afternoon)	18,000	Tabloid owned by El Mercurio.	Byron Gigoux (*Dir.*)
La Noticias de Ultima Hora (evening)	20,000	Left, independent.	Luis L. Rodriguez (*Ed.*)
Las Ultimas Noticias (evening)	25,000	Tabloid owned by El Mercurio.	Estate of Agustín Edwards (*Prop.*) Byron Gigoux (*Dir.*)
Ercilla (weekly)	50,000	Pictorial news magazine.	J. Lanzarotti (*Dir.*)
Topaze (weekly)	30,000	Satirical; independent.	René Olivares (*Dir.*)
Zig Zag (weekly)	20,000	Pictorial news magazine.	Raúl Aldunate (*Ed.*)
South Pacific Mail (weekly)	7,000	Independent; printed in English.	Kevin Bannon (*Dir.*)
Vistazo (weekly)	10,000	Communist; pictorial news review.	Edeciro Alvarado (*Ed.*)
El Mercurio (Antofagasta)	25,000	Formerly connected with El Mercurio of Santiago and Valparaiso; independent.	Sociedad Chilena de Publicaciones (*Prop.*) Luis Fernando Navas (*Ed.*)
Vea (weekly)	125,000	Pictorial news magazine.	Genaro Medina (*Dir.*)
La Discusión (Chillán)	6,000	Independent; second oldest paper in Chile.	Estate of Alfonso Lagos Villar (*Prop.*)
La Patria (Concepción)	30,000	Catholic rightist.	Sociedad Periodistica del Sur (*Pub.*) Alfredo Pacheco (*Dir.*)
El Sur (Concepción)	35,000	Radical, independent.	Aurelio Lamas (*Prop.*) Armando Lascano (*Ed.*)
El Tarapacá (Iquique)	5,000	Rightist liberal.	Manuel Fernandez Rios (*Ed.*)
La Prensa (Osorno)	10,000	Independent, rightist.	Roberto Luna (*Ed.*)
La Prensa Austral (Punta Arenas)	8,000	Independent.	Carlos Aracena (*Ed.*)
La Mañana (Talca)	3,000	Rightist liberal.	Vicente Ignacio Rojas (*Prop. and Dir.*)
El Diario Austral (Temuco)	8,000	Independent.	Raúl Gallardo (*Dir.*)
El Correo de Valdivia (Valdivia)	6,000	Rightist tendency.	Luis Alfaro (*Ed.*)
La Estrella (evening) (Valparaiso)	15,000	Evening tabloid of El Mercurio.	Francisco Le Dantec (*Dir.*)
El Mercurio (Valparaiso)	25,000	Independent.	Francisco Le Dantec (*Dir.*)
La Unión (Valparaiso)	28,000	Conservative Catholic.	Alfredo Silva (*Prop. and Dir.*)

CHINA

Capital: Nanking
Temporary Capital: Taipei, Taiwan (Formosa)
Area: 4,278,352 square miles (Chinese Post Office estimate)
Mainland population: 602,320,000 (1955 Communist estimate)
Taiwan population: 9,870,000 (1956 census)

GOVERNMENT OF THE REPUBLIC OF CHINA*

President
GENERALISSIMO CHIANG KAI-SHEK
Re-elected March 22, 1954, for six-year term

Vice-President
CH'EN CH'ENG

Premier (President of Executive Yüan)
CH'EN CH'ENG
Appointed by the President with the consent of the
Legislative Yüan on July 4, 1958

NATIONAL ASSEMBLY

The National Assembly met in Nanking on March 28, 1948, and elected the President and Vice-President of the Republic. The Assembly also amended the Constitution to give the President of the Republic wide powers of government by decree for the duration of the Civil War. The Assembly then adjourned. It reconvened in Taipei on February 19, 1954, elected the President and Vice-President and extended the President's emergency powers. Of the 3,045 members of the Assembly, 1,578 attended the session.

The Government is composed of five Yüan and the office of the President, to which are attached such organs as: National Defense Council (Secretary-General, Chang Ch'un), Mainland Recovery Planning Committee (Chairman, Ch'en Ch'eng), and Military Strategy Advisory Committee (Chairman, Ho Ying-ch'in).

FIVE YÜAN (BRANCHES) OF THE GOVERNMENT
EXECUTIVE YÜAN
President: Ch'en Ch'eng (appointed by the President with the consent of the Legislative Yüan)

---

* The National Government of the Republic derived its original mandate from the Organic Law promulgated at Nanking on October 8, 1928, by the authority of the Kuomintang. It is by virtue of this basic law that the National Government functioned during the "period of tutelage" of the Chinese people. A draft Constitution was published on May 5, 1936.

A National Assembly was convened on November 15, 1946, to establish a Constitutional régime. The Communists refused to participate in the Assembly. A new Constitution was adopted on December 23, 1946, and was promulgated by President Chiang Kai-shek on New Year's Day, 1947, and put into effect on December 25, 1947. Elections for a National Assembly were held in November, 1947. The National Assembly was inaugurated on March 28, 1948, amended the Constitution and elected the President and Vice-President of the Republic.

Vice-President: Wang Yun-wu

Members of the Executive Yüan Council:
  Tien Chun-chin (concurrently Minister of Interior)
  S. K. Huang (concurrently Minister of Foreign Affairs)
  Yu Ta-wei (concurrently Minister of National Defense)
  C. K. Yen (concurrently Minister of Finance)
  Y. C. Mei (concurrently Minister of Education)
  Ku Feng-hsiang (concurrently Minister of Justice)
  Yuan Shou-ch'ien (concurrently Minister of Communications)
  Yang Chi-tseng (concurrently Minister of Economic Affairs)
  Li Yung-hsin (concurrently Chairman of the Mongolian and Tibetan Affairs Commission)
  C. M. Chen (concurrently Chairman, Commission on Overseas Chinese Affairs)
  Ch'en Ch'ing-yu (Comptroller General)
  Sampson C. Shen (Director of Government Information)

Ministers Without Portfolio:
  Wang Shih-chieh
  Ts'ai P'ei-huo
  Hsueh Yueh
  Yu Ching-t'ang
  Chiang Ching-kuo

Legislative Yüan

President: Chang Tao-fan
Vice-President: Huang Kuo-shu
(Elected by members of the Legislative Yüan from among themselves)

The Legislative Yüan, the highest law-making body, is composed of 773 members elected by the people on a regional and occupational basis. There are now 12 committees in the Yüan, namely: domestic affairs, foreign affairs, national defense, finance, budget, economic affairs, education, communications, frontier affairs, overseas Chinese affairs, civil, criminal, and commercial law, and law codification; about 500 members of the Yüan are in Taiwan. The term of office of the Yüan has been extended indefinitely during present emergency.

Judicial Yüan

President: Hsieh Kuan-sheng
Vice-President: Fu Ping-chang
(Both appointed by the President with the consent of the Control Yüan)

There are 17 Grand Justices in the Judicial Yüan, appointed by the President with consent of the Control Yüan. In addition to the two already in Taiwan, seven new Grand Justices were appointed on March 19, 1952, thus making the necessary quorum. The appointment of 15 Grand Justices was made by the President on September 16, 1958.

Under the Judicial Yüan are the Supreme Court (President, Hsieh Ying-chou), the Administrative Court (President, Ma Shou-hua), and the Committee on the Discipline of Public Functionaries (President, Fu Ping-chang).

CHINA

EXAMINATION YÜAN

President: Mo Te-hui
Vice-President: Cheng Tien-fong
(Appointed by the President with the consent of the Control Yüan)

There are 19 members of the Examination Yüan, appointed by the President with the consent of the Control Yüan.

Under the Examination Yüan are the Ministry of Personnel (Minister, Lei Fa-chang) and the Ministry of Examination (Minister, Huang Chi-lu).

CONTROL YÜAN

President: Yu Yu-jen
Vice-President: Li Szu-ts'ung
(Both elected by members of the Control Yüan from among themselves)

The Control Yüan, the highest supervisory body, is composed of 223 members, elected by the provincial, municipal, Mongolian, Tibetan councils and overseas Chinese communities. About 155 of the members actually elected are now in Taiwan. There are 10 committees in the Control Yüan. Under the Yüan is the Ministry of Audit (Minister of Audit, Tsai Ping-fan).

PARTY PROGRAMS AND LEADERS

THE KUOMINTANG OR NATIONALIST PARTY: Advocates program supporting the late Dr. Sun Yat-sen's Three People's Principles (Principles of Nationalism, People's Rights and People's Livelihood).

The party underwent a drastic reorganization on July 22, 1950 when Generalissimo Chiang Kai-shek (Tsung-Ts'ai or Director-General) ordered the formation of a "Central Reform Committee" to replace the Central Executive Committee of the Kuomintang as its highest organ of political direction. On October 10, 1952, a new Central Committee was named by the 7th National Kuomintang Congress.

At the 7th National Congress of the Party on October 10–12, 1952, Generalissimo Chiang Kai-shek was elected Director General, together with 48 consultative members, 23 Central Committee members, and 16 alternates. The Congress also issued a new political platform which contained the following policies: to fight against Russian aggression and Chinese Communists and restore territorial integrity of China; to unite with all anti-Communist forces at home and abroad to form a united front against communism and Soviet imperialism; to practice democracy; to uphold the U. N. Charter and world peace; to strengthen relations with anti-Communist and non-Communist countries in the Pacific; to prepare for a military counter-offensive against the mainland; to strive for economic rehabilitation, and make good use of foreign aid; and to proceed with land reform.

The 8th National Congress of the Kuomintang was held on October 10–24, 1957. Chiang Kai-shek was re-elected Director General of the Party, and Vice-President Ch'en Ch'eng was selected as Deputy Director General. The Central Committee was expanded from 32 to 50 members, and alternates were increased from 16 to 25. It elected a Standing Committee as follows: O. K. Yui, Chou Chih-jou, Chiang Ching-kuo, Ku Cheng-kang, Chang Chi-yun, Chang Tao-fan, Tao Hsi-sheng, Huang Shao-ku, Ma Chi-chuang, Chen Hsueh-ping, Yuan Shou-chien, Shen Chang-huan, Ku Feng-hsiang, Hu Chien-chung, Chiu Nien-tai.

OTHER PARTIES: The only two parties besides the Kuomintang now represented in the Government (National Assembly, Legislative Yüan, Control Yüan, Executive Yüan and other branches of the Government)are the Young China Party (Leaders: Li Huang and Tso Shun-sheng) and the Democratic Socialist Party which has split into several factions (Leaders: Chien I-chao and Shih Chih-chuan).

Other Chinese parties include the Communist Party (Leader, Mao Tse-tung) which has carried on an armed rebellion against the Government and has now gained control of the mainland of China; and the China Democratic League which was outlawed by the Government in the latter part of 1947 for collusion with the Communists, and is now collaborating in the Peking Communist régime.

POLITICAL EVENTS SINCE 1945

The long-standing conflict between the Nationalists and the Communists in China did not subside during the eight-year war with Japan. Civil strife quickly followed Japan's surrender in 1945, as Nationalists and Communists alike did their best to seize localities liberated from the Japanese.

In the meantime, the proposed National Assembly met on November 15, 1946. The Constitution drawn up by this body was approved on December 25, 1946, and entered into effect a year later. As provided by the Constitution, a National Assembly was elected in November, 1947, and, convening in March 1948, it chose Chiang Kai-shek as China's President. He was inaugurated on May 20, 1948.

Civil warfare went on relentlessly during 1948 and 1949, the Communists winning victory after victory. Chiang Kai-shek retired on January 21, 1949, shortly after the fall of Tientsin, and the Vice-President, General Li Tsung-jen, became Acting President. Peiping surrendered January 31, 1949. On March 8 Dr. Sun Fo resigned as Prime Minister. He was succeeded by General Ho Ying-chin, under whom a Cabinet was formed on March 21. Nanking fell to the Communists in April, and Hangchow and Shanghai were taken in May. On May 30 the Cabinet resigned, and Marshal Yen Hsi-shan was made Prime Minister on June 3. On June 11, 1949, a Supreme Policy Committee was set up by the Central Political Council with Generalissimo Chiang Kai-shek as its head. Later Changsha fell, as did Foochow, Canton and Chungking.

Acting President Li Tsung-jen left China for the United States on November 4, 1949, ostensibly for medical treatment. He refused to return despite repeated requests of the National Assembly and the Control Yüan. The National Government withdrew to Taiwan on December 8, 1949. Ex-Shanghai Mayor K. C. Wu (Wu Kuo-chen) was appointed Governor of Taiwan on December 16, 1949; he was succeeded by O. K. Yui on April 16, 1953. C. K. Yen succeeded O. K. Yui in 1954, and he in turn was succeeded in 1957 by Chou Chih-jou. On March 1, 1950, Generalissimo Chiang Kai-shek resumed the Presidency and appointed General Ch'en Ch'eng as Premier to replace Yen Hsi-shan. Following election of President Chiang for a second term in 1954, O. K. Yui was appointed Premier. On February 25, 1953, the Government abrogated the 1945 Sino-Soviet Treaty of Friendship and Alliance.

Hainan Island was taken by the Chinese Communists in April, 1950. The Nationalists evacuated the Chusan Archipelago in the middle of May, 1950. The Chinese Communists' control of the entire China mainland, with the exception of scattered rural areas chiefly in Central and South China occupied by anti-Communist guerrilla elements, was complete. In 1950 and 1951 the Communist army invaded Tibet and established a new régime, retaining the Dalai Lama as nominal ruler.

PEOPLE'S REPUBLIC OF CHINA (COMMUNIST)
Capital: Peking

On October 1, 1949, the Communist leader, Mao Tse-tung, proclaimed the inauguration of the Central People's Government of the People's Republic of China. This announcement was made in Peking at the close of the meeting of the Chinese People's Political Consultative Council. This government is described in the following paragraphs.

ORGANIZATION

The Government of Communist China, officially known as the Central People's Government of the People's Republic of China, was originally founded on October 1, 1949. Since that time, its organization has undergone considerable change. Its present structure is based on a national constitution and four organic laws, adopted at the first session of the National People's Congress, September 1954. Its capital is Peking.

The Chinese Communist Government is essentially a one-party dictatorship, in which all power resides in the Chinese Communist Party. However, a façade of "democracy" is provided by a United Front composed of several small political parties, which are nominally represented in major government agencies, but are in fact dominated and controlled by the Chinese Communist Party. Further, "democratic" trimmings are provided by a system of elections and "people's congresses" which lend an appearance of popular approval to the régime.

The formal structure of the Chinese Communist government is similar in many respects to the governments of the USSR and its Eastern European satellites. In theory, the highest organ of government is a large national assembly known as the National People's Congress, which is scheduled to meet once a year. The National People's Congress elects a Standing Committee, composed of a chairman, 12 vice-chairmen, and 66 members, which is vested with broad supervisory and legislative powers.

The National People's Congress also elects a single national executive, known as the Chairman of the People's Republic, who enjoys broad appointive powers, commands the armed forces of the nation, and presides over two important national agencies, the National Defense Council, and the Supreme State Conference. The Defense Council is headed by the Chairman and consists of 15 vice-chairmen and 81 members nominated by the Chairman. The Supreme State Conference is convened by the Chairman and includes ranking government leaders. It has functioned as a sounding-board for important policy statements by Chairman Mao and other government leaders. In theory, the Chairman and the Standing Committee exercise "joint leadership" of the Government and comprise a "collective" head of state.

The center of day-to-day government administration is a body known as the State Council, headed by a Premier appointed by the Chairman of the People's Republic, and composed of a Secretary-General and 12 vice-premiers. The

Council, analogous to the Council of Ministers in the USSR, directs the work of 41 ministries and 7 commissions, and supervises the activities of provincial and local government councils.

The judicial and control functions of the state are vested in a Supreme People's Court and an Office of Supreme People's Procurator General, both of which are under the supervision of the Standing Committee of the National People's Congress. The Supreme People's Court supervises the work of judicial bodies throughout the nation, while the office of Procurator General enforces uniform observance of governmental laws.

PERSONNEL

Following are the leading figures in the Communist Government.

Chairman of the People's Republic
MAO TSE-TUNG†

Vice-Chairman
CHU TEH

Premier
CHOU EN-LAI

NATIONAL PEOPLE'S CONGRESS, STANDING COMMITTEE

Chairman: Liu Shao-ch'i
Secretary General: P'eng Chen
Vice Chairmen: 12, Members: 66

STATE COUNCIL

Premier: Chou En-lai
Vice Premiers (12: Ch'en Yün, P'eng Te-huai, Lin Piao, Ho Lung, Ch'en I, Teng Hsiao-p'ing, Teng Tzu-hui, Ulanfu, Li Fu-ch'un, Li Hsien-nien, Nieh Jung-chen, Po I-po.
Secretary-General: Hsi Chung-hsün
Members: Include heads of ministries and commissions

NATIONAL DEFENSE COUNCIL

Chairman: Mao Tse-tung
Vice-Chairmen: 15, Members: 81

SUPREME PEOPLE'S COURT

President: Tung Pi-wu

OFFICE OF SUPREME PEOPLE'S PROCURATOR GENERAL

Chief Procurator: Chang Ting-ch'eng

MINISTRIES UNDER STATE COUNCIL

Ch'en I (Foreign Affairs), Li Hsien-nien (Finance), P'eng Te-huai (National Defense), Liao Lu-yen (Agriculture), Lo Jui-ch'ing (Public Security), T'eng Tai-yüan (Railways), Ch'en Yun (Commerce), Yang I-chen (Second Ministry of Commerce), Yeh Chi-chuang (Foreign Trade), Hsieh Chüeh-tsai (Interior), Wang Shou-tao (Communications), Shih Liang (Justice), Yang Hsiu-feng (Education), Shen Yen-ping (Culture), Ma Wen-jui (Labor), Chu Hsüeh-fan (Posts and Telecommunications), Li Chu-chen (Light Industry), Chao

---

†Mao has indicated his decision not to stand for re-election, but will continue as "leader of the Communist Party, and the people."

CHINA

Erh-lu (First Machine Industry), Sung Jen-ch'iung (Second Machine Industry), Liu Hsiu-feng (Building), Chiang Kuang-nai (Textile Industry), Ch'ien Ying (Supervision), Li Te-ch'uan (Public Health), Li Ssu-kuang (Geology), Liang Hsi (Forestry), Sha Chien-li (Food), Chang Lin-chih (Coal Industry), Fu Tso-yi (Water Conservancy and Electric Power), Yu Chiu-li (Petroleum Industry), Hsu Te-heng (Marine Products), Wang Hao-shou (Metallurgical Industry), Chang Lin-chih (Power Equipment), P'eng T'ao (Chemical Industry), Wang Chen (Land Reclamation).

Commissions Under State Council
State Planning Commission: Li Fu-ch'un (Director)
Nationalities Affairs Commission: Ulanfu (Director)
Overseas Chinese Affairs Commission: Ho Hsiang-ning (Director)
Physical Culture & Athletics Commission: Ho Lung (Director)
National Economic Commission: Po I-po (Director)
State Technological Commission: Huang Ching (Director)

PRESS

Name of Paper	Political Affiliation	Proprietor, Editor, etc.
TAIWAN		
Chung Yang Jih Pao (Taipei, Taiwan)	Kuomintang organ.	Kuomintang (*Prop.*)
Hsin Sheng Pao (Taipei)	Pro-Kuomintang.	Taiwan Gov't (*Prop.*)
Kung Lun Pao (Taipei)	Independent; Taiwanese.	Li Wan-chu (*Prop.*)
Lien Ho Jih Pao	Independent; Taiwanese.	Wang Tih-wu (*Prop.*)
Chung Hua Jih Pao (Taipei)	Kuomintang.	Kuomintang (*Prop.*)
China News (Taipei)	Independent; in English.	Stanway Cheng (*Ed.*)
China Post (Taipei)	Independent; in English.	Nancy Yu Huang (*Prop.*)
MAINLAND		
Chieh Fang Jih Pao (Shanghai)	Communist organ.	Communist Party (*Prop.*)
Nan Fang Jih Pao (Canton)	Communist organ.	Communist Party (*Prop.*)
Ta Kung Pao (Peking)	Pro-Communist.	CCP-controlled
Tien Ching Jih Pao (Tientsin)	Communist organ.	Communist Party (*Prop.*)
Jen Min Jih Pao (Peking)	Communist organ.	Communist Party Central Committee (*Prop.*)
Kung Jen Jih Pao (Peking)	Communist trade union organ.	Trade Unions Fed. (*Prop.*)
Chung Kuo Ch'ing Nien Pao (Peking)	Communist youth organ.	Young Communist League (*Prop.*)
Chung Kuo Shao Nien Pao (Peking)	Communist youth organ; large circulation.	Young Communist League (*Prop.*)
Kuang Ming Jih Pao (Peking)	Pro-Communist.	China Democratic League (*Prop.*)
Chang Chiang Jih Pao (Hankow)	Communist organ.	Communist Party (*Prop.*)
HONGKONG		
Hongkong Times	Kuomintang.	Hsu Hsiao-yen (*Pub.*)
Hsing Tao Jih Pao	Pro-Kuomintang.	Ch'en Meng-yin (*Ed.*)
Ta Kung Pao	Communist.	CCP controlled
Wah Kiu Yat Po	Independent.	T'sen Wo-hsiu (*Pub.*)
Kung Shang Jih Pao	Pro-Kuomintang.	
NEWS AGENCIES		
Central News Agency (Taipei, Taiwan)	Kuomintang; official.	Tseng Hsu-pai (*Dir.*)
New China News Agency (Peking and other cities)	Communist; official.	Wu Leng-hsi (*Dir.*)

COLOMBIA

Capital: Bogotá
Area: 447,536 square miles
Population: 13,000,000 (1956 estimate)

President
ALBERTO LLERAS CAMARGO (Liberal)
Elected by popular vote on May 4, 1958
Took office on August 7, 1958, for four-year term

Cabinet
Bipartisan (Liberal and Conservative)
Appointed August 7, 1958

PARLIAMENT
(*Congreso*)

Colombia's Congress consists of a popularly-elected Senate and House of Representatives, the former with a four-year term and the latter with a two-year term. The present Congress was elected on March 16, 1958 and convened on July 20, 1958—constituting the first Congressional session since 1952 and the first bipartisan Congress since 1949. Under the "parity" formula described below, the Senate consists of 40 Liberals and 40 Conservatives and the House of 74 Liberals and 74 Conservatives. The Liberal membership is largely united, while the Conservatives are split into three factions, the "Laureanistas" being the majority faction and the "Valencistas" and "Independents" being minority factions, the last in outright opposition to the National Front Government.

RECENT POLITICAL EVENTS

Since the time of Bolívar, Colombia has had two major political parties, the Conservatives and the Liberals.

A long period of relative political stability ended in 1948. From that date until 1958, except for a few months in 1949, the country was governed under a state of siege. In June 1953, responding to widespread desire for peace and strong government, General Rojas Pinilla overthrew the ultra-Conservative ruling element and took power. Widespread opposition, however, was aroused by the announcement in February 1957 that military leaders had determined on another term to commence in 1958 for President Rojas. Public demonstrations forced Rojas to resign on May 10, 1957. A military junta was appointed to take over power. The Junta dismantled the machinery of the Rojas dictatorship. It was supported by the "National Front," an alliance of the Liberal and Conservative parties which had opposed Rojas.

On December 1, 1957, a national plebiscite affirmed a "parity" formula of bi-partisan government to end a decade of dictatorship. Under it the Conservative and Liberal Parties, during 12 years, will hold an equal number of Cabinet posts, and have equal representation in the National Congress, state legislatures and city councils.

COLOMBIA

PARTY PROGRAMS AND LEADERS

At present there is little difference between the political, economic and social programs of the Liberal Party and of the Conservative factions supporting the National Front—generally progressive in outlook—while the "Independent" Conservatives, opponents of the National Front, are generally authoritarian minded.

Liberal Party Leaders: Alberto Lleras Camargo, Carlos Lleras Restrepo, Darío Echandía, Alfonso López, Eduardo Santos, Roberto García Peña, Julio César Turbay Ayala, Antonio Rocha, Alberto Jaramillo Sanchez.

Conservative Party Leaders: Laureanistas: Laureano Gómez, Alfredo Araújo Grau, Belisario Betancourt, Alvaro Gómez Hurtado, Guillermo Amaya Ramírez. *Valencistas:* Guillermo Leon Valencia, Mariano Ospina Pérez, Roberto Urdaneta Arbelaez, José Antonio Montalvo, José María Bernal. *Independents:* Jorge Leyva, Gilberto Alzate Avendaño.

THE CABINET

The members of the Cabinet are: Guillermo Amaya Ramírez (Conservative), Minister of Government; Julio César Turbay Ayala (Liberal), Foreign Relations; Germán Zea Hernández (Liberal), Justice; Hernando Agudelo Villa (Liberal), Finance & Public Credit; Brig. Gen. Alfonso Saiz Montoya (non-partisan), War; Augusto Espinosa Valderrama (Liberal), Agriculture & Cattle Raising; Raimundo Emiliani Román (Conservative), Labor; Alejandro Jiménez Arango (Conservative), Public Health; Rafael Delgado Barreneche (Conservative), Development; Jorge Ospina Delgado (Conservative), Mines & Petroleum; Reinaldo Muñoz Zambrano (Conservative), National Education; Hernán Echavarría Olozaga (Liberal), Communications; Virgilio Barco Vargas (Liberal), Public Works.

PRESS

Unless otherwise noted, papers are published in the capital city.

Name of Paper	Circulation	Political Affiliation	Proprietor, Editor, etc.
El Tiempo (morning)	150,000	Liberal.	Roberto García Peña (*Dir.*)
El Espectador (morning)	80,000	Liberal.	Gabriel Cano (*Dir.*)
El Espectador (evening)	80,000	Liberal.	Guillermo Cano (*Dir.*)
El Siglo (morning)	60,000	Conservative.	Guillermo Gómez Moncayo (*Dir.*)
La República (morning)	40,000	Conservative.	Silvio Villegas (*Dir.*)
Diario del Caribe (Barranquilla) (morning)	8,000	Conservative.	Luis Paccini Santodomingo (*Dir.*)
El Heraldo (Barranquilla) (morning)	5,000	Liberal.	Juan B. Fernández (*Dir.*)
La Prensa (Barranquilla) (morning)	4,000	Conservative.	Carlos Martínez Aparicio (*Dir.*)
Vanguardia Liberal (Bucaramanga) (morning)	4,000	Liberal.	Alejandro Galvis Galvis (*Dir.*)
El País (Cali) (morning)	60,000	Conservative.	Alvaro Lloreda (*Dir.*)
El Relator (Cali) (morning)	25,000	Liberal.	Luis Zornosa Falla (*Dir.*)
Diario de la Costa (Cartagena) (morning)	2,000	Conservative.	Rafael Escallón Villa (*Dir.*)
Diario de la Frontera (Cúcuta) (morning)	2,000	Conservative.	Luis Parra Bolívar (*Dir.*)
La Tribuna (Ibagué) (morning)	8,000	Liberal.	Flavio De Castro (*Dir.*)
La Patria (Manizales) (morning)	10,000	Conservative.	Arturo Gómez Jaramillo (*Dir.*)
El Colombiano (Medellín) (morning)	50,000	Conservative.	Fernando Gómez Martínez (*Dir.*)
El Correo (Medellín) (morning)	20,000	Liberal.	Adolfo L. Gómez (*Dir.*)

COSTA RICA

Capital: San José
Area: 32,000 square miles
Population: 1,081,300 (1958 estimate)

President of the Republic
MARIO ECHANDI JIMÉNEZ
Assumed office May 8, 1958, for term
ending May 8, 1962

Cabinet
Appointed May, 1958

PARLIAMENT

Elections of February 2, 1958, for term May 1, 1958–April 30, 1962.

Parties	Representation
National Liberation	20
Republican (Calderonista)	11
National Union	10
Independent	3
Civic Revolutionary Union	1
Total	45

PARTY PROGRAMS AND LEADERS

General elections took place on February 2, 1958. A President, the 45-man membership of the unicameral legislature and municipal authorities for the entire republic were elected for a four-year period. The new Legislative Assembly took office on May 1, 1958, and President Mario Echandi Jiménez was inaugurated May 8, 1958. Despite the intensity of the election campaign, the elections were held in an orderly and democratic manner. President Echandi received 46.4% of the valid votes cast as compared to the 42.8% received by his principal opponent, National Liberation Party candidate Francisco Orlich.

The results of the congressional elections present a different picture: the National Liberation Party of former President José Figueres secured 20 seats which gave it the largest representation, though not a clear majority, in the Legislative Assembly.

The National Republican Party of ex-President Rafael Angel Calderón Guardia, who had been in exile for ten years, demonstrated its actual and potential strength by obtaining 11 seats; President Echandi's own National Union Party gained 10; the "splinter" of National Liberation led by Independent candidate Rossi won 3; and the Civic Revolutionary Party of Mr. Frank Marshall 1. As the Calderonista Republican Party supported Echandi for the presidency, he is faced with a difficult legislative situation.

President Echandi is regarded as a representative of the more conservative elements. However, it is predicted that he will support and maintain most of the social and economic measures instituted by his predecessors. Mr. Echandi's foreign policy is based upon the maintenance of friendly relations with all other nations and a policy of non-interference in other nations' domestic affairs.

THE CABINET

The Cabinet is composed as follows: José Joaquín Peralta Esquivel (First Vice-President), Abelardo Bonilla Baldares (Second Vice-President), Alfredo Vargas Fernández (Minister of Foreign Affairs), Alfredo Hernández Volio (Minister of Economy and Finance), Joaquín Vargas Gené (Minister of Government), Espíritu Santo Salas (Minister of Public Works), Estela Quesada Hernández (Minister of Public Education), Franklin Solórzano Salas (Minister of Labor), Jorge Borbón Castro (Minister of Agriculture and Industries), Dr. José Quirce Morales (Minister of Public Health), and Luis Demetrio Tinoco Castro (Minister without Portfolio and Secretary of the Cabinet).

PRESS

Unless otherwise noted, papers are published in the capital city.

Name of Paper	Circulation	Character	Proprietor, Editor, etc.
Diario de Costa Rica	20,000	Pro-Government.	Otilio Ulate (*Prop.*) Mariano Sanz (*Ed.*)
La Gaceta	12,000	Official Gov't. gazette.	The Government (*Prop.*)
La Hora	12,000	Owned by *Diario de Costa Rica*.	Guillermo Calvo Navarro (*Ed.*)
La Nación	32,000	Pro-Government.	Ricardo Castro Beeche (*Ed.*)
La Prensa Libre	16,000	Independent.	Andrés Borrasé (*Ed.*)
La República	10,000	Opposition.	Gonzalo Solórzano (*Ed.*)
La Última Noticia	5,000	Opposition.	Francisco Zeledón (*Ed.*)
El Heraldo (Puntarenas)		Independent.	F. L. Enríquez (*Prop. and Ed.*)
Diario Nacional (weekly)	8,000	Independent; owned by *La Prensa Libre*.	José A. Zavaleta (*Ed.*)
Eco Católico (weekly)		Catholic.	Victor Manuel Arrieta (*Ed.*)
Voz del Atlántico (Puerto Limón) (weekly)		Independent.	Joseph R. Thomas (*Adm.*)
Repertorio Americano (monthly)		Literary.	
Revista de Agricultura		Agricultural.	Luis Cruz (*Prop.*)
Revista de la Cámara de Comercio (monthly)		Commercial.	Chamber of Commerce (*Pub.*)

CUBA

Capital: Havana
Area: 44,400 square miles (including Isle of Pines and surrounding keys)
Population: 6,421,161 (1957 estimate)

Provisional President
MANUEL URRUTIA LLEO
Named by leader of the rebellion, Fidel Castro,
following resignation of Fulgencio Batista on January 1, 1959
Assumed office on January 2, 1959

Head of the Armed Forces
FIDEL CASTRO

PARLIAMENT
Election of November 1, 1954.*

UPPER CHAMBER
(Senate)

Four-year term.

President: ANSELMO ALLIEGRO MILÁ
(Acción Progresista)

Parties	Representation
Government:	
Acción Progresista	26
Unión Radical	5
Liberal	4
Demócrata	1
	36
Opposition:	
Revolucionario Cubano (A.)	18
Total	54

LOWER CHAMBER
(House of Representatives)

Renewed by halves every two years.

President: GASTON GODOY Y LORET DE MOLA

Parties	Representation
Government:	
Acción Progresista	60
Liberal	24
Demócrata	15
Unión Radical	15
	114
Opposition:	
Revolucionario Cubano (Auténtico)	11
Independents	5
	16
Total	130

* Elections were held on November 3, 1958, but the official returns have not been announced.

RECENT POLITICAL EVENTS

President Fulgencio Batista, the strong-man in Cuban politics for twenty-five years, resigned his office on January 1, 1959, and fled to exile in the Dominican Republic. His downfall was brought about by the growing success

(48)

of the months-old rebellion led by Fidel Castro. Col. Ramon Barquin, who had been imprisoned for conspiring against the Batista Government, was freed and brought to Havana by military plane and named chief of the joint staffs. He immediately sent out a call to Señor Castro to come to Havana.

Meanwhile, the forces of Fidel Castro moved swiftly to seize power throughout the island. They took Santiago and Santa Clara. Early in the morning on January 2, at Santiago, Castro announced the appointment of Manuel Urrutia Lleo as Provisional President. Urrutia immediately named Castro as head of the nation's armed forces and appointed a Cabinet of seven ministers. Then he outlined the program of the new régime—to restore Cuba's economy, to rebuild democracy and to oppose dictatorship throughout Latin America. He announced that constitutional guarantees, suspended by General Batista during the two-year rebellion, would be restored at once, that complete freedom of press and radio would be re-established and that the harvesting of the sugar crop would be started on schedule.

THE CABINET

The following are the members of the Cabinet: Dr. Roberto Agramonte (Minister of State), Dr. Angel Fernandez (Minister of Justice), Raúl Chibas (Minister of Finance), Raúl Cepero Bonilla (Minister of Commerce), Dr. Martinez Paiz (Minister of Health), Manuel Fernandez (Minister of Labor), Faustino Perez Hernández (Minister in Charge of Recovering Stolen Government Property).

PRESS

Unless otherwise noted, papers are published in the capital city.

Name of Paper	Circulation	Character*	Proprietor, Editor, etc.
Alerta	10,000	Pro-Batista.	Emilio Palomo (*Dir.*)
Ataja	32,000	Pro-Batista.	Alberto Salas Amaro (*Dir.*)
Avance	26,880	Pro-Batista.	Esther Menéndez Vda de Zayas (*Dir.*)
El Crisol	47,185	Pro-Batista.	Dr. Renato Villaverde (*Dir.*)
Diario de la Marina	30,000	Independent; conservative.	José I. Rivero (*Dir.*)
Diario Nacional	22,000	Liberal.	José R. Rivero (*Dir.*)
Finanzas	15,000	Independent; business journal.	Manuel Camío (*Dir.*)
Havana Post	11,607	Independent; in English.	Mrs. Clara Park Pessino (*Gen. Mgr.*)
Información	45,000	Independent.	Dr. Santiago Claret (*Ed.*)
Mañana	55,000	Pro-Batista.	J. López Vilaboy (*Ed.*)
El Mundo	30,000	Independent.	Dr. Raoul Alfonso Gonsé (*Dir.*)
El País	65,790	Liberal.	Alfredo Hornedo Suárez (*Prop.*)
Excelsior	52,000	Liberal.	Alfredo Hornedo Suárez (*Prop.*)
Prensa Libre	95,000	Independent.	Sergio Carbó (*Dir.*)
Pueblo	28,000	Pro-Batista.	Octavio R. Costa (*Dir.*)
Tiempo	16,000	Pro-Batista.	Rolando Masferrer (*Dir.*)
El Camagueyano (Camaguey)	10,000	Independent.	W. Rodríguez Blanca (*Dir.*)
El Comercio (Cienfuegos)	8,300	Independent.	Pedro A. Aragonés (*Ed.*)
La Correspondencia (Cienfuegos)	5,500	Independent.	Nicolás Machado Rodríguez (*Dir.*)

* As of December 31, 1958.

CUBA

Name of Paper	Circulation	Character	Proprietor, Editor, etc.
Diario de Cuba (Santiago de Cuba)	15,000	Independent.	Eduardo Abril Amores (*Dir.*)
Prensa Universal (Santiago de Cuba)	11,176	Independent.	Raul López Lacau (*Dir.*)
Bohemia (weekly)	280,000	Independent; anti-Batista.	Miguel A. Quevedo (*Dir.*)
Carteles (weekly)	100,000	Independent; anti-Batista.	Antonio Ortega (*Dir.*)
Cuba Económica y Financiera (monthly)	25,000	English language mercantile monthly.	J. B. Suris (*Dir.*)

PRESS GROUPS

Asociación de la Prensa de Cuba	Association of Reporters.	Lorenzo de Castro (*Pres.*)
Bloque de Prensa	Association of Newspaper owners.	Ing. Cristóbal Díaz (*Pres.*)
Colegio Nacional de Periodistas de Cuba	Newspapermen's union.	Leandro Carbajal Rodríguez (*Pres.*)

CZECHOSLOVAKIA

Capital: Praha (Prague)
Area: 49,330 square miles
Population: 13,470,000 (1958 estimate)

President
ANTONÍN NOVOTNÝ (Communist)
Elected by National Assembly on November 19, 1957

Cabinet
National Front, dominantly Communist

Premier
VILIAM ŠIROKÝ (Communist)

NATIONAL ASSEMBLY
Elected November 28, 1954, on a single list of candidates of the National Front.
Speaker: ZDENĚK FIERLINGER (Communist, former Social Democrat)
Number of Members 368

POLITICAL EVENTS SINCE 1945

President Beneš, who had headed the Czechoslovak Government in London during World War II, was able to return to Prague on May 16, 1945. On April 4, 1945, he named a new government headed by Zdeněk Fierlinger, former Czechoslovak Ambassador to the Soviet Union. The Cabinet included eight Communists, members from the other principal parties, and several non-partisans.

On October 28, 1945, a Provisional National Assembly was convened. Its first act was to confirm Dr. Beneš in office as President of Czechoslovakia.

A Constituent National Assembly was elected on May 26, 1946, primarily to revise the Constitution but also to perform interim legislative functions.

The power of the Communists in the Government increased gradually during 1946. After gaining the vital post of Prime Minister, and the control of the Ministry of the Interior and of the army through a friendly Minister of National Defense, the stage was set for taking over the administration. This was accomplished in February 1948, with the help of "action committees" which seized the headquarters of opposition parties and newspapers, and led mass demonstrations. A new Cabinet of Communists and left-wing Social Democrats was installed, in which sympathetic members of other parties were included.

Communist control was then quickly consolidated. On May 9, 1948, the Constituent National Assembly unanimously adopted a new Constitution.

On May 30, 1948, a new National Assembly was elected on a single list of candidates.

On June 7, 1948, President Beneš, refusing to sign the new Constitution, resigned. Klement Gottwald, acting as Premier, signed it, and it was promulgated on June 9, 1948. Gottwald was unanimously elected President by the new National Assembly on June 14, 1948. On June 15, 1948, a new Cabinet with Antonín Zápotocký as Prime Minister, and with twelve Communist and three Social Democratic members out of a total of twenty-two, was installed. On June 27, 1948, the Communists absorbed the Social Democratic Party.

During 1948 there was increasing political, economic and cultural orientation toward the USSR. Although formally other political parties of the National Front continued to function, they were subordinate to the Communist Party and acknowledged its leadership.

In September 1951, the Czechoslovak Government and Communist Party underwent an extensive reorganization. The posts of Secretary General and Deputy Secretaries General of the CP were abolished, a political and an organizational secretariat were established, and the Praesidium of the Party's Central Committee completed.

The reorganization of the Government and Party was followed by a far-reaching purge of high level officials, the most prominent of whom was Rudolf Slansky, former Secretary General of the Czechoslovak Communist Party.

After Gottwald's death in 1953, Antonín Novotný was entrusted with the management of the Central Committee. Novotný was elected First Secretary of the Central Committee in September 1953. He was elected President of Czechoslovakia by the National Assembly in November 1957, to succeed Antonín Zápotocký.

In June 1954, the Tenth Congress of the Communist Party was convened in Prague. Its deliberations resulted in confirming the decision to delay the inception of the second Czechoslovak Five Year Plan until 1956, thus bringing it into synchronization with those of the USSR and the majority of the other People's Democracies. The Congress also approved Party directives placing greater emphasis on agricultural and consumers goods production, stressing that the previous emphasis placed on the development of heavy industrial capacity had seriously warped the natural pattern of the Czechoslovak economy. Organizationally it abolished the former Praesidium of the Party and established the Politburo of the Central Committee as the governing body.

The present Politburo is composed of Karol Bacílek (also First Secretary of the Central Committee of the Communist Party of Slovakia), Rudolf Barák, David Pavol, Jaromír Dolanský, Zdeněk Fierlinger, Jiří Hendrych, Václav Kopecký, Antonín Novotný (First Secretary of Czechoslovak Communist Party), Otakar Simůnek and Viliam Siroký. Candidate members are Jan Hlína, Ludmila Jankovcová and Rudolf Strechaj. There are also five "secretaries" of the Central Committee: Jiří Hendrych, Bruno Koehler, Vlatislav Krutina, Oldřich Černik and Vladimír Koucký. The Central Committee consists of 94 members and 50 candidates. The Control Commission is chaired by Jan Harus.

Elections to the local administrative bodies (the National Committees) were held on May 16, 1957, with the National Front candidates (the only candidates) achieving an average vote of 99.12%. Elections to the National Assembly and the Slovak National Council were held on November 28, 1954. As usual, only a single slate of candidates was available to the voters.

The Eleventh Congress of the Party, held in June 1958, approved a plan to expand production through 1965 and to complete agricultural collectivization

CZECHOSLOVAKIA

within two years. On January 1, 1958, the Party had 1,422,199 members and candidate members.

THE CABINET

The members of the present Cabinet are: Viliam Široký, Prime Minister (Communist); Jaromír Dolanský, First Deputy Prime Minister (Communist); Václav Kopecký, Deputy Prime Minister (Communist); Ludmila Jankovcová, Deputy Prime Minister (Communist); Karel Poláček, Engineering (Communist); Michal Bakula, Agriculture and Forestry (Communist); Rudolf Barák, Interior (Communist); Oldřich Beran, Construction (Communist); Josef Reitmajer, Heavy Engineering (Communist); Václav David, Foreign Affairs (Communist); Július Ďuriš, Finance (Communist); Richard Dvořák, Foreign Trade (Communist); Josef Jonáš, Fuel (Communist); František Kahuda, Education and Culture (Communist); František Krajčír, Internal Trade (Communist); Josef Krosnář, State Control (Communist); Jozef Kyselý, Without Portfolio (Slovak Regeneration Party); Bohumír Lomský, Defense (Communist); Božena Machačová-Dostálová, Consumer Industries (Communist); Zdeněk Nejedlý, Without Portfolio (Communist); Alois Neumann, Communications (Socialist Party); Josef Plojhar, Health (People's Party); Antonín Pospíšil, Power (People's Party); Jozef Púčik, Chemical Industry (Communist); Václav Cerný, Foundries and Ore Mines (Communist); Otakar Simůnek, State Planning (Communist); Václav Škoda, Justice (Communist); Jindřich Uher, Food Processing and Crop Collection (Communist); Franisek Vlasák, Transport (Communist); Emanuel Šlechta, State Committee for Construction (Socialist Party); Josef Tesla, Without Portfolio.

PRESS

The press is Government-controlled. Unless otherwise noted, papers are published in Prague.

Name of Paper	Sponsor	Editor
Rudé Právo	Central Committee of Czechoslovak Communist Party.	Oldrich Svestka
Práce	Revolutionary Trade Union Movement.	Antonín Zázvorka
Obrana Lidu	Ministry of National Defense.	Jiří Kubka
Mladá Fronta	Youth League.	Ivo Kalvínský
Zemědělské Noviny	Ministry of Agriculture and Forestry.	Jaroslav Šmid
Svobodné Slovo	Socialist Party.	Ladislav Technik
Lidová Demokracie	People's Party.	Rostislav Petera
Večerní Praha	Prague Region.	Jan Zelenka
Literární Noviny	Writers Union.	Jan Pilař
Lud (Bratislava)	Slovak Regeneration Party.	Jozef Gajdošik
Pravda (Bratislava)	Central Committee, Slovak Communist Party.	Ondrej Klokoč
Sloboda (Bratislava)	Slovak Freedom Party.	František Štefánik
Večerník (Bratislava)	Slovak Trade Union Council.	Michal Lanko
Rovnost (Brno)	Brno Region, Communist Party Committee.	Oldrich Jarušek
Nová Mysl	Theoretical and Political Journal of Central Committee, Communist Party of Czechoslovakia.	Editorial Board
Život Strany	Information magazine of Central Committee of the Communist Party of Czechoslovakia.	Josef Valenta
Statistický Obzor	Magazine of State Office of Statistics.	Editorial Board
Zahraniční Obchod	Czechoslovak Chamber of Commerce.	Otto Růžička

DENMARK

Capital: Copenhagen
Area: 16,576 square miles
Population: 4,479,000 (1957 estimate)

Sovereign
KING FREDERIK IX
Born March 11, 1899; ascended throne April 20, 1947

Cabinet
Coalition: Social Democrats—9, Radical Liberals—4,
Single-Taxers—3.
Appointed May 27, 1957

Prime Minister
H. C. HANSEN
Appointed February 1, 1955

PARLIAMENT
(Folketing)
Election of May 14, 1957 (for four years)
Speaker: GUSTAV PEDERSEN (Social Democrat)

Parties	Representation
Social Democratic	70
Moderate Liberal	45
Conservative	30
Radical Liberal	14
Single Tax (Liberal Georgeists)	9
Communist	5
Faroe Representatives	2
Greenland Representatives	2
German Minority Representative	1
Socialist Peoples Party	1
Total	179

POLITICAL EVENTS SINCE 1945

Denmark was liberated from the Germans by Allied troops in May 1945, and on May 5 King Christian in a radio talk to the Danish people declared that the oppressive years of German occupation were over, and thanked the Allies and the leaders of the resistance movement. Vilhelm Buhl was appointed Premier and formed a coalition Cabinet.

Elections for the Lower Chamber were held on October 30, 1945, and Premier Buhl, because his Social Democratic Party lost ground, submitted his resignation on the following day.

The Moderate-Liberal (Agrarian) Party took over and formed the Knud Kristensen (minority) government, supported in Parliament by Conservatives and Radical Liberals. However, a split on the Prime Minister's policy toward the South Schleswig question developed and, the Radical Liberals withdrawing their support, Knud Kristensen was defeated in the House on October 4, 1947. After the general election on October 28, 1947, a Social Democratic Government (minority) was formed.

Due to disagreement over defense and national economy issues, the Rigsdag was dissolved in September 1950, and new elections were held. They were inconclusive, leaving the Social Democrats' position intact. After a defeat by one vote in Parliament, the Social Democratic Cabinet resigned in October 1950, and was succeeded by a Moderate-Liberal and Conservative coalition.

On June 5, 1953, there went into effect a new Danish Constitution which introduced a unicameral Parliament and the possibility of female succession to the throne. Due to failure to secure continued Radical Liberal support, the Moderate Liberal-Conservative coalition resigned after the elections on September 22, to be succeeded by a Social Democratic minority Government.

Following the general election of May 1957, the Social Democrats, the Radical Liberals and the Single-Taxers formed a coalition government.

PARTY PROGRAMS AND LEADERS

SOCIAL DEMOCRATIC PARTY: Represents mainly industrial labor. *In foreign policy:* favors United Nations, Atlantic Pact, European Recovery Program, and Scandinavian collaboration. *In domestic policy:* advocates government planning in economic life so that full employment, social security and industrial democracy are assured, and supports adequate national defense.

Leaders: H. C. Hansen (Prime Minister), Alsing Andersen (former Minister of Defense), Gustav Pedersen (Speaker of the Folketing), Viggo Kampmann (Minister of Finance), J. O. Krag (Minister of Foreign Affairs).

MODERATE LIBERAL PARTY: Represents mainly farmers and professional groups. *In foreign policy:* favors United Nations, Atlantic Pact, European Recovery Program and Scandinavian collaboration. *In domestic policy:* stands for individualism as against socialism in industry and business, reduction of taxation by strict governmental economy, relaxation of economic restrictions, and adequate defense.

Leaders: Erik Eriksen (former Prime Minister), Jens Sønderup (former Minister of Agriculture), Professor Thorkil Kristensen (former Minister of Finance).

CONSERVATIVE PARTY: Represents financial, industrial, and business groups, and farmers. *In foreign policy:* favors United Nations, Atlantic Pact, European Recovery Program, and Scandinavian collaboration. *In domestic policy:* supports adequate defense, protection of private property, protective tariff duties to aid industry, sound fiscal policy, and lower taxation. Opposes parcelling of large estates; stands for personal initiative as against socialism, and for taxation of cooperative enterprises and consumer associations.

Leaders: Einar Foss (Party Chairman), Poul Sørensen (chairman of Folketing Group), Poul Møller (political spokesman).

RADICAL LIBERAL PARTY: Represents mainly small landowners and urban intellectual and professional elements. *In foreign policy:* favors United Nations, restriction of armaments, European Recovery Program, and Scandinavian collaboration. Opposed Denmark joining Atlantic Pact. *In domestic policy:* advocates strengthening of private enterprise along Radical Liberal lines.

Leaders: Hans Jeppesen (Chairman of Party), Jørgen Jørgensen (Minister of Education), Bertel Dahlgaard (Minister of Economics).

COMMUNIST PARTY: *Foreign Policy:* opposed Atlantic Pact, favors close political and economic relations with USSR and satellite countries. *Domestic policy:* favors state ownership of means of production, opposes defense expenditures.

Leaders: Knud Jespersen (Chairman) and Villy Fuglsang (political spokesman).

SOCIALIST PEOPLES PARTY: Formed in 1958 after Aksel Larsen's expulsion from the Communist Party. Advocates Danish Communism independent of Soviet Russia, and disarmament.

Leaders: Aksel Larsen.

SINGLE TAX (Liberal Georgeists): *Foreign policy:* favors United Nations and Atlantic Pact. *Domestic policy:* advocates Henry George's doctrine of single tax on land, professional army, free trade, abolition of economic restrictions, reduction of public expenditures.

Leaders: Dr. Viggo Starcke (Minister without Portfolio), Oluf Pedersen (Minister of Fisheries).

THE CABINET

The members of the present Cabinet are: H. C. Hansen, Prime Minister (Social Democrat); Jens Otto Krag, Minister for Foreign Affairs (Social Democrat); Viggo Kampmann, Minister for Finance (Social Democrat); Jørgen Jørgensen, Minister for Education (Radical Liberal); Viggo Starcke, Minister without Portfolio (Single-Tax Party); Bertel Dahlgaard, Minister for Economic Affairs (Radical Liberal); Julius Bomholt, Minister for Social Affairs (Social Democrat); Mrs. Bodil Koch, Minister for Ecclesiastic Affairs (Social Democrat); Hans Haekkerup, Minister for Justice (Social Democrat); Kai Lindberg, Minister for Public Works and Minister for Greenland (Social Democrat); Poul Hansen, Minister for Defense (Social Democrat); Oluf Pedersen, Minister for Fisheries (Single-Tax Party); Kaj Bundvad, Minister for Labour and Housing (Social Democrat); Karl Skytte, Minister for Agriculture (Radical Liberal); Søren Olesen, Minister for the Interior (Single-Tax Party); Kjeld Philip, Minister for Commerce (Radical Liberal).

PRESS

Unless otherwise noted, papers are published in the capital city.

Name of Paper	Circulation	Political Affiliation	Proprietor, Editor, etc.
Aftenbladet	20,000	Independent.	G. Lund Henriksen and Poul Barentzen (*Eds.*)
B. T.	138,000	Conservative.	Carl Th. Jensen (*Ed.*)
Berlingske Aftenavis	23,000	Conservative.	T. M. Terkelsen, Svend Aage Lund, Otto Fog Petersen (*Eds.*)
Berlingske Tidende	163,000	Conservative.	T. M. Terkelsen and Svend Aage Lund (*Eds.*)
Børsen	10,000	Conservative; commercial.	P. Koch-Jensen (*Ed.*)
Ekstrabladet	66,000	Liberal.	Harald Mogensen, Flemming Hasager (*Eds.*)

DENMARK

Name of Paper	Circulation	Political Affiliation	Proprietor, Editor. etc.
Information	25,000	Independent.	Børge Outze, E. Seidenfaden, Knud Bidstrup (Eds.)
Kristeligt Dagblad	17,000	Independent; Lutheran.	Edv. Petersen (Ed.)
Land og Folk	10,000	Communist.	Martin Nielsen (Ed.)
Dagens Nyheder	26,000	Conservative.	Jens Søltoft-Jensen and Eigil Steinmetz (Eds.)
Politiken	154,000	Liberal.	Hakon Stephensen, Svend Tillge-Rasmussen (Eds.)
Social-Demokraten	39,000	Social Democratic Party.	Peder Tabor (Ed.)
Aalborg Amtstidende (Aalborg)	22,000	Moderate Liberal.	A. Juhl Andersen (Ed.)
Aalborg Stiftstidende (Aalborg)	39,000	Independent, Conservative.	A. Schiøttz-Christensen (Ed.)
Aarnuus Stiftsidende (Aarhus)	49,000	Conservative.	E. Schmidt (Ed.)
Jyllands-Posten (Aarhus)	65,000	Conservative.	Lasse Egebjerg (Ed.)
Vestkysten (Esbjerg)	37,000	Moderate Liberal.	Knud Ree (Ed.)
Flensborg Avis (Flensborg, Germany)	9,500	Independent; organ of Danish minority.	L. P. Christensen (Ed.)
Frederiksborg Amts Avis (Hillerød)	23,000	Moderate Liberal.	H. Brix (Ed.)
Vendsyssel Tidende (Hjørring)	26,000	Moderate Liberal.	E. Glerup (Ed.)
Fyens Stifstidende (Odense)	30,000	Conservative.	Knud Secher (Ed.)
Fyns Tidende (Odense)	35,000	Moderate Liberal.	S. P. Qvist (Ed.)
Sorø Amtstidende (Slagelse)	20,000	Moderate Liberal.	Erhardt Larsen (Ed.)
Vejle Amts Folkeblad (Vejle)	22,000	Moderate Liberal.	G. Skytte Nielsen (Ed.)
Finanstidende (weekly)	5,000	Political, economic, and financial.	Carl Thalbitzer & Svend Thiberg (Eds.)
Ugeskrift for Landmænd (weekly)	5,000	Agricultural.	Axel Pedersen (Ed.)
Tidsskrift for Industri	5,000	Industrial.	Jørgen Jensen and Poul Melgaard (Eds.)
Fremtiden (monthly)	3,000	Foreign Policy.	Sten Gudme, Erik Seidenfaden and Johan Wilhjelm (Eds.)
Ökonomi og Politik (quarterly)	3,500	Economics and political science.	Institutet for Historie og Samfundsøkonomi (Prop.)

NEWS AGENCY

Ritzau		Danish news agency.	G. Naesselund (Mg. Dir.)

PRESS ORGANIZATIONS

Danske Dagbades Faellesrepraesentation	Federation of Danish Newspapers.	Svend Aage Lund (Ch.)
Danske Journalisters Fællesrepræsentation	The Joint Danish Journalists Assn.	Andreas Elsnab (Ch.)
Dansk Journalistforening	Soceity of Danish Journalists. (Provincial).	Andreas Elsnab (Ch.)
Københavns Journalistforbund	Assn. of Copenhagen Journalists.	Carsten Nielsen (Ch.)
Socialdemokratisk Presseforening	Social-Democratic Press Union.	Aage Petersen (Ch.)
Journalistforeningen i København	Society of Journalists in Copenhagen.	Carl Th. Jensen (Ch.)

DOMINICAN REPUBLIC

Capital: Ciudad Trujillo (formerly Santo Domingo)
Area: 19,332 square miles
Population: 2,693,914 (1957 estimate)

President
GENERALÍSIMO HECTOR B. TRUJILLO MOLINA
Re-elected May 16, 1957
Assumed office August 16, 1957, for term ending in 1962

Vice-President
DR. JOAQUIN BALAGUER

Cabinet
Partido Dominicano

PARLIAMENT
(Congreso Nacional)
Last regular election, May 17, 1957

UPPER CHAMBER (Senado)	LOWER CHAMBER (Cámara de Diputados)
President: PORFIRIO HERRERA	President: JOSÉ RAMON RODRIGUEZ SÁNCHEZ
The Senado is composed of 26 members, one for each province and one for the District of Santo Domingo, elected for five years. A vacancy is filled by the body itself from a list of three names submitted by the chief of the party with which the retiring member was affiliated.	The Cámara is composed of 55 members, one for each 60,000 of population, or fraction of more than 30,000, with the provision that no province shall be represented by less than two. They are elected for five years and vacancies are filled in the same manner as in the Senado.

POLITICAL PARTIES AND LEADERS

Following the revolution of 1930, the old political organizations disappeared with the formation of the single government party—Partido Dominicano—which is headed by Generalísimo Dr. Rafael Leonídas Trujillo Molina, whose official title given by Congress is Benefactor of the Fatherland. Generalísimo Trujillo did not run for President in 1938, his candidate, Dr. Jacinto B. Peynado, being elected.

A presidential election was held in May 1942. Generalísimo Trujillo, who was the only candidate, and was President for the terms 1930-34 and 1934-38, was elected. He was re-elected for a new five-year term on May 16, 1947.

During 1946 a labor group of working class leaders and a few intellectuals with leftist tendencies (Partido Laborista), and a "democratic youth" group (Juventud Democrática) were organized. The National Democratic Party was organized before the elections in May 1947. These parties have now disappeared and the Partido Dominicano remains the only one in active existence. All members of Congress and the Cabinet belong to it.

Generalísimo Trujillo refused to run for another term in 1952, but supported the nomination of his brother General Hector B. Trujillo Molina.

THE CABINET

The following are the members of the President's Cabinet: General José García Trujillo, Armed Forces; Luis Ruiz Trujillo, Presidency; Porfirio Herrera Báez, Foreign Affairs; Pedro M. Hungría, Interior; Manuel V. Ramos, Agriculture; César A. Cortina, Public Works; J. A. Turull, Finance; Víctor Garrido, Education and Fine Arts; Mario Abreu Penzo, Justice; Juan O. Velázquez, Industry and Commerce; Dr. José G. Sobá, Public Health; José A. Castellanos, Labor; Virgilio Alvarez Pina, Worship; R. Paíno Pichardo, Communications and Transport; Virgilio Alvarez Sánchez, Banking and Credit.

PRESS

Unless otherwise noted, papers are published in the capital city.

Name of Paper	Circulation	Political Affiliation	Proprietor, Editor, etc.
La Nación	20,000	Pro-Government; founded in 1940.	Manuel Valldeperes (*Dir.*)
El Caribe	30,000	Pro-Government; founded in 1947.	Rafael Herrera (*Dir.*)
La Información (Santiago)	8,000	Pro-Government; founded in 1915.	Luis A. Franco (*Dir.*)
El Diario de Macorís (San Pedro de Macorís)	1,000	Pro-Government; founded in 1922.	Néstor Febles (*Dir.*)
The Herald (weekly)	3,500	Independent; in English.	William Johnson (*Ed.*)

ECUADOR

Capital: Quito
Area: 116,270 square miles
Population: 4,080,000 (1958 estimate)

President

DR. CAMILO PONCE ENRIQUEZ
Elected on June 3, 1956, for four-year term

Cabinet

Coalition of Conservatives, Social Christians, Liberals and Independents; appointed in September 1956

PARLIAMENT
(Congreso)

Congress consists of an Upper Chamber (Senado) and a Lower Chamber (Cámara de Diputados).

PARTY PROGRAMS AND LEADERS

THE CONSERVATIVE PARTY: United in a coalition with the Social Christian Party and elected Camilo Ponce Enriquez President in the June 3, 1956, Presidential election, thus giving Ecuador its first conservative-oriented administration in 61 years. Dr. Ponce won by a margin of 3,000 votes over his closest rival, Dr. Raúl Clemente Huerta of the coalition National Democratic Front of Liberals and Socialists. Final official vote was: Ponce, 178,424 and Huerta 175,378.

Leaders: Manuel Jijon Caamaño y Flores, Enrique Arroyo Delgado, Enrique Arizaga Toral, José Gabriel Teran Varea.

LIBERAL RADICAL PARTY: Held power practically continuously from the late nineteenth century until the Revolution of May 1944. Opposes participation by the Church in politics and secular control of education. It joined the Socialist Party to form the National Democratic Front coalition for the June 3, 1956, Presidential elections.

Leaders: Raúl Clemente Huerta (National Director), Julio Moreno Espinosa, Rodrigo Jacome Moscoso, Leonardo Cornejo, Caton Cardenas, Carlos Plaza Dañin.

SOCIALIST PARTY: Divided into two factions, right-wing and left-wing. The right-wing group advocates a conventional Socialist program, and has joined in a united front with the Liberal Party and independents in recent elections. The left-wing Socialists have joined in pacts with the Communist Party, and in general follow the Communist line.

Leaders: Right-wing: Ricardo Cornejo Rosales (Secretary General), Eliecer Irigoyen, Jaun Isaac Lovato. Left-wing: Manuel Agustin Aguirre, Miguel Angel Arauz, Victor Zuñiga.

NATIONAL VELASQUISTA MOVEMENT (Velasquistas): A group of supporters of three-time former President José Maria Velasco Ibarra, who is now living in Montevideo, Uruguay.

ECUADOR

Leaders: Manuel Araujo Hidalgo, Jaime Nebot Velasco, Carlos Julio Arosemena.

COMMUNIST PARTY: Advocates a conventional Communist program.
Leaders: Pedro Saad (Secretary General), Oswaldo Albornoz Peralta (Secretary for Propaganda), Rafael Echeverria Flores (Secretary for Organization), Jose Maria Roura Cevallos (Treasurer), Marco Tulio Ormas (Secretary for Trade Unions), Enrique Gil Gilbert, Ricardo Paredes, Jorge Arellano.

NATIONAL REVOLUTIONARY ACTION (ARNE): Formed in the early forties after the pattern of the Spanish Falangist Party. Exercised greater influence during the recent Velasco Administration than at any time since its founding. Advocates nationalism, military preparedness, an authoritarian type of democracy, and social and agrarian reforms.
Leader: Jorge Luna Yepez.

CONCENTRATION OF POPULAR FORCES (CFP): Its founder and leader, Dr. Carlos Guevara Moreno, former Mayor of Guayaquil, ran for the Presidency in the June 3, 1956, election on the CFP ticket, and came in third with 149,935 votes. The Party's greatest strength is in the Guayaquil area.
Leader: Carlos Guevara Moreno.

THE CABINET

The members of the Cabinet are: Dr. Carlos Bustamante Pérez (Government), Carlos Tobar Zaldumbide (Foreign Affairs), Dr. José Basquerizo Maldonado (Public Education), Sixto Durán Ballén (Public Works), Alfonso Calderón (Defense), Dr. Gonzalo Cordero Crespo (Social Welfare and Labor), Luis Gómez Izquierdo (Treasury), Gustavo Mortensen Gangotena (Production), and Isidro Icaza Plaza (Economy).

PRESS

Unless otherwise noted, papers are published in the capital city.

Name of Paper	Circulation	Political Affiliation	Proprietor, Editor, etc.
El Comercio	25,000	Independent: commercial; founded in 1906, widely read.	Carlos Mantilla & Son (*Props. and Eds.*)
Diario del Ecuador	15,000	Independent; liberal.	Francisco Illescas (*Prop.*) Eduardo Borja (*Ed.*)
La Tierra	1,500	Leftist; Socialist.	José Jaramillo Hidalgo (*Dir.*)
Ultimas Noticias	5,000	Independent.	Published as afternoon daily by *El Comercio*
Crónica (Ambato)	1,500	Independent.	Dr. Tarquino Toro Navas (*Prop. and Ed.*)
El Globo (Bahia de Caráquez)	1,700	Independent.	Carlos V. Palau (*Prop. and Ed.*)
El Mercurio (Cuenca)	1,500	Conservative.	Miguel Merchán (*Prop.*)
La Hora (Guayaquil)	5,000	Liberal.	Simon Cañarte B. (*Dir.*)
La Nacíon (Guayaquil)	8,000	Liberal.	Simon Cañarte B. (*Prop.*)
La Prensa (Guayaquil)	5,000	Independent.	Pompilio Ulloa (*Prop. and Ed.*)
El Telégrafo (Guayaquil)	25,000	Liberal; dean of Ecuadorian newspapers.	Castillo & Sons (*Props.*)
El Universo (Guayaquil)	45,000	Independent.	Sucre Pérez Castro (*Prop. and Ed.*)
La Provincia (Portoviejo)	4,000	Independent; liberal.	Felipe Saul Morales (*Prop.*)

FINLAND

Capital: Helsinki (Helsingfors)
Area: 130,148 square miles (after the cession of 16,548 square miles to the Soviet Union)
Population: 4,375,340 (92% Finnish Speaking, 8% Swedish Speaking, 1958 estimate)

President
URHO KALEVA KEKKONEN
Elected February 15, 1956
Inaugurated March 1, 1956, for six-year term

Cabinet
Five Party Coalition
Appointed August 29, 1958
This Cabinet resigned on December 4, 1958,
but continues as Caretaker Government

Premier
K. A. FAGERHOLM (Social Democrat)

PARLIAMENT
(Eduskunta)
Election of July 6–7, 1958 (four-year term)
Speaker: V. J. SUKSELAINEN (Agrarian)

Parties	Representation
Finnish People's Democratic Union (Dominated by Finnish Communist Party)	50
Agrarian	48
Social Democratic	38
Coalition Conservative Party	29
Swedish People's Party	14
Social Democratic Opposition	13
Finnish People's Party	8
Total	200

RECENT POLITICAL EVENTS

Economic difficulties had a strong effect on the political life in Finland in 1958. This was evident in the elections held in July 1958. The Social Democrats and the Agrarians, who for nearly a decade had shared jointly or separately the responsibility of government, suffered a loss, whereas the opposition parties both on the right and left gained ground. A split in the Social Democratic Party also contributed to their loss. The Communists gained seven seats, the Coalition Conservative Party five, and the Swedish People's Party one. The Agrarian Party and the Finnish People's Party lost five seats each. The two Social Democratic groups got three seats less than their previously unified party had held.

FINLAND

After negotiations for two months, K. A. Fagerholm was able to form a coalition cabinet with strong parliamentary support. In this cabinet all parties, except the Communists and the Social Democratic Opposition, are represented. The main objective of the new government is the stabilization of economic conditions.

PARTY PROGRAMS AND LEADERS

SOCIAL DEMOCRATIC PARTY: Constitutional socialistic program; mainly supported by the working class, with some support among small farmers.

Leaders: Vainö Tanner, Chairman of Party; Kaarlo Pitsinki, Secretary of Party; Gunnar Henriksson, Chairman of Diet Group; Karl-August Fagerholm, Premier; Väinö Leskinen.

SOCIAL DEMOCRATIC OPPOSITION: After the 1958 parliamentary election this group became a separate faction. Some notable leaders of the Trade Unions belong to this Social Democratic Opposition.

Leaders: Aarre Simonen, Chairman of the Diet Group, Eero Antikainen, Chairman of the Finnish Trade Unions; Emil Skog.

AGRARIANS: A center party founded to promote the interests of the rural population, especially those of the numerous small farmers, on the line of individual enterprise.

Leaders: V. J. Sukselainen, Chairman of Party; Johannes Virolainen, Vice-Chairman of Party; Arvo Korsimo, Secretary of Party; Kauno Kleemola, Chairman of Diet Group; Mrs. Kerttu Saalasti.

FINNISH PEOPLE'S DEMOCRATIC UNION (SKDL): Communist-controlled organization for promoting collaboration among all leftist groups. The SKDL includes the Communist Party and several semi-political organizations.

Leaders: Mrs. Hertta Kuusinen, Chairman of Diet Group (Communist); Yrjö Enne, Secretary of the Union (Communist); T. I. Kujala, First Vice-Speaker of Diet (Communist); Eino Kilpi, Vice-Chairman of Diet Group.

COMMUNIST PARTY: A conventional Stalinist-Leninist Communist party; represented in Diet through the SKDL.

Leaders: Aimo Aaltonen, Chairman of Party; Ville Pessi, Secretary of Party; Hertta Kuusinen.

COALITION CONSERVATIVE PARTY: Advocates democratic, social and legal order on conservative lines, and private enterprise.

Leaders: Jussi Saukkonen, Chairman of Party and Chairman of Diet Group; Päiviö Hetemäki; T. A. Wiherheimo; Kalevi Teräsalmi, Secretary of Party.

SWEDISH PEOPLE'S PARTY: Swedish-speaking minority party; divided on political and social questions, with liberals in majority.

Leaders: Lars-Erik Taxell, Chairman of Party; John Osterholm, Chairman of Diet Group; Ralf Törngren; Nils Meinander.

FINNISH PEOPLE'S LIBERAL PARTY: A new party, with a liberal democratic program.

Leaders: Veli Merikoski, Chairman of Party; Esa Kaitila, Chairman of Diet Group; Pekka Malinen, Secretary of Party.

FINLAND

THE CABINET

The members of the Cabinet are: Karl-August Fagerholm, Social Democrat (Premier); Johannes Virolainen, Agrarian (Deputy Premier and Foreign Affairs); Sven Högström, Swedish People's Party (Justice); Atte Pakkanen, Agrarian (Interior); T. A. Wiherheimo, Conservative (Defense); Päiviö Hetemäki, Conservative (Finance); Kaarlo Kajatsalo, Finnish People's Party (Education); Urho Kähönen, Agrarian (Agriculture); Kustaa Eskola, Agrarian (Communications); Onni Hiltunen, Social Democrat (Trade and Industry); Väinö Leskinen, Social Democrat (Social Affairs).

PRESS

Unless otherwise noted, papers are published in the capital city.

Name of Paper	Political Affiliation	Proprietor, Editor, etc.
Helsingin Sanomat	Independent, liberal.	Yrjö Niiniluoto (*Ed.*)
Uusi Suomi	Conservative.	E. Petäjäniemi (*Ed.*)
Kansan Uutiset	SKDL and Communist.	Jorma Simpura (*Ed.*)
Hufvudstadsbladet	Swedish People's.	Egidius Ginström (*Ed.*)
Suomen Sosialidemokraatti	Social Democrat.	Atte Pohjanmaa (*Ed.*)
Ilkka (Vaasa)	Agrarian.	Veikko Pirilä (*Ed.*)
Ilta-Sanomat	Independent, liberal.	Teo I. Mertanen (*Ed.*)
Maakansa	Agrarian.	Pentti Sorvali (*Ed.*)
Maaseudun Tulevaisuus	Independent, agricultural.	Onni Koskikallio (*Ed.*)
Nya Pressen	Swedish People's.	Axel Grönvik (*Ed.*)
Ny Tid	Democratic Union.	Mikael Romberg (*Ed.*)
Svenska Demokraten	Social Democrat.	Gunnar Henriksson (*Ed.*)
Kauppalehti	Commercial, Independent.	Pentti Poukka (*Ed.*)
Aamulehti (Tampere)	Conservative.	Jaakko Hakala (*Ed.*)
Kansan Lehti (Tampere)	Social Democrat.	Arvo Tuominen (*Ed.*)
Savon Sanomat (Kuopio)	Agrarian.	E. Lappalainen (*Ed.*)
Kansan Tahto (Oulu)	Democratic Union.	Into Kangas (*Ed.*)
Turun Sanomat (Turku)	Independent.	Weikko Puro (*Ed.*)
Uusi Aura (Turku)	Conservative.	Sakari Talvitie (*Ed.*)
Vaasa (Vaasa)	Conservative.	Ilmari Laukkonen (*Ed.*)
Keskisuomalainen (Jyväskylä)	Agrarian.	M.E. Juusela (*Ed.*)
Vasabladet (Vaasa)	Swedish People's.	E. Sundquist (*Ed.*)
Talouselämä (weekly)	Economic.	Jaakko Kahma (*Ed.*)
Mercator (weekly)	Economic.	Eige Cronström (*Ed.*)
Bank of Finland Monthly Bulletin (monthly)	Economic (in English).	Reino Rossi (*Ed.*)
Economic Review (quarterly)	Economic (in English).	Tuure Junnila (*Ed.*)
Unitas (quarterly)	Economic (in English).	Göran Stjernschantz (*Ed.*)

NEWS AGENCIES

Suomen Tietotoimisto (STT)	Semi-official.	E. A. Berg (*Mgr.*)
Työväen Sanomalehtien Tietotoimisto (TST)	Social Democrat.	Eino Kalkkinen (*Mgr.*)
Demokraattinen Lehtipalvelu (DLP)	Democratic Union.	Timo Koste (*Mgr.*)
Maaseutulehtien Uutiskeskus (UK)	Agrarian.	Matti Hakkarainen (*Mgr.*)
Oikeiston Sanomapalvelu (OSP)	Conservative.	Leo Lahtinen (*Mgr.*)
Suomen Kansanpuolueen Uutistoimisto (K)	People's Party.	Lauri Kuntijärvi (*Mgr.*)

FRANCE

Capital: Paris
Area: 212,659 square miles
Population: 44,289,000 (1958 estimate)

President

GENERAL CHARLES DE GAULLE
Elected by Electoral College on December 21, 1958
Assumed office on January 8, 1959, for seven-year term

Cabinet

Union for The New Republic—7, Popular Republican—4,
African Democratic Rally—1, Radical—1, Algerian Group—1,
Independent and Non-Party—12
Appointed January 8, 1959

Premier

MICHEL DEBRÉ (Union for the New Republic)

NATIONAL ASSEMBLY

Elected November 23 and 30, 1958 (for five years)
President: JACQUES CHABAN-DELMAS (Union for the New Republic)

Parties	Representation
Union for the New Republic	189
Independents and Moderates	136
Socialists, Left Center, and Miscellaneous Left	66
MRP and Christian Democracy	57
Radicals, Radical Socialists and Left Republicans	16
Communists	10
Extreme Right	1
Elected in Algeria	71
Total	546†*

† Thirty-nine deputies from overseas continue to sit temporarily until new institutions are set up by the new Constitution.
* The "Journal Officiel" has not yet published the list of the party groups and of their members in the new National Assembly. The grouping indicated above may therefore be subject to change.

(65)

SENATE

Elected May 18, 1952, and June 19, 1955 (for six years; one-half renewable every three years).

President: GASTON MONNERVILLE (Radical Socialist)

Parties		Representation
Communists	14	
affiliated	1	15
Democratic Left	57	
affiliated	1	58
U.D.S.R.—R.D.A.	10	10
Union pour la Nouvelle Rep.	29	29
Independent Republicans	63	
affiliated	3	66
Republican Center Group	3	3
Republican Center Group of Social & Rural Action	21	21
M.R.P.	22	22
Socialists	51	
affiliated	12	63
Total		287*

* List of the members of political groups submitted to the Presidency of the Senate on December 10, 1958 in accordance with the motion passed by the Senate on December 9, 1958. The difference between the present number of Senators (287) and the number of Senators previously seated in the Council of the Republic (320) is due to the following facts: 1) Some Senators have been appointed to governmental positions, 2) Some Senators were elected deputies on November 30, 1958, 3) Some Senators are not seated in the present Senate (Guinea) 4) Some Senate seats fell vacant. The senatorial body will be entirely re-elected in April 1959.

THE FOURTH FRENCH REPUBLIC

By a referendum on October 13, 1946, France adopted a new Constitution that had been worked out by the Second Constituent Assembly, which had been elected by proportional representation. It established two houses of Parliament, the National Assembly and the Council of the Republic. Of these, nearly all the power was held by the Assembly, which was elected by universal suffrage. It voted the budget, and the Government was directly responsible to it.

Under this Constitution, the President of the Republic fulfilled for the most part ceremonial functions. It was he, however, who designated the Prime Minister who, in turn, in order to take office, must, together with his Cabinet, be "invested" by a voting majority of the members of the National Assembly. The President also presided over the Council of Ministers and could demand that the Assembly reconsider a law before he promulgated it. The Assembly could remove a Government from office when more than one-half of the deputies voted against it in a vote of confidence or if they voted a motion of censure. The Government, on the other hand, could dissolve the Assembly only if there were two adverse votes of confidence within 18 months, and after the first 18 months of the life of an Assembly. Premier Faure used this provision to dissolve the Assembly in 1955.

The Council of the Republic, elected indirectly, had limited powers. Bills examined in first reading by either chamber of Parliament were "shuttled" back and forth between the two bodies until they approved identical texts. However, failing agreement within a period of one hundred days from the day on which the bill was submitted to the Council of the Republic for a second reading, the National Assembly could rule definitely.

POLITICAL EVENTS DURING THE FOURTH REPUBLIC

The first National Assembly, elected on November 10, 1946, showed the Communists to be numerically the strongest party (5.5 million votes, 166 deputies), closely followed by the MRP (Popular Republicans), a new Catholic liberal party which obtained 5.1 million votes (158 deputies). The Socialists, with 3.4 million votes (90 deputies) were the third strongest party. (All figures of votes pertain to Metropolitan France only.) In the first phase of the Assembly's life, the Communists, Socialists, and MRP governed together. The Radical Socialists, Peasants, Independents, and PRL had between them only a third of the seats in the National Assembly.

The Communists in May 1947, ceased their cooperation and reverted to their original role of opposition, with full emphasis on the class-struggle and on alignment with Soviet Russia. The re-emergence of de Gaulle as the leader of the new political movement, the Rally of the French People (RPF), also profoundly changed the political line-up, although this was not fully reflected in the National Assembly until 1951. From 1947 to 1951 the government was one based on the center parties (Socialists, MRP, Radical Socialists —then called "Third Force"—plus miscellaneous rightists), with the Communists on the left and the Gaullists on the right constituting the opposition.

New national elections were held in June 1951. Whereas the 1946 elections to the Assembly had still been held under a system of proportional representation, the 1951 elections featured a limited form of majority voting. It resulted in a loss of seats by the Communists and MRP and the advent of the Gaullists.

By popular votes, the Communists were still the strongest party in the 1951 elections (5.0 million votes) but they had lost about 10 per cent of their supporters and obtained only 101 seats in the Assembly. The Gaullists, with 4.1 million votes, obtained 120 seats.

After the election of 1951 the Socialists finally went into outright opposition and a new majority was achieved when M. Pinay presented himself for investiture in March 1952. His government, which was accompanied by a relative stabilization of the economic situation, saw a further development of the trend toward cooperation among the Gaullists.

After Pinay was overthrown in December 1952, the RPF finally made a complete break with its past, accorded support to the Government of René Mayer and subsequently not only supported but also participated in the Government of Joseph Laniel. The Laniel Government, which lasted from June 28, 1953, to June 18, 1954, represented the final stages of the post-war trend to the right.

With the advent of Pierre Mendès-France to the Premiership in June 1954, a new and heterogeneous majority was formed consisting largely of the Radicals, the Social Republicans (Gaullists), the Socialists and scattered deputies from other parties. Opposition to Mendès-France consisted primarily of the MRP, the conservative groups (Independents, Peasants and ARS), and also the Communists. In view of the Prime Minister's own policies and of Socialist support, although they did not participate in the Cabinet, the Government and its majority tended to have a center-left orientation.

Mendès-France was voted out of office by the National Assembly on February 5, 1955, on his North African policy. He was succeeded by Edgar Faure on February 23rd. Faure received a vote of no confidence on November 29, 1955, and invoked the procedure provided by the Constitution for dissolving the Assembly, and called for new elections on January 2, 1956. This election was fought by four main political groups: the Communists on the Left, the Left-of-Center following of Mendès-France, the Right-of-Center group behind caretaker Premier Edgar Faure, and the anti-tax rightists.

Guy Mollet, the Socialist leader, succeeded Edgar Faure on January 31, 1956, with a Left-of-Center Minority Cabinet made up largely of Socialists and Radicals, and joined later by the Social Republicans. The Mollet régime received shifting support—from the Left on internal and on economic and social issues, and from the Right on Algerian and foreign policy. Its forceful stand on the Suez nationalization united all parties, except the Communists, behind the Government.

Mollet was defeated in the Assembly on May 22, 1957. He was replaced on June 12, 1957, by Maurice Bourgès-Maunoury, Radical Socialist. The Bourgès-Maunoury government completed action on the ratification of the Euratom and Common Market treaties. It then set about the task of drafting a basic law for Algeria. The Parliament was called back into Special Session in September. After considerable attempts to find common ground for the proposed Algerian legislation, Bourgès-Maunoury was forced to ask for a confidence vote. The government fell on September 30. After a 36-day crisis, Radical Socialist Félix Gaillard was invested with a majority running from Socialists through Moderates. Gaillard was succeeded by Pierre Pflimlin on May 15, 1958, and by General de Gaulle on June 1, 1958.

THE FIFTH FRENCH REPUBLIC

The political situation, which had been deteriorating in France for many months, came to a head in the spring of 1958, with dissidence in Algeria and resurgent Gaullism at home. The National Assembly declared a state of emergency in May. The situation continued to deteriorate, however, and on June 1st General de Gaulle was invested as Premier by the Assembly which accepted his terms, that included: a) six-month full decree power to take legislative measures necessary for the nation's recovery, b) right to propose and submit to popular referendum a new Constitution based on these principles: 1) Universal suffrage is the source of power; 2) Separation of the Executive and Legislative powers; 3) Government responsibility to Parliament; 4) Independence of the Judiciary; 5) Definition of a new association with the Overseas Territories.

A revision of the Constitution was made and approved by a referendum on September 28, 1958. A new National Assembly was elected on November 23 and 30, 1958, and General de Gaulle was elected President of the Fifth Republic on December 21st to take office on January 8, 1959. The new National Assembly will convene for business in April, 1959.

The new Constitution gives much more power to the President and the Premier than they enjoyed under the Fourth Republic. The President is not required to submit his Premier and Cabinet for formal investiture. Nor can he or the Cabinet be easily overthrown. In a dispute with the Assembly the President can appeal to the electorate by referendum. He also holds the power to dissolve the Assembly and call for new elections.

POLITICAL PARTIES AND LEADERS

The programs and leadership of the parties in the new assembly, which has as yet met only to elect its President, are not yet clear. The following descriptions therefore refer mostly to the past, but are given as a matter of record. Many of the party leaders were not elected to the new Assembly which will assemble in April 1959.

UNION FOR THE NEW REPUBLIC: Formed in 1958 to support General de Gaulle in the establishment of the Fifth Republic. It was the leaders of this group who worked shrewdly and patiently to bring the General back to power. The Gaullists have sworn to refrain from joining other groups, to remain faithful to the party's objectives, to sustain actions of General de Gaulle in Parliament and in their districts, and to accept voting discipline on major questions.

Leaders: Michel Debré, Jacques Soustelle, Jacques Chaban-Delmas.

COMMUNIST PARTY: The largest party in Parliament during the Fourth Republic. In the 1958 election for the new Assembly, however, its representation was reduced from 144 to 10. While playing down communism and the dictatorship of the proletariat, the party's national program heavily emphasizes demands for peace and social betterment. It has endeavored to promote "unity of action" with the Socialists but without success because of its opposite foreign policy goals and opposition to the government's policy toward Algeria. It advocates some nationalization measures, but also the support of small industries and crafts, and "the defense of the peasant landowners against trusts." Because of their more decisive and more definitely left-wing policy, the Communists immediately after the war managed to win over many Frenchmen who formerly voted Socialist. They control France's largest labor organization, the Confédération Générale du Travail (CGT). They also exert some influence among the peasants. They emphasize the democratic and national character of their party. In *foreign policy:* opposed to American aid, to NATO, to the Schuman Plan and to German rearmament. Favors the Soviet-sponsored "peace" movements, uses nationalist slogans to warn against German association with Western Europe, and indirectly encourages "neutralist" propaganda and anti-colonialism.

Leaders: Maurice Thorez, Jacques Duclos, François Billoux and Etienne Fajon.

SOCIALIST PARTY: The party has consistently suffered from being out-bid by its less responsible neighbors on the Left. In the Provisional Government it had to play the role of a center party between the Communists and the MRP. As a result, it lost to the Right those members who feared too close a collaboration with the Communists; and it lost to the Communists those who feared it had become simply a party of compromise. Advocates state planning, full employment, collective bargaining, high wages, control of prices. Opposed to cooperation with the Communists. Approves defense expenditures. For industry it favors two sectors, one socialized and one free. In *foreign policy:* it favors NATO and European integration.

Leaders: Guy Mollet (Secretary-General), André Le Troquer, Albert Gazier, Christian Pineau, Daniel Mayer, Marcel-Edmond Naegelen, Charles Lussy and Jules Moch.

POPULAR REPUBLICAN MOVEMENT (MPR): This is a party which developed out of the Resistance. It is descended from the pre-war Parti Démocrate Populaire. Although it derives support from some conservatives who see in it a bulwark against communism, the party program has been moderately leftist in character. At the same time, however, the party contains strong Catholic elements. The party stands for limited nationalization, collective bargaining, full employment and development of exports. Until the advent of Mendès-France, the MRP had formed part of every Government coalition and participated in every Cabinet since the end of World War II, with either

Georges Bidault or Robert Schuman as Foreign Minister. It was in opposition to Mendès-France but participated in the Faure Cabinet, and the Gaillard Government. In *foreign policy:* it is the party that most strongly favors Western European integration.

Leaders: Pierre Pflimlin (Party Chairman), P. H. Teitgen, Georges Bidault, Maurice Schuman, Robert Schuman, André Colin, Robert Lecourt, François de Menthon.

REPUBLICAN RADICAL AND RADICAL SOCIALIST PARTY: The strength and prestige of the "great" party of the Third Republic was at its lowest ebb at the time of the liberation. It has participated in the coalition Governments since November 1947, and has had a part in the gradual return to free economy. With the advent of Radical-Socialist Mendès-France to the Premiership, the political orientation of the Party tended to left-center. The Party favors a return to the system of majority vote in single-member constituencies, constitutional reform and better distribution of taxes and reform of social security. After Edgar Faure became Premier, Mendès-France gained control of the Party and had him and other leading members, including René Mayer and Léon Martinaud-Déplat, expelled. In the 1956 election the Faure faction candidates appeared on the ballot of the Rally of the Republican Left. A dissident group of 14 deputies led by Henri Queuille and André Morice founded a new parliamentary group in October 1956, calling itself just "Radical Socialist."

Leaders: Edouard Daladier, Pierre Mendès-France, Félix Gaillard, Maurice Bourgès-Maunoury. André Morice and Vincent Badie (dissidents).

DEMOCRATIC AND SOCIALIST UNION OF RESISTANCE (USDR and RDA): A coalition of erstwhile Socialist and non-Communist resistance groups loosely affiliated with the Radical Socialist Party. Includes overseas deputies (RDA).

Leaders: François Mitterand (President), René Pleven, Eugène Claudius-Petit and Félix Houphouet-Boigny.

RALLY OF THE REPUBLICAN LEFT (RGR): This loose association of Radical-Socialists, UDSR, and minor parties formed a group in the Council of the Republic (now the Senate) called "Gauche Démocratique." Following the split in the Radical Socialist Party between Mendès-France and Faure, the latter retained control of the Rally and formed a new group in the National Assembly under its label.

Leader: Edgar Faure.

INDEPENDENTS AND PEASANTS FOR SOCIAL ACTION (IPAS): Rightist group, solidly devoted to defense of free enterprise, but state aid for certain branches of agriculture, constitutional reform, state support for church schools and administrative reform; includes the last legitimate Prime Minister of the Third Republic, Paul Reynaud. The IPAS includes the former Independent Republicans, Independent Peasants and the remnants of the RPF dissidents. A new dissident group of the Peasant Party, the Peasants for Social and Rural Action (PASR), is allied to it.

Leaders: Antoine Pinay, Roger Duchet (Secretary-General), Paul Reynaud, Jean Legendre, Raymond Marcellin, Jean Laborde, René Coty.

THE CABINET

The members of the Cabinet are: Michel Debré (Premier), Jacques Soustelle (Minister Delegate), Félix Houphouet-Boigny, Robert Lecourt, André

FRANCE

Malraux and Louis Jacquinot (Ministers of State), Edmond Michelet (Justice), Maurice Couve de Murville (Foreign Affairs), Jan Berthoin (Interior), Jean Guillaumat (Armed Forces), Antoine Pinay (Finance and Economic Affairs), André Bulloche (Education), Robert Buron (Public Works), Pierre Jeanneney (Industry and Commerce), Roger Houdet (Agriculture), Bernard Cornut-Gentille (Communications), Paul Bacon (Labor), Bernard Chenot (Health), Pierre Sudreau (Housing), Raymond Triboulet (Veterans), Roger Frey (Information). There are six Secretaries of State: Mlle. Nefissa sid Cara, Victor Chatenay, Max Vlechet, Joseph Fontanet, Valery Giscard d'Estaing, Maurice Bokanowsky.

PRESS

I. PARIS DAILIES—MORNING

Name of Paper	Circulation*	Political Affiliation	Proprietor, Editor, etc.
L'Aurore	475,000	Rightist.	Robert Lazurick (Dir.)
Combat	73,000	Independent.	Henry Smadja (Dir.)
Les Echos	40,000	Financial.	E. Servan Schreiber (Dir.)
Le Figaro	510,000	Conservative.	Pierre Brisson (Dir.)
Paris-Journal	105,000	Liberal.	E. Peju (Dir.)
L'Humanité	218,000	Communist.	Marcel Cachin (Dir.)
Libération	118,000	Crypto-Communist.	Emmanuel D'Astier de la Vigerie (Dir.)
Le Parisien Libéré	880,000	Independent; rightist.	Claude Bellanger (Ed.)
Le Populaire	15,000	Socialist.	René Naegelen (Dir.)

II. PARIS DAILIES—EVENING

Name	Circulation	Affiliation	Editor
France-Soir	1,345,000	Moderate.	Pierre Lazareff (Dir.)
La Croix	153,000	Catholic.	Joseph Matheron (Dir.)
Le Monde	210,000	Independent.	Hubert Beuve-Méry (Dir.)
L'Information	62,000	Business.	André Bollack (Ed.)
Paris-Presse-L'Intransigeant	185,000	Moderate.	Henri Massot (Ed.)

III. PARIS DAILIES—PUBLISHED IN ENGLISH

Name	Circulation	Affiliation	Editor
Daily Mail (London)	22,000	British, Continental edition.	Noel Barber (Ed.)
New York Herald-Tribune	59,000	American, European edition.	Ogden Reid (Pres.)

IV. PROVINCIAL NEWSPAPERS

Name	Circulation	Affiliation	Place of Publication
Résistance de l'Ouest	86,000	Moderate.	Nantes
Le Courier de l'Ouest	100,000	Rightist.	Angers
La Liberté du Massif Central	65,000	Moderate.	Clermont Ferrand
La Nouvelle République du Centre Ouest	249,000	Socialist.	Tours
La Nouvelle République	126,000	Left.	Bordeaux
Sud-Ouest	345,000	Moderate.	Bordeaux
Liberté de Lille	62,000	Communist.	Lille
Nord Eclair	73,000	MRP.	Lille
Nord Matin	172,000	Socialist.	Lille
Voix du Nord	353,000	Moderate.	Lille
L'Echo-Liberté	56,000	Center Left.	Lyon
Le Progrès de Lyon	375,000	Left.	Lyon
Le Dauphiné Libéré	341,000	Independent.	Grenoble
Le Dépêche de Saint-Etienne	60,000	Center Left.	Saint-Etienne
La République du Centre	65,000	UDSR.	Orleans
La Tribune du Centre et du Sud Est	89,000	Radical Socialist.	Saint-Etienne
Le Télégramme de Brest	125,000	Moderate.	Morlaix

Name of Paper	Circulation*	Political Affiliation	Place of Publication
La Marseillaise	90,000	Communist.	Marseilles
Le Provençal	208,000	Socialist.	Marseilles
Le Méridional-La France	107,000	Rightist.	Marseilles
Le Républicain Lorrain	172,000	Independent.	Metz
Midi Libre	169,000	Independent.	Montpellier
Nice-Matin	116,000	RGR.	Nice
L'Est Républicain	247,000	Independent.	Nancy
L'Union	152,000	Independent.	Reims
Ouest France	577,000	MRP.	Rennes
Paris Normandie	157,000	Left.	Rouen
Courrier Picard	76,000	Independent.	Amiens
Les Dernières Nouvelles d'Alsace	140,000	Independent.	Strasbourg
L'Alsace	95,000	Independent.	Mulhouse
La Dépêche du Midi	296,000	Radical Socialist.	Toulouse
La Montagne	148,000	RGR.	Clermont-Ferrand

V. LEADING PERIODICALS

Name of Publication	Character	Proprietor, Editor, etc.
Carrefour	Political-Gaullist.	Félix Garas (*Dir.*)
Figaro Littéraire	Literary-Conservative.	Pierre Brisson (*Ed.*)
Force Ouvrière	Syndical CGT-FO (non-Communist)	Robert Bothereau (*Dir.*) André Viot (*Ed.*)
France Nouvelle	Political-Communist.	Florimond Bonté (*Dir.*)
Point de Vue—Images du Monde	Rightist.	Charles Giron (*Dir.*)
Lettres Françaises	Communist.	Louis Aragon (*Dir.*) Pierre Daix (*Ed.*)
Nouvelles Littéraires	Literary-moderate.	André Gillon (*Dir.*) G. Charensol (*Ed.*)
Paris-Match	Moderate.	M. Lebreton (*Ed.*)
Témoignage Chrétien	Catholic; liberal.	J. Gérard-Libois (*Ed.*)
L'Express	Pro-Mendès-France.	Jean-Jacques Servan-Schreiber (*Ed.*)
La Terre	Agricultural; Communist.	Waldeck-Rochet (*Ed.*)
La Terre Nouvelle	Agricultural; conservative.	Jean Delcroix (*Ed.*)
Tribune des Nations	Leftist.	Joseph Dubois (*Ed.*)
France-Dimanche	Sensational.	Paul Guyot (*Dir.*)
Réalités	Conservative.	Didier W. Remon (*Dir.*)
Syndicalisme	Catholic Workers, C.F.T.C.	Maurice Bouladoux (*Dir.*)
Observateur	Neutralist.	Claude Bourdet (*Ed.*)
Climats	Overseas affairs; conservative.	Maurice Chevance (*Ed.*)
Aspects de la France et du Monde	Royalist.	Lionel Moreux (*Dir.*)
Le Peuple	Communist; Syndical C.G.T.	Jacques Marion (*Dir.*)

NEWS AGENCY

Agence France Presse	Independent.	Jean Marin (*Dir.*)

* The circulation figures are estimates derived from French sources.

GERMANY

Area: 137,607 square miles
Approximate area comprising pre-1938 Germany minus the area administered
by the USSR and Poland
Population: 71,171,200 (1957 estimate)

POLITICAL EVENTS SINCE 1945

As a consequence of unconditional surrender on May 8, 1945, the governments of the United States, the Soviet Union, Great Britain and France assumed full executive power in Germany. Germany was divided into four zones of occupation under American, British, French and Soviet control. The territories east of the Oder and Neisse Rivers were placed under Polish administration, East Prussia partly under Soviet and partly under Polish administration. Pending final settlement of borders by a Peace Treaty the Saar was attached economically to France. The four occupying powers pledged themselves to treat Germany as an economic entity and to safeguard parallel political developments in the four zones towards restoration of truly democratic institutions.

As the Soviet representative in the Allied Control Council failed to cooperate for fulfilment of the above mentioned pledges, the Federal Republic of Germany was formed on the initiative of the three Western occupation powers, following the decisions of the London Foreign Ministers Conference of 1948, which provided for the creation of a democratic state, based on federal principles. A Parliamentary Assembly went into session at Bonn on September 1, 1948, to draft a provisional Constitution or Basic Law. This instrument was approved by the Bonn Assembly on May 8, 1949, and signed on May 23, 1949. The Federal Republic consisting of the American, British and French zones, was proclaimed, with Bonn as its provisional capital. On the Saar a new agreement was reached between France and Germany in October 1956 following preceding elections. Effective January 1, 1957, the Saar became the tenth Land of the Federal Republic politically; economically a transition period is allowed lasting to January 1, 1960. In October 1949, the so-called German Democratic Republic (DDR) was proclaimed in the Soviet Zone. Berlin, however, remained divided into the sectors of the four occupying powers, with the Government of the DDR located in the Soviet Zone.

Elections for the West German Parliament were held on August 14, 1949 and resulted in a victory for the Christian Democratic Union, led by Dr. Konrad Adenauer. The Social Democratic Party under Dr. Kurt Schumacher, polled the next highest vote.

On September 12, 1949, Dr. Theodor Heuss, leader of the Free Democratic Party, was elected first President of the German Federal Republic. On September 15 the newly-elected Bundestag chose Dr. Adenauer as Chancellor, and he in turn selected a coalition Cabinet. General elections were again held on September 6, 1953, and on September 15, 1957, returning the Government Parties to power.

Step by step, the former military occupation of Western Germany was converted into a contractual relationship: final measures toward the restoration of sovereignty to the Federal Republic were taken at a Nine-Power Conference held in London from September 28 to October 3, 1954, and at a series of conferences in Paris from October 18 to October 23, 1954. With the ratification of the Bonn Conventions and the treaties regarding the admission of the Federal Republic to the Western European Union and its participation in the North Atlantic Treaty Organization on May 5, 1955, the Federal Republic became a sovereign state.

FEDERAL REPUBLIC OF GERMANY

Capital: Bonn
Area: 95,918 sq. mi. (including West Berlin and the Saar)
Population: 53,339,000 (including West Berlin and the Saar)

President
Dr. THEODOR HEUSS
Re-elected by the Federal Assembly on June 17, 1954, for five-year term

Cabinet
Coalition (Christian Democrats—16, German Party—2)
Appointed on October 28, 1957

Chancellor
Dr. KONRAD ADENAUER (Christian Democrat)
Elected by the Bundestag on September 15, 1949
Re-elected October 9, 1953, and October 22, 1957

PARLIAMENT
(Bundestag)
Election of September 15, 1957
President: Dr. EUGEN GERSTENMAIER (CDU)

Name of Party	Representation
Christian Democratic Union (CDU) and Christian Social Union (CSU)	270
Social Democrat (SPD)	169
Free Democrat (FDP)	41
German Party (DP)	17
Total	497

There are 22 representatives of West Berlin with only consultative status.
There is an Upper House or Bundesrat composed of 41 members appointed by State Governments, with the heads of State Governments alternating as President.

PARTY PROGRAMS AND LEADERS

THE CHRISTIAN DEMOCRATIC UNION (CDU) and its Bavarian affiliate, the CHRISTIAN SOCIAL UNION (CSU), emerged as the strongest party from the elections to the West German Bundestag in 1949, 1953, and again in 1957. It furnishes the Federal Chancellor.

The CDU is an inter-denominational middle-of-the-road party which seeks to solve political, social and economic problems by applying to them the principles of Christianity. It stands for the concept of the state being founded on the inviolable rights of the individual and of property, and for a social market economy with emphasis on free competition and enterprise. It defends rights of individual states of the Federal Republic.

Leaders: Dr. Konrad Adenauer (Chairman of Party), Theodor Blank (Vice-Chairman), Heinrich Krone, Dr. Eugen Gerstenmaier, Kai Uwe von Hassel, Heinrich von Brentano and Franz-Josef Strauss.

THE SOCIAL DEMOCRATIC PARTY (SPD), runner-up in the 1949, 1953, and 1957 elections to the Bundestag, is the principal opposition party and the most tightly organized of the democratic political groups in the Federal Republic. Founded in 1863, it derives from Marxist roots but may in practice be compared to the British Labor Party. The SPD advocates a strong, central German government, while respecting the federal structure of the West German Republic, equal chance in education for every citizen without respect to his religion, co-determination of labor in industry, public control of key industries and a national budget.

Leaders: Erich Ollenhauer (Chairman of Party), Waldemar von Knoeringen (Deputy Chairman), Herbert Wehner (Deputy Chairman). Dr. Kurt Schumacher, former leader, died on August 20, 1952.

THE FREE DEMOCRATIC PARTY (FDP) was formerly known as the Liberal Democratic Party. It stands on the moderate right. Professor Theodor Heuss, ex-Chairman of the FDP, was elected Federal President in 1949, and re-elected July 17, 1954. The party leaders stress the sanctity of private property, advocate unfettered free enterprise without state interference. They advocate a centralized federal government, particularly with regard to economics and finance, and non-denominational public education. They reject Socialistic experiments and state capitalism.

Leaders: Dr. Reinhold Maier (Chairman of Party), Dr. Erich Mende.

THE GERMAN PARTY (DP) is the most conservative element in the Federal Parliament and is merged now with the Free People's Party, a group that split from the FDP. The party did not succeed in polling 5% of the vote cast in the last elections, which is the prerequisite for representation in Parliament. However, as six of its candidates were elected by direct vote, this 5% clause was ruled out, so that the party is now represented in the Bundestag.

Leaders: Heinrich Hellwege (Chairman of Party), Heinrich Schneider, Dr. Hans-Joachim von Merkatz.

THE ALL-GERMAN BLOC—Bloc of Expellees and Victims of Injustice (GB-BHE) demands particularly indemnities for expellees and refugees and compensation for war damage as well as peaceful recovery of the Eastern territories. It ran in the 1953 elections and was the third largest party in the Coalition. In October 1955 it left the Government. In the 1957 elections it failed to win a seat, polling only 4.6% of the votes cast. The GB-BHE continues on the State and local levels.

Leaders: Frank Seiboth (Chairman of Party), Willi Guthsmuths, Dr. Alfred Gille, Gotthard Franke.

The Communist Party was outlawed as unconstitutional in September 1956 by the Federal Constitutional Court (as was the "Neo-nazi" Socialist

Reichsparty in 1953). In the 1953 elections it polled only 2.2% of the votes cast and therefore was not represented in the Federal Parliament.

All parties join in calling for the reunification of Germany. They favor all attempts to bring about a united Europe and are represented in the European organizations.

THE CABINET

The members of the Cabinet are: Dr. Konrad Adenauer, Chancellor (CDU); Prof. Dr. Ludwig Erhard, Vice-Chancellor and Economic Affairs (CDU); Dr. Heinrich von Brentano, Foreign Affairs (CDU); Dr. Gerhard Schröder, Interior (CDU); Franz-Josef Strauss, Defense (CSU); Franz Etzel, Finance (CDU); Fritz Schäffer, Justice (CSU); Dr. Hermann Lindrath, State-Owned Enterprise (CDU); Dr. Heinrich Lübke, Food and Agriculture (CDU); Theodor Blank, Labor and Social Security (CDU); Dr. Hans-Christoph Seebohm, Transport (DP); Paul Lücke, Housing (CDU); Ernst Lemmer, All-German Affairs (CDU); Dr. Hans-Joachim von Merkatz, Bundesrat and State Affairs (DP); Richard Stücklen, Post and Telecommunications (CSU); Dr. Theodor Oberländer, Expellees and War Victims (CDU); Dr. Franz-Josef Wuermeling, Family and Youth Affairs (CDU); Dr. Siegfried Balke, Atomic Energy and Water Supply (CSU).

THE PRESS

Name and Circulation of Paper	Political Orientation	Editor
WEST BERLIN		
Berliner Morgenpost 236,991	Independent.	Helmut Meyer-Dietrich
Telegraf 104,336	Independent; Socialist.	Arno Scholz
Der Abend 100,344	Independent.	M. Müller-Jabusch
Der Tagesspiegel 102,216	Independent.	Dr. Karl Silex
Der Kurier 32,843	Independent; Christian.	Dr. Karl Friedrich Grosse
BADEN-WURTTEMBERG		
Stuttgarter Zeitung 142,478 (Stuttgart)	Independent.	Josef Eberle
Schwäbische Zeitung 115,677 (Leutkirch/Allgau)	Independent; Pro-CDU.	T. Walterscheid
Mannheimer Morgen 121,801 (Mannheim)	Independent.	Dr. E. Frhr. von Schilling
Badische Neueste Nachrichten 126,701 (Karlsruhe)	Independent.	Wilh. Baur
Stuttgarter Nachrichten 80,323 (Stuttgart)	Independent.	H. Bernhard
Südkurier 86,042 (Konstanz)	Independent.	A. Gerigk
Rhein-Neckar-Zeitung 64,867 (Heidelberg)	Independent.	Dr. H. Knorr
BAVARIA		
Süddeutsche Zeitung 209,298 (Munich)	Independent.	Werner Friedmann
Schwäbische Landeszeitung 168,183 (Augsburg)	Independent; Pro-CDU.	Curt Frenzel
Münchner Merkur 166,562	Independent; Pro-CDU.	Dr. F. Buttersack
Nürnberger Nachrichten 166,257 (Nürnberg)	Independent; Pro-SPD.	Roland Buschmann
BREMEN		
Weser-Kurier 110,355 (Bremen)	Independent.	Dr. Karl Bachler
Bremer Nachrichten 46,396 (Bremen)	Independent.	W. Schmalfeldt

GERMANY

HAMBURG

Name and Circulation of Paper	Political Orientation	Editor
Hamburger Abendblatt 339,370 (Hamburg)	Independent; Pro-CDU.	Otto Siemer
Die Welt 232,936 (Hamburg)	Independent.	Hans Zehrer
Hamburger Morgenpost 281,779 (Hamburg)	Independent; Pro-SPD.	H. Braune

HESSEN

Abendpost 180,499 (Frankfurt/M.)	Independent.	Emil Frotscher
Frankfurter Rundschau 114,662 (Frankfurt/M.)	Independent; Pro-SPD.	Karl Gerold
Frankfurter Neue Presse 104,439 (Frankfurt/M.)	Independent; Pro-CDU.	Marcel Schulte
Frankfurter Allgemeine 220,341 (Frankfurt/M.)	Independent; liberal.	Editorial Board

LOWER SAXONY

Hannoversche Presse 151,277 (Hanover)	Independent; Pro-SPD.	
Hannoversche Allgemeine Zeitung 122,346 (Hanover)	Independent.	Wolfgang Köpker

NORTH RHINE-WESTPHALIA

Westdeutsche Allgemeine 414,200 (Essen)	Independent.	
Westfälische Rundschau 242,343 (Dortmund)	Pro-SPD.	Walter Poller
Rheinische Post 253,913 (Düsseldorf)	CDU.	Heinrich Darius
Neue Ruhr-Zeitung 229,966 (Essen)	Independent; Pro-SPD.	Klaus Besser
Kölnische Rundschau 152,388 (Cologne)	CDU.	Edmund Posch
Ruhr-Nachrichten 303,380 (Dortmund)	Pro-CDU.	Robert Schmelzer
Westfalenpost 115,718 (Hagen/Westf.)	CDU.	T. Fritzen
Freie Presse 97,264 (Bielefeld)	SPD.	Georg Strutz

SAARLAND

Saarbrücker Zeitung, 130,000 (Saarbrücken)	Independent.	Wilhelm Gries
Saarbrücker Neueste Nachrichten 30,000 (Saarbrücken)	CDU	Fritz Fiala
Saarländische Volkszeitung 30,000 (Saarbrücken)	CSU.	Ludwig Schnur
Saarbrücker Allgemeine Zeitung 15,000 (Saarbrücken)	SPD.	Friedrich Regitz

RHINELAND-PALATINATE

Die Rheinpfalz 197,143 (Ludwigshafen)	Independent.	Editorial Board
Rhein-Zeitung 171,934 (Koblenz)	Independent.	Michael Weber
Allgemeine Zeitung 100,882 (Mainz)	Independent.	Dr. Heinrich Toetter

SCHLESWIG-HOLSTEIN

Kieler Nachrichten 96,124 (Kiel)	Independent; Pro-CDU.	Theodor Dotzer
Lübecker Nachrichten 78,544 (Lübeck)	Independent; Pro-CDU.	Hans Schrem
Flensburger Tagblatt 56,310 (Flensburg)	Independent.	Dr. Hanno Schmidt

PERIODICALS

Name of Journal	Character	Proprietor, Editor, etc.
Allgemeine Wochenzeitung der Juden in Deutschland (Duesseldorf) (semi-weekly)	Jewish interests.	Karl Marx
Deutsche Zeitung und Wirtschaftszeitung (Stuttgart) (semi-weekly)	Independent, finance.	Helmut Cron
Das Parlament (Bonn) (weekly)	Governmental, Parliament reports.	F. Kippenberg
Rheinischer Merkur (Cologne) (weekly)	Catholic, CDU.	Dr. Otto Roegele
Sonntagsblatt (Hamburg) (weekly)	Lutheran, independent.	Axel Seeberg
Der Spiegel (Hamburg) (weekly)	Independent, news magazine.	Rudolf Augstein
Welt der Arbeit (Cologne) (weekly)	Trade Unions, progressive.	Artur Saternus
Die Zeit (Hamburg) (weekly)	Independent, national.	I. Müller-Marein
Aussenpolitik (Stuttgart) (monthly)	International affairs, independent.	Dr. Herbert von Borch
Deutsche Rundschau (Baden-Baden) (monthly)	Political affairs, independent.	Dr. Rudolf Pechel
Europa Archiv (Frankfurt) (semi-monthly)	International affairs.	Wilhelm Cornides (*Pub.*)
Frankfurter Hefte (monthly)	Political affairs, independent.	Eugen Kogon
Die Gegenwart (Frankfurt) (semi-monthly)	Liberal, independent.	Benno Reifenberg
Merkur (Stuttgart) (monthly)	Independent.	Dr. J. Moras
Der Monat (monthly)	Progressive, international.	Melvin J. Lasky
Zeitschrift für Politik (Berlin) (monthly)	Political affairs	Prof. Dr. A. Grabowsky
Vierteljahrshefte für Zeitgeschichte (Munich) (quarterly)	Historical and political.	Dr. H. Krausnick

NEWS AGENCY

Deutsche Presse-Agentur (Hamburg)	Cooperative news agency in the Federal Republic.	Fritz Saenger

SOVIET OCCUPATION ZONE
(German Democratic Republic)

Capital: East Berlin
Area: 41,645 sq. mi.
Population: 17,410,670 including East Berlin (1957 estimate)

The establishment of the Federal Republic in Western Germany, which was the result of Soviet frustration of plans for a united Germany, was followed, on October 7, 1949, by the proclamation of the East German "Democratic Republic," the seat of which was to be in the Soviet Sector of Berlin. A Constitution had been formulated by the People's Council of the Soviet Zone and was adopted May 30, 1949, by the Third People's Congress under the Presidency of Wilhelm Pieck. The People's Council became the lower house of Parliament, or People's Chamber, and promulgated the Constitution.

President

WILHELM PIECK (Communist—SED)
Elected by joint session of the two Houses of Parliament on October 11, 1949; re-elected October 7, 1953, and October 7, 1957, for a four-year term

GERMANY

Cabinet
Communist-controlled Coalition
Re-appointed on November 19, 1954

Minister President
OTTO GROTEWOHL (Communist—SED)
Appointed on October 7, 1949; named by People's Chamber on October 15, 1950; re-named on November 16, 1954, for four-year term

PARLIAMENT

UPPER CHAMBER† (Laenderkammer)	LOWER CHAMBER (Volkskammer)
Selected by the 14 district conventions of Soviet Zone.	*Selected by way of electoral approval of a single "unity list."*
President: AUGUST BACH (CDU)	President: JOHANNES DIECKMANN (Liberal Democrat)
Number of members 63	Number of members 400

† A law was passed in December 1958 abolishing the Laenderkammer.

PARTY PROGRAMS AND LEADERS

THE SOCIALIST UNITY PARTY (SED) was founded under pressure from the Soviet Occupation Authorities in April 1946 by merging the Communist Party (KPD) and the Social Democratic Party (SPD) in the Soviet Zone. It has become all-powerful in East Germany. All political parties and mass organizations are under the sway of the SED.

Leaders: Walter Ulbricht (First Secretary). *Politburo:* Friedrich Ebert, Otto Grotewohl, Erich Honecker, Bruno Leuschner, Hermann Matern, Erich Mückenberger, Alfred Neumann, Albert Norden, Wilhelm Pieck, Heinrich Rau, Willi Stoph, Walter Ulbricht, Herbert Warnke.

THE CHRISTIAN DEMOCRATIC UNION OF THE SOVIET ZONE (CDU), founded in the summer of 1945, is completely dependent on the SED. Its ideological conception, as defined by former Secretary General Goetting, is "Christian realism."

Leader: August Bach.

Other parties which have also ceased to have any importance are the Liberal Democratic Party (LDPD), National Democratic Party (NDPD) and Democratic Farmer Party (DBD).

THE CABINET

Otto Grotewohl, Minister President (Communist—SED); Walter Ulbricht, First Deputy President (Communist—SED); Dr. Hans Loch, Deputy President, All-German Affairs (LDPD); Dr. Lothar Bolz, Deputy President, Foreign Affairs (NDPD); Paul Scholz, Deputy President, Agriculture (DBD); Willi Stoph, Deputy President, Minister of Defense (SED); Heinrich Rau, Deputy President, Foreign and Interzonal Trade (SED); Fred Oelssner, Deputy President, Supply (SED); Bruno Leuschner, Deputy President, State Planning Commission (SED); Max Sefrin, Deputy President.

Ministers: Karl Maron, Interior (SED); Erich Mielke, State Security (SED); Hans Reichelt, Agriculture and Forestry (DBD); Willi Rumpf, Finance (SED); Kurt Wach, Commerce and Supply (SED); Luitpold Steidle, Public Health (CDU); Erwin Kramer, Traffic (SED); Friedrich Burmeister, Post and Telecommunications (CDU); Dr. Werner Winkler, Chemical Industry (SED); Ernst Scholz, Reconstruction (CDU); Fritz Lange, Education (SED); Dr. Johannes Becher, Culture (SED); Dr. Hilde Benjamin, Justice (SED).

The following independent departments have heads who are all called State Secretaries: Hermann Streit, Control and Purchase (SED); Dr. Wilhelm Girnus, University Affairs (SED); Dr. Hans Schuster, Sports and Physical Training (SED); Ernst Wabra, State Control (SED); Franz Peplinski, Affairs of the Local Councils (SED); Werner Eggerath, Church Affairs (SED).

THE PRESS
EAST BERLIN

Name of Paper	Circulation	Political Affiliation	Editor
Tribüne	200,000	FDBG	Editorial Board
Berliner Zeitung	120,000	SED	Erich Henschke
Neues Deutschland	400,000	SED	Hermann Axen
Neue Zeit	50,000	East-CDU	Alwin Schaper

SOVIET ZONE

Name of Paper	Circulation	Location	Editor and Party
Lausitzer Rundschau	90,000	Cottbus	Paula Acker (SED)
Die Union	50,000	Dresden	Max Karg (East-CDU)
Sächsische Zeitung	400,000	Dresden	Carl Bobach (SED)
Freiheit	185,000	Halle	R. Singer (SED)
Der Neue Weg	30,000	Halle	Herbert Reinelt (CDU)
Freie Erde	220,000	Neubrandenburg	Karl-Heinz Karge (SED)
Märkische Volksstimme	110,000	Potsdam	Hans Ortmann (SED)
Schweriner Volkszeitung	220,000	Schwerin	Hans Mahle (SED)
Das Volk	280,000	Erfurt	Erich Richter (SED)

PERIODICALS

Deutsche Aussenpolitik (Berlin, monthly)	Political affairs, SED	Editorial Board
Einheit (Berlin, monthly)	Communist ideology, SED	Editorial Board

NEWS AGENCY

Allgemeines Deutsches Nachrichtenbureau (ADN) — Government-owned news agency in the Soviet Occupation Zone.

UNITED KINGDOM OF GREAT BRITAIN AND NORTHERN IRELAND[1]

Capital: London
Area: 94,214 square miles (including Northern Ireland)
Population: 51,455,000 (1957 estimate including Northern Ireland)

Sovereign
QUEEN ELIZABETH II
Born April 21, 1926; proclaimed Queen February 6, 1952
Crowned June 2, 1953

Cabinet
Conservative
Assumed office October 26, 1951
Re-elected May 26, 1955

Prime Minister
HAROLD MACMILLAN (Conservative)

PARLIAMENT
UPPER CHAMBER
(House of Lords)

Lord Chancellor: VISCOUNT KILMUIR

Peers of the Royal Blood	4
Archbishops	2
Dukes	21
Marquesses	27
Earls	132
Viscounts	107
Bishops	24
Barons	547[2]
Baronesses for Life[3]	4
Scottish Representative Peers	16
Irish Representative Peers	1
Total	885

[1] See also section on Northern Ireland, page 88.
[2] Including 10 Barons for Life created under the Life Peerages Act, 1958.
[3] Created under the Life Peerages Act, 1958.

LOWER CHAMBER
(House of Commons)
Last general election May 26, 1955, for five-year term, subject to dissolution of Parliament
Speaker: WILLIAM SHEPHERD MORRISON

Parties	Representation	
Government		
Conservative	311	
Conservative Supporters (Nat. Lib-Con.)	18	
Ulster Unionist	12	
		341
Opposition		
Labor and Cooperative		281
Others		
Liberal	6	
Independents	2	8
Total		630

Note: In the General Election of May 1955 the number of votes cast was: Conservative and Supporters 13,285,519; Labor 12,405,254; Liberal 722,402; Communist 33,144; Others 313,410; Grand Total 26,759,729.

PARTY PROGRAMS AND LEADERS

For the history of the National Government, August 1931—May 1940; the Coalition Government, May 1940—May 1945, and the Labor Government, 1945—October 1951, and the alignment of parties, see previous issues of the POLITICAL HANDBOOK OF THE WORLD.

CONSERVATIVE PARTY: Likewise called the Unionist Party; formed the large majority of the supporters of the National Government; successor to the Tory Party of the 18th and 19th centuries. Elected to office, 1951, and returned with increased majority in 1955.

The Party policy aims at respecting the freedom and dignity of the individual in all walks of life and providing opportunity in which all can develop their aptitudes to the full, within the limits of law and social justice, and guaranteed by democratic parliamentary institutions. To this end, the Party's policy proposes to give confidence and responsibility to local government and stop meddlesome State interference with it; encourage the small man in industry and prevent abuses by monopolies, whether private or public; give the British farmer first place in the home market and secure guaranteed prices for him; see that every family has a separate and proper home; safeguard the social services and maintain a basic minimum below which none shall fall; strengthen family life; take the lead in organizing a move towards a world-wide system of freer world trade and freer payments; strive for closer consultation within the Commonwealth; see that developments in the Empire and Commonwealth have first claim on what is available for investment overseas, and enable private enterprise to play its part in colonial development; strengthen trading links within the Commonwealth and Empire and reserve the right to retain Imperial Preferences; improve education, health and agriculture in the colonies, uphold the principle of racial partnership, guide them along the road to self-government within the British Empire and Commonwealth; strive to uphold the ideals and to support the authority of the U.N. and to make the conception of European unity a reality; work for the maintenance of peace through strength, increasing cooperation with the

United States, understanding in the Middle East, and security in Southeast Asia; and to increase the standard of the Regular Forces by improving their conditions of service, carry on a suitable re-equipment program, and coordinate defense within the Empire.

The Conservative Party is opposed to further nationalization and advocates, where practicable, restoration of free enterprise and overhauling of the organization of nationalized industries to improve their efficiency.

Leaders: Harold Macmillan (Leader of the Party), Viscount Hailsham, (Chairman of the Party Organization), Viscount Kilmuir, Heathcote Amory, A. T. Lennox-Boyd, Sir David Eccles, Selwyn Lloyd, Duncan Sandys, R. A. Butler, Earl of Home (Leader in the House of Lords), E. R. G. Heath (Chief Whip in Commons), Earl St. Aldwyn (Chief Whip in Lords).

LABOR PARTY (Socialist): Composed of the membership of national organizations (trade unions, socialist, and cooperative societies) and local organizations (constituency and local labor parties), the constituent organizations nominating and financing candidates who, following endorsement by the National Executive, run as official Labor candidates; also has a working relationship with the Cooperative Party (representing the interests of consumers organized in cooperative societies), whose members in Parliament form part of the Labor Party.

Labor was a full partner in the Coalition Government, whose war aims it supported. It came to power as a result of the election of July 1945. It immediately introduced, and carried through, a bold social program. By planned production for common use it provided full employment; social services to ensure adequate health, nutrition, and care in old age for everybody; and full educational opportunities for all. It gave freedom to India, Pakistan, Ceylon and Burma. The aim of Labor's policy for the Colonies is to enable them to achieve democratic self-government under conditions which ensure for their peoples both a fair standard of living and freedom from oppression from any quarter. It recognizes the obligation to give all possible help to the political, economic and social development of the colonial territories.

Labor has stated that the principle of collective security against aggression must be given its appropriate methods and institutions.

Labor fought the 1955 election on its three-fold policy for peace, i.e. disarmament, relaxing world tension, and help for under-developed areas; on the cost of living; housing; fair shares; the need for increased production by planning and the public ownership of certain industries; and a policy for an expanding and efficient farming industry.

The party was returned to power by a small majority in the 1950 general election, but lost in the general elections of 1951 and 1955. The Labor Party is one of the Parties of the Socialist International.

Officers: Parliamentary Labor Party: Hugh Gaitskell (Leader of the Party), James Griffiths (Deputy Leader), Herbert Bowden (Chief Whip), Carol Johnson (Secretary), Lord Alexander (Leader of Labor Peers). *Labor Party National Executive Committee:* Mrs. Barbara Castle (Chairman), Ian Mikardo (Vice-Chairman), Aneurin Bevan (Treasurer), Morgan Phillips (Secretary).

NATIONAL LIBERAL PARTY: Originally composed of a group of Liberal members of Parliament who believed that the National Government should have complete freedom in approaching national problems without the restraint of party views. Formed a separate party in 1931.

At the annual conference of the Party in 1948 the name was changed from Liberal National to National Liberal. In its manifestoes for recent elections the Party stated that there was no contemporary difference of principle or aim between Conservatives and Liberals.

Leaders: Sir Leighton Seager, Lord Teviot (Chief Whip in Lords), Sir Herbert Butcher, Lord Ennisdale, John Maclay (Leader of Parliamentary Party), Viscount Lambert, Sir Geoffrey Shakespeare, Earl of Rosebery and P. Ensor Walters (General Secretary and Treasurer).

LIBERAL PARTY: Successor to Whig Party. The Liberal Party participated in the Coalition Government from May 1940 until May 1945.

In the 1955 elections the Party won 6 seats in the House of Commons.

Leaders: Jo Grimond (Leader of Parliamentary Party), Deryck Abel (Chairman of Party Executive), Lord Rea (Leader of Liberal Peers), Lord Amulree (Chief Whip in Lords), Donald Wade (Chief Whip in Commons), Frank Byers, Sir Andrew McFadyean, Lord Stamp, Elliott Dodds, Lord Beveridge, Lady Violet Bonham-Carter, Lord Layton, Philip Fothergill and Leonard Behrens.

COMMUNIST PARTY: At the 1955 general election only 17 Communist candidates ran. All of them were defeated.

THE CABINET

The following are members of the Cabinet: Harold Macmillan (Prime Minister, First Lord of the Treasury); Selwyn Lloyd (Secretary of State for Foreign Affairs); Viscount Hailsham (Lord President of the Council); Earl of Home (Secretary of State for Commonwealth Relations); Viscount Kilmuir (Lord Chancellor); R. A. Butler (Secretary of State for the Home Department); D. Heathcoat Amory (Chancellor of the Exchequer); A. T. Lennox-Boyd (Secretary of State for the Colonies); John Maclay (Secretary of State for Scotland); Duncan Sandys (Minister of Defense); Iain Macleod (Minister of Labor and National Service); Henry Brooke (Minister of Housing and Local Government and Welsh Affairs); Sir David Eccles (President of the Board of Trade); John Hare (Minister of Agriculture, Fisheries & Food); Geoffrey Lloyd (Minister of Education); Lord Mills (Minister of Power); Harold Watkinson (Minister of Transport and Civil Aviation); Dr. Charles Hill (Chancellor of Duchy of Lancaster); Reginald Maudling (Paymaster General).

MINISTERS NOT IN THE CABINET

Earl of Selkirk (First Lord of the Admiralty); Christopher Soames (Secretary of State for War); George Ward (Secretary of State for Air); Aubrey Jones (Minister of Supply); John Boyd-Carpenter (Minister of Pensions and National Insurance); Ernest Marples (Postmaster-General); Allan Noble and D. Ormsby-Gore (Ministers of State for Foreign Affairs); Earl of Perth (Minister of State for Colonial Affairs); D. Walker-Smith (Minister of Health); Hugh Molson (Minister of Works); Lord Forbes (Minister of State, Scottish Office); Lord Brecon (Minister of State for Wales); J. K. Vaughan-Morgan (Minister of State, Board of Trade); Earl of Dundee (Minister without Portfolio). *Law Officers:* Sir Reginald Manningham-Buller (Attorney-General); W. R. Milligan (Lord Advocate); Sir Harry Hylton-Foster (Solicitor-General); William Grant (Solicitor-General for Scotland).

GREAT BRITAIN

PRESS

Name & Circulation of Paper	Political Orientation	Proprietor, Editor, etc.

I. DAILIES—LONDON

Daily Express 4,040,572	Independent.	Beaverbrook Newspapers Ltd. E. D. Pickering (*Ed.*)
Daily Herald 1,523,334	Organ of the Labor Party, TUC.	Odhams Press, Ltd. (*Pub.*) D. B. Machray (*Ed.*)
Daily Mail 2,105,988	Independent; conservative.	Viscount Rothermere (*Chairman*) Assoc. Newspapers Ltd. Arthur Wareham (*Ed.*)
Daily Mirror 4,526,453	Independent; of the Left.	Daily Mirror Newspapers Ltd. J. S. Nener (*Ed.*)
Daily Sketch 1,223,948	Independent; conservative.	Assoc. Newspapers Ltd. Herbert Gunn (*Ed.*)
Daily Telegraph & Morning Post 1,108,514	Independent; conservative.	Daily Telegraph Ltd. Colin Coote (*Ed.*)
Daily Worker (Circ. not available)	Supports the policy of the Communist Party.	Daily Worker Co-operative Society (*Pub.*) J. R. Campbell (*Ed.*)
Evening News 1,225,013	Independent; conservative.	Viscount Rothermere (*Chairman*) Assoc. Newspapers Ltd. C. R. Willis (*Ed.*)
Evening Standard 589,706	Independent.	Beaverbrook Newspapers, Ltd. P. Elland (*Ed.*)
Financial Times 83,713	Independent.	Financial Times Ltd. Gordon Newton (*Ed.*)
News Chronicle and Daily Dispatch 1,267,341	Independent; liberal.	News Chronicle, Ltd. Norman Cursley (*Ed.*)
Star (evening) 789,485	Independent; liberal.	Star Newspaper Co., Ltd. R. McCarthy (*Ed.*)
Times 248,248	Independent; moderate conservative; correspondence from all parties.	Lord Astor; John Walter (*Chief Dirs.*) Sir Wm. Haley (*Ed.*)

II. DAILIES—ENGLAND & WALES

Birmingham Post and Gazette (Birmingham) 78,787	Independent.	W. Vaughan Reynolds (*Ed.*)
South Wales Echo 146,762	Independent; conservative.	Ivor Lewis (*Ed.*)
Western Mail (Cardiff) 93,051	Independent; conservative.	David Cole (*Ed.*)
Yorkshire Post (Leeds) 112,729	Independent.	Sir Linton Andrews (*Ed.*)
Liverpool Daily Post (Liverpool) 73,273	Independent.	Ian Hosie (*Ed.*)
Manchester Guardian (Manchester) 178,692	Independent; liberal.	H. A. Hetherington (*Ed.*)
Newcastle Journal (Newcastle) 132,889	Independent; conservative.	Kemsley Newspapers Ltd. R. Clough (*Ed.*)
Western Morning News (Plymouth) 64,104	Independent.	N. A. T. Vinson (*Ed.*)
Sheffield Telegraph (Sheffield) 95,510	Independent; conservative.	Kemsley Newspapers Ltd. W. Lyth (*Ed.*)

III. DAILIES—SCOTLAND

Press & Journal (Aberdeen) 82,817	Independent; conservative.	Kemsley Newspapers Ltd. K. J. Peters (*Ed.*)
Scotsman (Edinburgh) 58,550	Independent.	R. Thomson (*Chairman*) Alastair M. Dunnett (*Ed.*)
Daily Record & Mail (Glasgow) 428,361	Independent.	Daily Mirror Newspapers Ltd. Alex Little (*Ed.*)
Glasgow Herald (Glasgow) 75,853	Independent.	George Outram & Co., Ltd. James Holburn (*Ed.*)

Name & Circulation of Paper   *Political Orientation*   *Proprietor, Editor, etc.*

IV. SUNDAY NEWSPAPERS
Published in London unless otherwise stated.

Name & Circulation	Political Orientation	Proprietor, Editor, etc.
News of the World 6,767,348	Independent.	Reginald Cudlipp (*Ed.*)
The Observer 638,074	Independent.	The Observer Ltd. Hon. David Astor (*Ed.*)
The People 4,899,748	Independent.	Odhams Press Ltd. Stuart Campbell (*Ed.*)
Reynolds News 367,635	Labor & Co-operative.	Co-operative Press Ltd. W. R. Richardson (*Ed.*)
Sunday Dispatch 1,834,857	Independent; conservative.	Assoc. Newspapers Ltd. Walter Hayes (*Ed.*)
Empire News and Sunday Chronicle 2,161,230	Independent.	Kemsley Newspapers Ltd. L. Harton (*Ed.*)
Sunday Express 3,397,913	Independent.	Beaverbrook Newspapers Ltd. John Junor (*Ed.*)
Sunday Graphic 952,781	Independent; conservative.	Kemsley Newspapers Ltd. J. G. McKenzie (*Ed.*)
Sunday Mail (Glasgow) 616,550	Independent.	Scottish Daily Record & Evening News, Ltd. E. R. Wason (*Ed.*)
Sunday Pictorial 5,378,242	Independent; of the Left.	Sunday Pictorial Newspapers (1920) Ltd. Colin G. Valdar (*Ed.*)
Sunday Times 795,192	Independent; conservative.	Kemsley Newspapers Ltd. H. V. Hodson (*Ed.*)

V. NEWS AGENCIES

The Associated Press Ltd. (Great Britain)	Independent.	John Lloyd (*London Chief of Bureau*) Lloyd Stratton (*Mg. Dir.*)
British United Press Ltd.	Independent.	Paul Eve (*News Editor*) F. H. Fisher (*Mg. Ed.*)
Exchange Telegraph Co. Ltd.	Independent.	William C. Stevens (*Mg. Dir.*) Edward J. Gelling (*Ed.*)
Press Association Ltd.	Non-political.	E. W. Davies (*Gen. Mgr.*) C. E. Jervis (*Ed. in Chief*)
Reuters Ltd.	Independent.	J. L. Burgess, Harry Lindley, Cecil H. King, Gavin Astor, Lord Burnham, Sir Harold Campbell, L. P. Scott (*Directors*) Sir Christopher Chancellor (*Gen. Mgr.*) Walton A. Cole (*Ed.*)

VI. PERIODICALS

Name of Periodical	*Character*	*Proprietor, Editor, etc.*
Contemporary Review (m)	Liberal.	Dr. G. P. Gooch (*Ed.*)
The Economist (w)	Independent; liberal.	Shares so distributed between Financial News Ltd. and individual shareholders as to ensure editorial independence. Donald Tyerman (*Ed.*)
International Affairs (q)	Independent; international relations.	Royal Institute of International Affairs (*Pub.*) Muriel Grindrod (*Ed.*)
Journal of the Parliaments of the Commonwealth (q)	Summaries of proceedings of general interest in Commonwealth Parliaments.	Commonwealth Parliamentary Association. Sir Howard D'Egville (*Ed.*)
Listener (w)	Reprints of B. B. C. talks including speeches of all parties.	British Broadcasting Corporation (*Pub.*) A. E. W. Thomas (*Ed.*)

Name of Periodical	Character	Proprietor, Editor, etc.
New Statesman (w)	Independent socialist political and literary review.	Kingsley Martin (*Ed.*)
Parliamentary Affairs (q)	Devoted to all aspects of parliamentary democracy.	Cdr. Sir Stephen King-Hall (*Hon. Ed.*) Ann Dewar (*Ed.*) Hansard Society (*Pub.*)
Political Quarterly	Independent; progressive.	Leonard Woolf and W. A. Robson (*Ed.*)
Quarterly Review	Political, literary and general.	Sir John Murray (*Ed.*)
The Round Table (q)	Politics of the British Commonwealth.	The Round Table Ltd. (*Prop.*) Sir Ivison S. Macadam (*Hon. Sec.*) Dermot Morrah (*Ed.*)
Spectator (w)	Non-partisan; conservative tendency.	Ian Gilmour (*Ed.*)
Statist (w)	Financial and economic.	T. J. Hickey (*Ed.*)
The Tablet (w)	Catholic.	Douglas Woodruff (*Ed.*)
Time and Tide (w)	Independent.	E. A. Lejeune (*Ed.*)
Tribune (w)	Socialist.	Michael Foot (*Ed.*)
Twentieth Century (m)	Independent.	Hon. David Astor (*Prop.*) Bernard Wall (*Ed.*)
The World Today (m)	Independent; international affairs.	Royal Institute of International Affairs (*Pub.*) Muriel Grindrod (*Ed.*)

NORTHERN IRELAND

Capital: Belfast
Area: 5,238 square miles
Population: 1,398,500 (1958 estimate)

Sovereign
QUEEN ELIZABETH II
Born in 1926; proclaimed Queen in 1952

The Government of Northern Ireland was established in conformity with the provisions of the Government of Ireland Act of 1920 (sometimes referred to as the Irish Home Rule Act of 1920). This Act, which has since been amended several times, was passed by the British Parliament and grants certain powers to the Government of Northern Ireland which are somewhat comparable to those of a State in the American Federal Union. The Government consists of a Governor, who represents the Queen, a Cabinet, and a legislative branch consisting of a Senate and a House of Commons. In other respects, the organization of the Government is almost identical with that in Westminster.

In addition to the semi-independent status of the Government of Northern Ireland in the United Kingdom, it is represented in the Parliament in London by 12 elected members.

Governor
BARON WAKEHURST OF ARDINGLY
Appointed in 1952

Prime Minister
VISCOUNT BROOKEBOROUGH OF COLEBROOKE
Appointed in 1943

PARLIAMENT

UPPER CHAMBER (Senate)

The Lord Mayor of Belfast and the Mayor of Londonderry and 24 members elected by the House of Commons.

Number of Members 26

LOWER CHAMBER (House of Commons)

Last general election, March 20, 1958, for five-year term, subject to dissolution of Parliament.

Parties	Representation
Unionists	37
Nationalists	7
Labor	4
Independent Nationalists	1
Independent Labor	1
Republican Labor	1
Independent	1
Total	52

NORTHERN IRELAND

THE CABINET

The composition of the Cabinet is as follows: Viscount Brookeborough (Prime Minister), Captain T. M. O'Neill (Finance), W. W. B. Topping (Home Affairs), Lord Glentoran (Commerce), Rev. Robert Moore (Agriculture), W. M. May (Education), J. L. O. Andrews (Health and Local Government), Maj. I. Neill (Labor and National Insurance), Lt. Col. A. R. G. Gordon (Minister in the Senate).

PRESS

Unless otherwise noted, papers listed are published in the capital city.

Name and Circulation of Paper		Political Orientation	Proprietor, Editor, etc.
Belfast News Letter	42,000	Unionist.	Belfast News-Letter, Ltd. (*Prop.*) R. G. Hamilton (*Ed.*)
Belfast Telegraph (evening)	195,510	Unionist.	W. & G. Baird, Ltd. (*Prop.*) J. E. Sayers and T. McMullan, (*Mg. Eds.*)
Irish News and Belfast Morning News	44,453	Nationalist.	Irish News, Ltd. (*Prop.*) Robert Kirkwood (*Ed.*)
Northern Whig and Belfast Post	43,328	Unionist.	Northern Whig, Ltd. (*Prop.*) B. F. Proudfoot (*Ed.*)
Derry Journal (Londonderry) (bi-weekly)	17,420	Nationalist.	Derry Journal, Ltd. (*Prop.*) T. Cassidy (*Ed.*)
Londonderry Sentinel (Londonderry) (weekly)	16,800	Unionist.	Londonderry Sentinel, Ltd. (*Prop.*) S. D. M. Buchanan (*Ed.*)
Northern Constitution (Coleraine) (weekly)	23,782	Independent.	Northern Constitution, Ltd. (*Prop.*), Robert Acheson (*Ed.*)

GREECE

Capital: Athens
Area: 51,843 square miles
Population: 8,130,000 (1957 estimate)

Ruler
KING PAUL
Born in 1901; succeeded to throne April 1, 1947, on the death of his brother, George II; took oath as sixth King of Greece on April 21, 1947

Cabinet
National Radical Union (ERE)
Took office May 17, 1958

Premier
CONSTANTINE KARAMANLIS
Took office on October 6, 1955, after death of Field Marshal Alexander Papagos
Formed National Radical Union which won elections of 1956 and 1958

PARLIAMENT
Election of May 11, 1958 (four-year term)

Parties	Representation
National Radical Union (ERE)	170
*United Democratic Left (EDA)	63
Liberal Party	33
**Democratic Union	12
Agrarian Party	6
**New Agrarian Movement (NAK)	4
Populist Party	2
Social Populist Party	2
Progressive Party	1
Democratic Party (DKEL)	1
National Progressive Union of the Center (EPEK)	1
Independent	5
Total	300

* Communist-front.
** Post-electoral offshoots of EDA.

PARTY PROGRAMS AND LEADERS

NATIONAL RADICAL UNION (ERE): Formed in January, 1956, by Prime Minister Constantine Karamanlis. In the 1956 elections received 47.5% of the popular vote, and won a majority in Parliament. In the 1958 elections secured 41.2% of the vote and increased its majority in Parliament.

Leader: Prime Minister Constantine Karamanlis.

UNITED DEMOCRATIC LEFT (EDA): Extreme left-wing party, founded in 1951 as a substitute for the Communist Party (KKE) outlawed in 1947. Running in the 1958 elections with a number of "independents" EDA received 24.4% of the popular vote increasing its parliamentary seats to 79. Twelve Deputies elected on EDA tickets later founded the EDA sponsored *"Democratic Union"* led by Elias Tsirimokos while 4 more joined the EDA sponsored *"New Agrarian Movement"* (NAK) set up shortly before the 1958 election.

Leaders: Committee headed by John Passalidis.

LIBERAL PARTY: After the re-union of the Liberal Democratic Union led by Venizelos and the Liberal Party under Papandreou in 1957, the party ran independently in the 1958 elections but lost half its seats in Parliament and now ranks third.

Leader: Sophocles Venizelos (former Prime Minister).

AGRARIAN PARTY: Draws most of its strength from the rural regions of Northern Greece. It was the only small party to hold its ground in the 1958 election.

Leader: Alexander Baltadzis.

OTHER PARTIES: *Populist Party* led by former Prime Minister Constantine Tsaldaris; the *Social Populist Party* founded by former Minister S. Stefanopoulos; the *Democratic Party of Working People* (DKEL) created by G. Kartalis and A. Svolos (both deceased); the *Progressive Party* established by Spyros Markezinis in 1955; the *National Progressive Union of the Center* (EPEK) led by S. Papapolitis.

THE CABINET

The members of the present Cabinet are: Constantine Karamanlis (Prime Minister and Minister of National Defense), Constantine Tsatsos (Minister to Prime Minister), Aristides Protopapadakis (Coordination), Constantine Papaconstandinou (Finance), Evangelos Averof (Foreign Affairs), Demetrios Makris (Interior), Constantine Kallias (Justice), George Voyadzis (Education), Solon Gikas (Communications and Public Works), Constantine Adamopoulos (Agriculture), Leonidas Dertilis (Commerce), Nicholas Martis (Industry), Andrew Stratos (Social Welfare), George Andrianopoulos (Merchant Marine), Augustus Theologitis (Northern Greece), Aristidis Demetratos (Labor), George Themelis (Under-secretary of Defense), Demetrios Alibrandis (Under-secretary for Finance), Evangelos Kalantzis (Under-secretary of Interior), Demetrios Thanopoulos (Under-secretary of Agriculture), Themistocles Konitsas (Under-secretary of Communications), Emmanuel Kefaloyannis (Under-secretary of Housing), John Psarreas (Under-secretary of Social Welfare), Constantine Chryssanthopoulos (Under-secretary of Commerce).

GREECE

PRESS

Unless otherwise noted, papers are published in Athens.

Name of Paper	Circulation	Political Orientation	Proprietor, Director or Editor
Acropolis	50,000	Conservative, Pro-Govt.	A. and N. Botsis (*Props.*) S. Grigoriadis (*Ed.*)
Apogevmatini	16,000	Conservative, Pro-Govt.	S. Constandopoulos (*Dir.*)
Athens News	2,500	Independent, in English.	Yannis Horn (*Ed.*)
Athinaiki	25,000	Center.	I. Papageorgiu (*Prop.*)
Avghi	35,000	Communist.	E. Glezos (*Prop. & Ed.*)
Eleftheria	19,000	Center.	P. Kokas (*Prop.*)
Ethnikos Kyrix	6,000	Conservative, Pro-Govt.	A. Paraschos (*Dir.*)
Ethnos	16,000	Center, Pro-Govt.	C. Nicolopoulos and D. Kyriazis (*Props.*) C. Oikonomides (*Dir.*)
Estia	8,000	Conservative.	K. Kyrou (*Dir.*)
Kathimerini	43,000	Conservative, Pro-Govt.	Mrs. E. Vlachou (*Prop. & Ed.*)
Messager d'Athènes		Semi-Official (in French).	
Ta Nea	52,000	Center, Pro-Govt.	Ch. Lambrakis (*Prop.*) Costas Nitsos (*Ed.*)
To Vima	13,000	Center, Pro-Govt.	Ch. Lambrakis (*Prop.*) G. Syriotis (*Dir.*)
Vradyni	15,000	Conservative, Pro-Govt.	Mrs. Nina Aravandinou (*Prop.*) L. Bortolis (*Dir.*)
Neologos (Patras)		Conservative, Pro-Govt.	Pan. Papandropoulos (*Prop.*)
Makedonia (Salonica)		Center.	G. Vellides (*Prop.*)
To Phos (Salonica)		Conservative, Pro-Govt.	J. Spatharis (*Dir.*)
Economikos Tachydromos (weekly)	4,000	Economic.	P. Tzannetakis (*Ed.*)
Embros (weekly)	30,000	Conservative, Pro-Govt.	Alkis Kalapothakis (*Dir.*)
Tachydromos (weekly)	23,000	Center, Pro-Govt.	N. Yannaras (*Ed.*)

PRESS ASSOCIATIONS

Agence d'Athènes (News Agency)	S. Selinas (*Mg. Dir.*)
Agence Economique et Financière	George Stephopoulos (*Dir.*)
Association des Correspondents de la Press Etrangère	A. Sedgwick (*Pres.*)
Agence France-Presse (News Agency)	A. Clot (*Dir.*)
Agence de Presse Hellenews	G. Vassiliadis (*Dir.*)

GUATEMALA

Capital: Guatemala
Area: 42,042 square miles
Population: 3,300,000 (1957 estimate)

President
MIGUEL YDÍGORAS FUENTES
Elected on January 19, 1958; inaugurated on March 2, 1958, for six-year term

Cabinet
Appointed on March 3, 1958

PARLIAMENT
(Congreso Nacional)

Election of January 19, 1958 (four-year term: renewed by half every two years).
President: JULIO PRADO GARCÍA SALAS

Movimiento Democrático Nacionalista (MDN)	23
Reconciliación Democrática Nacional (Redención)	16
Democracia Cristiana Guatemalteca (DCG)	9
Partido Revolucionario (PR)	6
Independents	8
Others	4
Total	66

POLITICAL EVENTS SINCE 1944

Guatemala was governed from 1871 to 1944, with few interludes, by a succession of Liberal dictatorships. On October 20, 1944, the last of these was swept away by the "October Revolution." This was followed by administrations of Presidents Juan José Arévalo (1945–1951) and Jacobo Arbenz Guzmán (1951–54) in which social security, an extensive labor code, and agrarian reforms were introduced as the keystones of a general reform program. However, Guatemalan and foreign Communists with extensive contacts with the international Communist movement infiltrated the Revolutionary movement in which, by 1954, they had achieved a dominant position. On June 18, 1954, a revolt against the Government broke out under the leadership of Col. Carlos Castillo Armas, an exile living in Honduras. The National Army deposed President Arbenz and negotiated an agreement with Castillo Armas by which he became a member of a governing Junta. By September 2, 1954, all of the other members of the Junta had resigned and Castillo Armas assumed the Presidency. He was confirmed in this office by a popular referendum on October 10. At the same time, a Constituent Assembly was elected to set his term and to draw up a new Constitution. Elections for congressional and municipal offices were held on December 18, 1955. The new Congress took office on March 1, 1956, simultaneously with the promulgation of a new Constitution. President Castillo Armas was assassinated on July 26, 1957.

GUATEMALA

Elections for President and 33 members of Congress were held on October 20, 1957, but were voided by Congress on October 29, 1957, on the basis of "proven frauds," and after several days of rioting in the capital. A military Junta took control on October 24, appointed a new Cabinet and brought about the installation of Second Vice-President Guillermo Flores Avendaño as Provisional President. He served until Miguel Ydígoras Fuentes was elected on January 19, 1958, and installed on March 2, 1958.

PARTY PROGRAMS AND LEADERS

The Government of Castillo Armas dissolved the Guatemalan Communist Party and the leftist parties supporting the Arbenz régime. It also suspended the functioning of all political parties pending the new Constitution. However, it permitted anti-Communist parties and organizations to continue to operate as "civic" organizations and gave them the opportunity to become legalized shortly before the December, 1955, elections. The principal ones are:

PARTIDO RECONCILIACIÓN DEMOCRÁTICA NACIONAL (Redención): A middle of the road party which supports the policies of President Ydígoras.

Leader: Jorge Luis Zelaya Coronado (Secretary General).

MOVIMIENTO DEMOCRÁTICO NACIONALISTA (MDN): Built around the nucleus of the old Comité de Estudiantes Universitarios Anticomunistas (CEUA). It supported Castillo Armas, but is now in opposition.

Leader: Luis David Eskenassy (Secretary General).

PARTIDO REVOLUCIONARIO (PR): A party of the moderate left.

Leader: Mario Méndez Montenegro (Presidential Candidate in 1958).

PARTIDO UNIFICACIÓN ANTICOMUNISTA (PUA): Largest of the registered anti-Communist parties under the Arévalo and Arbenz Administrations.

Leader: Felipe Nery Barrientos (Secretary General).

GUATEMALTECA DEMOCRACIA CRISTIANA (DCG): The Catholic Party.

Leader: René de León S. (Secretary General).

THE CABINET

The members of the Cabinet are: Lic. Hernán Morales Dardón (Government), Col. Rubén Gonzáles Seguí (Defense), Jesús Unda Murillo (Foreign Affairs), Lic. Carlos Salazar Gatica (Finance), Enrique García Salas (Agriculture), Dr. Mariano López Herrarte (Public Health), Lic. Ramiro Flores (Labor and Economy), Col. Marco Aurelio Merida Sáenz (Education), Ing. Carlos Cipriani Krautwald (Communications and Public Works).

PRESS

All papers are published in the capital city.

Name of Paper	Circulation	Political Orientation	Proprietor, Editor, etc.
El Espectador	5,000	Center.	Héctor Quiñones (*Dir.*)
Diario de Centro América	5,000	Official daily.	Gustavo Martínez Nolasco
La Hora	6,000	Conservative.	Clemente Morroquín Rojas (*Prop. and Dir.*)
El Imparcial	30,000	Conservative.	David Vela (*Dir.*)
Impacto	7,000	Catholic weekly.	Antonio Dutail (*Dir.*)
Prensa Libre	30,000	Left of Center.	Pedro Julio García (*Dir.*)
La Hora Dominical (weekly)	12,000	Left of Center.	Oscar Marroquín Rojas (*Dir.*)
Verbo (semi-monthly)	7,000	Catholic.	Edited by clergy

HAITI

Capital: Port-au-Prince
Area: 10,700 square miles
Population: 3,500,000 (1957 estimate)

President
DR. FRANÇOIS DUVALIER
Took oath of office October 22, 1957

Cabinet
Reorganized November 7, 1958

NATIONAL ASSEMBLY

UPPER CHAMBER (Sénat)	LOWER CHAMBER (Chambre des Députés)
Elected September, 1957, six-year term.	Elected September, 1957, four-year term.
President: HUGUES BOURJOLLY	President: RAMEAU ESTIME
Number of Members 21	Number of Members 37

RECENT POLITICAL EVENTS

Between the fall from power of President Paul E. Magloire in December, 1956, and the inauguration of President François Duvalier for a six-year term in October 1957, Haiti experienced a series of interim Governments whose succession was marked by disorders and political crises. After two unsuccessful attempts to hold popular elections, the country, with women voting for the first time, on September 22, 1957, peacefully elected Dr. Duvalier President by an overwhelming majority.

THE CABINET

The members of the Cabinet, called Secretaries of State are: Michel Lamartinière Honorat (Coordination and Information), Frédéric Duvigneaud (Interior and National Defense), Dr. Louis Mars (Foreign Affairs and Worship), André Théard (Finances, Commerce and Industry), Jean A. Magloire (Public Works, Transportation and Communications), Lucien Bélizaire (Justice, Labor and Social Welfare), Henri Marc Charles (Agriculture, Natural Resources and Rural Development), Dr. Auguste Denizé (Public Health and Population), Reverend Jean Baptiste Georges (National Education), Aurel A. Joseph (Under-Secretary of State, Interior and National Defense), George Figaro (Under-Secretary of State, Commerce and Industry).

PRESS

Unless otherwise noted, papers are published in the capital city.

Name of Paper	Circulation	Political Affiliation	Proprietor, Editor, etc.
Haiti-Journal	1,500	Pro-Government.	A Committee.
Le Jour	1,500	Pro-Government.	A Committee.
Le Matin	4,000	Pro-Government.	Franck Magloire (Prop. and Ed.)
Le Moniteur (bi-weekly)	2,000	Official Gazette.	Augustin R. Viau (Dir.)
Le Nouvelliste	3,500	Pro-Government.	Max Chauvet (Prop.)
La Phalange	3,500	Catholic organ, conservative.	Franck St. Victor (Dir.)

HONDURAS

Capital: Tegucigalpa
Area: 44,880 square miles
Population: 1,800,000 (1958 estimate)

President

Dr. Ramon Villeda Morales
Elected by Constituent Assembly on November 15, 1957
Assumed office on December 21, 1957

PARLIAMENT

Elected as National Constituent Assembly on September 22, 1957**

President: Modesto Rodas Alvarado (Liberal)

Parties	Representation
Liberal	36
Nationalist	18
Reformist	3
Independent	1
Total	58

* After writing a new Constitution the Assembly converted itself into the National Congress.

PARTY PROGRAMS AND LEADERS

The present Liberal Government, which took office in December 1957, is the first for this party in 25 years. The Nationalists, under the leadership of party chief, General Tiburcio Carias Andino, dominated the political processes down to 1948. During the régime of Juan Manuel Galvez (1948–1954), also a Nationalist, a dissident group organized the Reformist Party with the re-election of Galvez as its objective. Galvez refused, however, and the elections of 1954 were inconclusive, leading to the assumption of the Chief of State's powers by Vice President Julio Lozano D., who restricted political activities and sought to perpetuate himself in power by using the new Reformist Party, and by holding elections which were widely criticized as fraudulent. In 1956 public dissatisfaction had reached such proportions that Lozano was forced to step down in favor of a military Junta. The Junta Government restored political prisoners to freedom, allowed all political exiles to return, and allowed a gradual return to free domestic political activity. It held elections in September 1957, generally considered to be the fairest in Honduran history. That election created the predominantly Liberal National Constituent Assembly from which the present Government has emerged.

The split between the Nationalist and Reformist groups in the opposition has persisted during this first year of Liberal rule. The titular and much of the real authority among the Nationalists remains in the hands of General Tiburcio Carias, now 82 years of age. The leadership of the Reformist Party continues to be held by General Abraham Williams, Vice-President under Carias and an aspirant for the Presidency.

HONDURAS

THE CABINET

The members of the Cabinet are: Lisandro Valle (Interior and Justice), Andrés Alvarado Puerto (Foreign Affairs), Lt. Col. Antonio Molina Ortiz (Defense), Juan Miguel Mejia (Public Education), Dr. Rafael Martinez (Public Health and Social Welfare), Fernando Villar (Economy and Finance), Roberto Martinez Ordoñez (Public Works and Communications), Oscar A. Flores Midence (Labor and Social Security), Francisco Milla Bermúdez (Natural Resources), Jorge Bueso Arias (Secretary of National Economic Council with rank of Minister without Portfolio), Alfredo Lara L. (Mayor of Tegucigalpa and Minister without Portfolio), and Rafael Diaz Chávez (Director of Procurement and Minister without Portfolio).

PRESS

Unless otherwise noted, papers are published in the capital city.

Name of Paper	Circulation	Political Affiliation	Proprietor, Editor, etc.
La Gaceta	3,000	Official gazette.	The Government (*Prop.*)
El Dia	10,000	Independent.	Julián López Pineda (*Prop. and Ed.*)
El Pueblo	4,000	Liberal.	Salvador Turcios h. (*Ed.*)
El Cronista	7,000	Independent-Liberal.	Alejandro Valladares (*Prop. and Ed.*)
Correo del Norte (San Pedro Sula)	5,000	Official.	The Government (*Prop.*) Pompeyo Melara (*Ed.*)

PRESS ASSOCIATION

Associación de la Prensa Hondureña   Independent.   Céleo Murillo Soto (*Pres.*)

HUNGARY

Capital: Budapest
Area: 35,911 square miles (prior to peace treaty)
Population: 9,800,000 (1957 estimate)

President of the Praesidium
ISTVAN DOBI
Elected to office on resignation of Sandor Ronai, August 15, 1952;
re-elected July 3, 1953

Cabinet
Communist-dominated Workers-Peasants Revolutionary Cabinet

Chairman of the Council of Ministers
FERENC MUENNICH (Hungarian Socialist Workers—HSWP)
Assumed office on January 28, 1958

NATIONAL ASSEMBLY
Election of November 16, 1958, for four-year term
President: SANDOR RONAI (HSWP)
Number of members (all of the People's Front) 336

POLITICAL EVENTS SINCE 1946

The Hungarian Republic was established on January 31, 1946, following elections of the preceding November which had resulted in a clear victory for the conservative Smallholders. Prime Minister Zoltan Tildy, a Smallholder, was elected President of the Republic, and Ferenc Nagy, also a Smallholder, became Prime Minister, taking office on February 4, 1946. His Coalition Cabinet included a minority of Communists, and they thereby secured the toe-hold which enabled them to begin their rise to power.

In May 1947, a Communist coup drove Nagy from office. He was replaced by Lajos Dinnyes, a left-wing Smallholder. And in the Communist-controlled national elections of August 31 of that year, the two large opposition parties having been dissolved, the Communists emerged as the strongest single party, having 22 per cent of the votes cast. In June 1948, the Hungarian Workers Party was formed through a merger of the Communists and Social Democrats.

President Tildy resigned on July 30, 1948, and on August 23, Parliament elected as his successor one of the deputy Vice-Premiers, Arpad Szakasits, formerly a Social Democrat. Dinnyes continued as Premier until December 9, when he resigned and was replaced by Istvan Dobi, another Smallholder.

Meanwhile, the Communists continued to consolidate their position. On February 1, 1949, Deputy Premier Rakosi announced the integration of all existing parties into the Independent People's Front and informed the public of the forthcoming establishment of the "People's Republic." This new Communist state came formally into being later, on August 20, when Parliament adopted the new Constitution; five days later, Arpad Szakasits was made

HUNGARY

Chairman of the Praesidium. Meanwhile, general elections had been held on May 15 on a single ticket. The vote went overwhelmingly to the Government's candidates. A new cabinet was formed on June 10, 1949.

After its accession to power, the Hungarian Workers' Government devoted all its energies to the transformation of Hungary into a "People's democracy" modeled after the Soviet Union.

In October 1956, following demonstrations by students and workers, a revolt against the Government, the secret police and the Russian occupying forces broke out. Ernoe Geroe lost the leadership of the Communist party, and on October 24th, Imre Nagy became Premier. After a temporary withdrawal from Budapest, Russian forces returned and attacked Budapest and other cities on November 4th. Imre Nagy and some of his associates sought refuge in the Yugoslav Legation, and on the same day a Government headed by Janos Kadar was set up. It has since extended its control over the Hungarian population under the presence of Soviet military forces in Hungary. Imre Nagy's execution was announced on June 16, 1958.

PARTY PROGRAMS AND LEADERS

HUNGARIAN WORKERS' PARTY: In June 1948, the Communist Party and the Social Democratic Party merged to form the Hungarian Workers' Party.

The Social Democratic Party represented primarily industrial workers of the skilled class. It advocated the nationalization of mines and utilities, and the gradual evolution of the state from liberal democracy to socialism. Its right-wing group favored a western orientation, while the left-wing was pro-Soviet. As a result of party purges, the left-wing got control, and the party subsequently lost its identity through the merger with the Communists.

In 1950, a majority of the Social Democrats were dismissed after being charged with sabotage to cause production difficulties and food shortages.

The Hungarian Workers' Party was reorganized by Janos Kadar on November 1, 1956, and thereafter was called the Hungarian Socialist Workers' Party. However, the new party is a continuation of the old. Membership is, however, much smaller, approximately 400,000, less than one-half of the old membership.

Leaders: Members of the Politburo: Janos Kadar, (First Secretary), Antal Apro, Bela Biszku, Lajos Feher, Jenoe Fock, Gyula Kallai, Karoly Kiss, Gyorgy Marosan, Ferenc Muennich, Sandor Ronai and Miklos Somogyi.

THE CABINET

The Council of Ministers is composed as follows: Dr. Ferenc Muennich, President; Antal Apro, First Vice-President; Janos Kadar, Gyula Kallai, and Gyorgy Marosan, Ministers of State; Endre Sik, Foreign Affairs; Bela Biszku, Interior; Geza Revesz, Defense; Imre Doegei, Agriculture; Valeria Benke, Culture; Dr. Frigyes Doleschall, Health; Istvan Kossa, Posts & Communications; Istvan Antos, Finance; Ferenc Nezval, Justice; Janos Csergoe, Metallurgy & Machine Industry; Sandor Czottner, Heavy Industry; Mrs. Jozsef Nagy, Light Industry; Jenoe Incze, Foreign Trade; Janos Tausz, Internal Trade; Imre Kovacs, Food Industry; Rezsoe Trautmann, Building Industry; Oedoen Kishazi, Labor; Arpad Kiss, National Planning.

HUNGARY

PRESS

Name of Paper	Character	Proprietor, Editor, etc.
DAILY NEWSPAPERS		
Nepszabadsag	HSWP; morning.	Dezso Nemes (*Ed.*)
Nepszava	Trade Union; morning.	Editorial Board
Magyar Nemzet	Specializes in foreign and cultural affairs; morning.	Erno Mihalyfi (*Ch. Ed. Bd.*)
Esti Hirlap	Political daily; evening.	Jeno Revesz (*Ed.*)
WEEKLIES		
Uj Ember	Catholic church paper.	Balduin Penzes (*Ed.*)
Reformatusok Lapja	Calvinist church paper.	Istvan Szamoskozi (*Ed.*)
Evangelikus Elet	Lutheran church paper.	Gyula Groo (*Ed.*)
Uj Elet	Jewish paper.	Dezso Rooz (*Ed.*)
Ludas Matyi	Political humor.	Laszlo Tabi (*Ed.*)
Szabad Fold	Working Peasants paper.	Janos Szentkiralyi (*Ed.*)
Magyar Ifjusag	Communist youth organ.	Editorial Board
Nok Lapja	Working women's organ.	Editorial Board.
Orszag-Vilag	Hungarian-Soviet relations.	Pal Alpari (*Ed.*)
Hetfoi Hirek	Political weekly.	Gyorgy Parragi (*Ed.*)
Radio es Televisio Ujsag	Radio-TV weekly.	Bela Levai (*Ed.*)
Katolikus Szo	Catholic paper.	Editorial Board
Erdekes Ujsag	Illustrated weekly.	Editorial Board
Jovendonk	Cooperatives weekly.	Vince Busi (*Ed.*)
MONTHLIES		
Tarsadalmi Szemle	Ideological organ of HSWP.	Gyula Kallai (*Ed.*)
Magyar Kozgazdasagi Szemle	Economic review.	Editorial Board
Nagy Vilag	International literature.	Laszlo Gerebelyes (*Ed.*)
Nemzetkozi Szemle	International political review.	Editorial Board
Kortars	Literary journal.	Jozef Davas and Gabor Tolnai (*Eds.*)
NEWS AGENCY		
Magyar-Tavirati Iroda (MTI)	Official.	Sandor Barcs (*Dir.*)

ICELAND

Capital: Reykjavik
Area: 39,709 square miles
Population: 166,831 (1957 estimate)

President
ÁSGEIR ÁSGEIRSSON
Declared elected unopposed May 19, 1956
Assumed office August 1, 1956

Cabinet
Social Democratic
Appointed December 23, 1958

Premier
EMIL JÓNSSON (Social Democrat)

PARLIAMENT
(Althing)
Election of June 24, 1956
President of the United Althing: EMIL JÓNSSON (Social Democrat)

UPPER CHAMBER
(Efri deild)
Speaker: BERNHARD STEFANSSON
(Progressive)

Parties	Representation
Independence Party	6
Progressive	6
Labor Union (Communist)	3
Social Democrat	2
Total	17

LOWER CHAMBER
(Nedri deild)
Speaker: EINAR OLGEIRSSON
(Labor Union-Communist)

Parties	Representation
Independence Party	13
Progressive	11
Social Democrat	6
Labor Union (Communist)	5
Total	35

PARTY PROGRAMS AND LEADERS

INDEPENDENCE PARTY: Formed by the fusion of the Conservative and Liberal Parties. It stands for a liberal economic policy. Representing commercial and fishing interests, the Party also has appreciable farmer and labor support. In *foreign affairs*, it advocates the continued presence in Iceland of NATO military forces in the present world situation.

Leaders: Olafur Thors (Chairman of Party), Bjarni Benediktsson (Vice-Chairman of Party) and Gunnar Thoroddsen (Mayor of Reykjavik).

PROGRESSIVE PARTY: Advocates general improvement in agriculture, better popular education, and extension of cooperative movement. Supports program of internal economic stabilization and national development. In *foreign policy*, expresses continued support for NATO. Advocated withdrawal of NATO forces, but has recently reversed this stand.

Leaders: Hermann Jonasson (former Prime Minister, Chairman of Party), Eysteinn Jónsson (former Minister of Finance).

SOCIAL DEMOCRATIC PARTY: Advocates program of internal economic stabilization and national development. Ideology is based on program of moderate socialism. In *foreign policy*, advocates continued support for NATO but favored withdrawal of NATO forces. It reversed this stand, however, in December 1956, because of troubled world conditions.

Leaders: Emil Jónsson (Chairman of Party, President of United Althing), Gylfi Th. Gislason (Minister of Education), and Gudmundur I. Gudmundsson (Minister for Foreign Affairs).

COMMUNIST PARTY: Formed new front party with left-wing Social Democrats prior to 1956 general elections, and appears in Althing under designation "Labor Union." Advocates a radical socialistic program in internal policy. In *foreign affairs*, advocates withdrawal from NATO as soon as possible, and return to neutrality. Consistently supports policies of world communism.

Leaders: Einar Olgeirsson (Speaker of Lower House of Althing, Chairman of Party), Ludvik Josefsson (Vice-Chairman of Party), Brynjolfur Bjarnason (former Minister of Education).

NATIONAL DEFENSE PARTY: Formed in 1953; main policy is removal of NATO military forces, withdrawal from NATO and return to neutrality. Its internal program is vaguely left-wing. Won two Althing seats in 1953, but lost them in 1956.

Leaders: Valdimar Johannsson, Gils Gudmundsson and Bergur Sigurbjörnsson.

THE CABINET

The members of the Cabinet are: Emil Jónsson, (Prime Minister, Minister of Fisheries and of Communications), Gudmundur I. Gundmundsson (Minister of Foreign Affairs and of Finance), Fridjon Skarphedisson (Minister of Justice, of Agriculture and of Social Affairs), Gylfi Th. Gislason (Minister of Education and of Commerce and Industry.

PRESS

Name of Paper	Political Affiliation	Proprietor, Editor, etc.
Althýdubladid	Social Democrat.	Helgi Saemundsson (*Ed.*)
Morgunbladid	Conservative.	Bjarni Benediktsson and Valtýr Stefansson (*Eds.*)
Thjódviljinn	Communist.	Magnús Kjartansson (*Ed.*)
Vísir	Conservative.	Hersteinn Palsson (*Ed.*)
Timinn	Progressive.	Thorarinn Thorarinsson (*Ed.*)
Frjáls Thjód (weekly)	National Defense Party.	Jón Helgason (*Ed.*)
Mánudagsbladid (weekly)	Independent.	Agnar Bogason (*Ed.*)

INDIA

Capital: New Delhi
Area: 1,269,640 square miles
Population: 384,000,000 (excluding Jammu and Kashmir, 1956 estimate)

President
DR. RAJENDRA PRASAD
Assumed office January 26, 1950
Re-elected in January, 1952, and in May, 1957

Prime Minister
JAWAHARLAL NEHRU
Assumed office August 15, 1947

GOVERNORS OF STATES

Andhra Pradesh: Bhimsen Sachar
Assam: Saiyid Fazl Ali
Bihar: Zakir Hussain
Bombay: Sri Prakasa
Jammu & Kashmir: Karan Singh (Sardr-i-Riyasat)
Kerala: Ramakrishna Rao
Madhya Pradesh: Hari Vinayak Pataskar
Madras: Bishnuram Medhi
Mysore: His Highness Jaya Chamaraja Wadiyar
Orissa: Y. N. Sukthankar
Punjab: Narhar Vishnu Gadgil
Rajasthan: Gurmukh Nihal Singh
Uttar Pradesh: Varahagiri Venkata Giri
West Bengal: Srimati Padmaja Naidu

RECENT POLITICAL EVENTS

The Dominion of India came into being on August 15, 1947, when, under the Indian Independence Act passed by the British Parliament in July 1947, the former Indian Empire was divided into the two dominions of India and Pakistan, both of which were granted full self-government. At a meeting of the Prime Ministers of the British Commonwealth in London in April of 1949, India agreed to continue its full membership in the Commonwealth. On January 26, 1950, a new Constitution was adopted which established India as a "Sovereign Democratic Republic" consisting of a "Union of States." At the same time the Constituent Assembly, elected for the purpose of framing the Constitution, transformed itself into the Provisional Indian Parliament.

The Constitution, which includes a bill of rights, provides that the President, to be elected every five years, is the head of the State. He is advised in the administration by a Prime Minister, who must enjoy majority support in Parliament. Parliament, composed of two Houses—Council of States (Rajya Sabha) and House of the People (Lok Sabha)—is to be elected after every five years on the basis of adult franchise. Every man and woman of the age of 21 is entitled to vote. The Council of States has 232 members, 12 nominated by the President, the rest elected by the members of State Legislative Assemblies. The Council is a permanent body, one-third of its members retiring every second year.

India's first election was held in January 1952, and resulted in a victory of Mr. Nehru's Congress Party, which won 362 out of the 489 contested seats in the new Parliament. The Independents won 41, and the Communists were in third place with 23. The remaining 63 seats were divided among minor factions. In the second general elections held in March 1957 nearly 106 million people voted out of an electorate of 193 million—the largest free electorate in the world. Out of the total of 494 contested seats the Congress won 369, the Communists 27, the Praja Socialist Party 21, Jan Sangh 4; and the remaining 73 seats were divided among Independents and minor parties.

THE STATES

The Indian Union, after the Reorganization of States which came into effect on November 1, 1956, now consists of 14 states and 7 centrally administered territories. Each state is headed by an appointed Governor (except in Jammu and Kashmir where the head of the state is called Sardr-i-Riyasat). The territories are headed by a Commissioner who is responsible to the President of India. The states follow the British parliamentary system with respect to division of powers, the same as is done at the center. The larger states have bicameral legislatures while the smaller ones have a single chamber. All the states are governed by the Congress Party except Kerala where the Government is run by the Communist Party.

PARTY PROGRAMS AND LEADERS

THE INDIAN NATIONAL CONGRESS: Party members form the Government at the center and in almost all States which have elected legislatures. The Congress advocates a democratic secular government and a left-of-center social and economic policy with a welfare state as its goal. The Congress aims at the settlement of Indo-Pakistan disputes by peaceful means, and endeavors to maintain a strictly independent position in world affairs.

Leaders: Jawaharlal Nehru, U. N. Dhebar (President of Party).

COMMUNIST PARTY: Organized in its present form in 1934. Has exerted from time to time considerable influence in the labor movement and succeeded temporarily in gaining control over a large territory in Andhra Pradesh. Its policy of violence and sabotage bordering on open revolt underwent revision in 1950 and 1958, but there is little indication that its basic program has been permanently modified. Indian Communists follow the orthodox international Communist line. Their leaders sit in Parliament as the largest opposition party.

Leaders: A. K. Ghosh, A. K. Gopalan, E. M. S. Namboodiripad and P. C. Joshi.

PRAJA-SOCIALIST PARTY: Formed the left-wing of the Indian National Congress until 1947, when its members broke away from the parent body and formed an independent organization. Socialists are poorly represented in the legislatures, but exert some influence through trade unions in industrial areas, especially Bombay. Party declares as its objective the establishment of a democratic socialist society in India.

INDIA

Leaders: J. B. Kripalani, Asoka Mehta, Ganga Saran Sinha (Chairman of Party).

AKHIL BHARATIYA JAN SANGH: A sectarian group pledged to work for the annulment of partition and for social and economic regeneration of the country in conformity with national traditions and Hindu culture.
Leader: D. P. Ghosh (President of the Party).

THE CABINET

The following are members of the Cabinet: Jawaharlal Nehru (Prime Minister, External Affairs and Atomic Energy), Govind Ballabh Pant (Home Affairs), Morarji Desai (Finance), Jagjivan Ram (Railways), Gulzarilal Nanda (Labor), Lal Bahadur Shastri (Commerce and Industry), Sardar Swaran Singh (Steel, Mines and Fuel), K. C. Reddy (Works, Housing and Supply), Ajit Prasad Jain (Food and Agriculture), V. K. Krishna Menon (Defense), S. K. Patil (Transport and Communications), Hafiz Mohammad Ibrahim (Irrigation and Power), A. K. Sen (Law). In addition, there are 14 Ministers of State with Cabinet rank, but not members of the Cabinet.

PRESS

English Language Publications

Name of Paper	Political Affiliation	Proprietor, Editor, etc.
Leader (Allahabad)	Liberal, Congress.	Newspapers, Ltd. (*Prop.*) Rameshwar Nath Zutshi (*Ed.*)
Tribune (Ambala)	Nationalist.	J. Natarajan (*Ed.*)
Deccan Herald (Bangalore)	Nationalist.	Pothan Joseph (*Ed.*)
Bombay Chronicle (Bombay)	Congress.	Bombay Chronicle Co., Ltd. (*Prop.*) D. C. Patole (*Ed.*)
Evening News of India (Bombay)	Evening edition of Times of India.	Bennett Coleman & Co., Ltd. (*Prop.*) N. J. Nanporia (*Ed.*)
Free Press Journal (Bombay)	Liberal; independent.	A. Hariharan (*Act. Ed.*)
Times of India (Bombay and Delhi)	Leading English daily of Western India.	Bennett Coleman & Co., Ltd. (*Prop.*) Jai Chand Jain (*Gen. Mgr.*)
Advance (Calcutta)	Congress.	Mool Chand Agarwal (*Prop.*) S. N. Roy (*Ed.*)
Amrita Bazar Patrika (Calcutta and Allahabad)	Oldest daily published by Indians; pro-Congress.	Tushar Kanti Ghosh (*Ed.*)
Hindustan Standard (Calcutta and Delhi)	Independent.	Sudhanshukumar Basu (*Ed.*)
Statesman (Calcutta and Delhi)	Represents Progressive British opinion.	The Statesman, Ltd. (*Prop.*) George Arthur Johnson (*Ed.*)
Hindustan Times (Delhi)	Congress.	Hindustan Times, Ltd. (*Prop.*) Durga Das (*Ed.*)
National Herald (Lucknow)	Nationalist, leftist.	M. Chalapathi Rau (*Ed.*)
Pioneer (Lucknow)	Represents landed interests.	The Pioneer Ltd. (*Prop.*) S. N. Ghosh (*Ed.*)
Hindu (Madras)	Pro-Congress; inclines toward moderation.	K. Srinivasan (*Ed.*)
Indian Express (Madras, Bombay and Delhi)	Nationalist.	Frank Moraes (*Ed.*)
The Mail (Madras)	Represents English opinion.	Allan Taylor (*Ed.*)
Hitavada (Nagpur)	Independent.	A. D. Mani (*Ed.*)

Name of Paper	Political Affiliation	Proprietor, Editor, etc.
The Eastern Economist (New Delhi) (weekly)	Finance and commerce.	E. P. W. da Costa (*Ed.*)
Indian Nation (Patna)	Independent.	Dr. Sachin Sen (*Ed.*)
Searchlight (Patna)	Conservative; Congress.	M. S. Mantreshwara Sharma (*Ed.*)
Capital (weekly) (Calcutta)	A leading financial weekly.	Capital, Ltd. (*Prop.*) George Barrell (*Ed.*)
Swarajya (weekly) (Madras)	Independent.	Khasa Subba Rao (*Ed.*)
Thought (weekly) (Delhi)	Independent.	Ram Singh (*Ed.*)
Modern Review (monthly) (Calcutta)	Pro-Congress.	Kedarnath Chatterji (*Ed.*)
Indian Review (monthly) (Madras)	Liberal Orthodox.	Manian Natesan (*Prop. and Ed.*)

NEWS AGENCIES

United Press of India (Calcutta, Delhi, etc.)	Independent.	B. Sen Gupta (*Mg. Ed.*)
Press Trust of India	Independent.	Press Trust of India, Ltd. (*Prop.*)
Agence France-Presse, Paris	Independent.	Felix Nagar (*Ed.*)
Associated Press, U.S.A.	Independent.	Charles Lane (*Ed.*)
Reuters, London	Independent.	Peter Jackson (*Mgr.*)
Tass, U.S.S.R.	Communist.	G. Efimov (*Mgr.*)
United Press International U.S.A.	Independent.	B. K. Tiwari (*Mgr.*)

INDONESIA

Capital: Djakarta
Area: 735,865 square miles
Population: 82,500,000 (1955 estimate)

President
DR. SUKARNO

Cabinet
Coalition: NU—5, PNI—4, IPKI—1, Murba—1,
Parkindo—1, Pantjasila—1, Non-Party—14
Assumed office on April 8, 1957

Premier
DR. H. DJUANDA (Non-Party)

PARLIAMENT
(Dewan Perwakilan Rakjat)
Election of September 29, 1955
Speaker: R. M. SARTONO (PNI)

Parties	Representation
Partai Nasional Indonesia (Indonesian Nationalist Party)—PNI	57
Masjumi (Indonesian Moslem Council)	57
Nahdatul Ulama (Muslim Schoolmen League)—NU	45
Partai Komunis Indonesia (Indonesian Communist Party)—PKI	39
Other Parties	63
Appointed Deputies (Irian and Minorities)	12
Total	273

THE ELECTIONS OF 1955

The first general election since independence was held, beginning September 29, 1955, for the selection of a Parliament (one member for every 300,000) under the system of proportional representation. In addition, three deputies for West Irian and thirteen deputies for Chinese, European, and Arab minority groups were appointed. Ninety organized groups and independent candidates participated. Approximately 87% of a registered electorate of 43 million voted. No party succeeded in gaining a majority. The PNI led with about 22+% of the popular vote, followed by the Masjumi with 21%, the Nahdatul Ulama with 18+%, and the Communists with 16+%.

Beginning December 15, 1955, a second election for a Constituent Assembly of 514 members to draft a permanent constitution was held. The results were: PNI—119, Masjumi—112, Nahdatul Ulama—91, Communists—80, Other Parties—112, Appointed (West Irian)—7, total, 520. The Constituent Assembly was installed and began its deliberations in November, 1956. The major issues facing the Constituent Assembly are a unicameral or bi-cameral legislature, techniques for ensuring greater decentralization and regional autonomy, the role of Islam in the state, and the position and powers of the President.

POLITICAL PARTIES AND LEADERS

The two largest parties, Masjumi and PNI, are both internally divided. The Masjumi traditionalist wing is headed by former premier Sukiman. The Masjumi progressive wing is mildly socialistic and is headed by former premier Natsir. Both wings are anti-communist. The PNI has a socialist, chauvinist wing, which is opposed by moderates within the party, who strengthened their position during the PNI party congress in July 1956, when a moderate compromise candidate, Suwirjo, was elected Chairman. The Nahdatul Ulama is an association of Moslem scholars based regionally in East-Central Java and South Kalimantan. It has not yet developed a full political ideology. Its leaders have had little acquaintance with the West or with foreign affairs in general. The Communist Party (PKI) under the leadership of 35-year-old D. N. Aidit has, since 1953, consistently pursued "national front" tactics, designed to lull Indonesian fears concerning its ultimate goals and orientation. Utilizing this technique the Communists have made considerable gains in the last few years. They have increased their membership, strengthened and expanded their organization, established and fostered "front" groups in various fields, and widened and tightened their control of the labor movement.

While Indonesia's diplomatic, economic, and cultural relations with the Communist bloc are increasing, all parties support a policy of non-alignment with either the East or West in keeping with Indonesia's "active independent" foreign policy.

As a result of the growing threat of National disintegration in 1957, the Masjumi and three minor parties withdrew their members from the Ali Sastroamidjojo Cabinet and it resigned. On April 9 Sukarno took a step unprecedented since the transfer of sovereignty from the Netherlands in 1949. He appointed the Cabinet himself, stating that the criterion for appointment was personal ability rather than political influence. The PNI and the Communist Party (PKI) announced their support of the new Cabinet, which is led by Djuanda, a non-party man. The Moslem Teachers Party (NU) while stating it would adopt a wait-and-see attitude has actually supported it. The Masjumi adamantly opposed it and has maintained that position.

In February 1958, a group of dissident political leaders and army officers in Central Sumatra issued an ultimatum to the Central Government demanding that a new cabinet be formed, made up of individuals suitable to them. The ultimatum was rejected and the dissidents proclaimed a rival government to which another dissident movement in North Sulawesi announced its allegiance. In a series of military campaigns carried on from March through June, the Central Government Army invaded Central Sumatra and North Sulawesi, driving the rebels from all major cities and the rebellion subsided into guerrilla warfare.

THE CABINET

Dr. H. Djuanda, Prime Minister and Defense (Non-Party); Dr. Hardi, First Deputy Premier (PNI); K. H. Idham Chalid, Second Deputy Premier (NU); Dr. J. Leimena, Third Deputy Premier (Parkindo); Dr. Subandrio, Foreign Affairs (Non-Party); Sanusi Hardjadinata, Interior (PNI); G. A.

INDONESIA

Maengkom, Justice (Non-Party); Sudibjo, Information (PSII); Dr. Sutikno Slamet, Finance (PNI); Dr. Sadjarwo, Agriculture (BTI); Dr. F. J. Inkiriwang, Industry (Non-Party); Dr. Sukardan, Communications (Non-Party); Colonel Nazir, Shipping (Non-Party); Dr. Pangeran Noor, Public Works and Energy (Non-Party); Dr. Samjono, Labor (Non-Party); Muljadi Djojomartono, Social Affairs (Non-Party); Prof. Dr. Prijono, Education (Murba); K. H. Iljas, Religion (NU); Dr. Azis Saleh, Health (IPKI); Dr. Sunarjo, Agrarian Affairs (NU); A. M. Hanafi, Without Portfolio (People's Congress); Chairul Saleh, Veterans Affairs (1945 Revolutionary Generation); Dr. F. L. Tobing, Transmigration (SKI); Wahib Wahab, Military & Civilian Cooperation (NU); Col. Suprajogi, Economic Stabilization (Non-Party); Prof. H. Mohammad Yamin, Without Portfolio (Non-Party); Rachmat Muljomiseno, Minister of Trade (NU).

PRESS

Unless otherwise noted, papers are in the capital city.

Name of Paper	Circulation	Political Orientation	Proprietor, Editor, etc.
Abadi	30,000	Masjumi.	H. S. M. Sjaaf (*Ed.*)
Bintang Timur	40,000	Leftist.	Tan Foe Khiong (*Ed.*)
Duta Masjarakat	10,000	Nahdatul Ulama (NU).	Aminuddin Aziz (*Ed.*)
Harian Rakjat	58,000	Communist (PKI).	Naibaho (*Ed.*)
Indonesian Observer	8,500	Pro-Nationalist (PNI); in English.	Soetomo Satiman (*Ed.*)
Indonesia Raya	28,000	Independent.	Hasjim Mahdan (*Ed.*)
Merdeka	25,000	Pro-Nationalist (PNI).	Asa Bafagih (*Prop.*)
Nieuwsgier	9,000	Independent; in Dutch.	T. D. Hayaz (*Ed.*)
Pedoman	40,000	Socialist (PSI).	Rosihan Anwar (*Ed.*)
Pos Indonesia	45,000	Pro-Socialist.	Umar Sanusi (*Ed.*)
Sin Po	30,000	Pro-Communist; Indonesian and Chinese editions.	Kwa Sien Siauw (*Ed.*)
Suluh Indonesia	45,000	Nationalist (PNI).	Moh. Isnaeni (*Ed.*)
Times of Indonesia	5,000	Independent; in English.	C. Tambu (*Ed.*)
Kedaulatan Rakjat (Jogjakarta)	10,000	Pro-PNI.	Wonohito (*Ed.*)
Nasional (Jogjakarta)	10,000	Independent.	P. Wardojo (*Ed.*)
Pedoman Rakjat	10,000	Pro-Socialist.	M. Basir (*Ed.*)
Mestika (Medan)	4–5,000	NU.	Tamzil Ja'coeb (*Ed.*)
Lembaga (Medan)	5–7,000	Masjumi.	Joesoef Sou'yb (*Ed.*)
Mimbar Umum (Medan)	12,500	Independent (PSI).	Sjamsuddin Manan (*Ed.*)
Waspada (Medan)	14,000	Pro-PNI.	Moh. Said (*Ed.*)
Java Post (Surabaya)	8,000	Independent, anti-Communist.	Thio Oen-Sik (*Ed.*)
Surabaya Post	3,500	Independent.	A. Aziz (*Prop. and Ed.*)
Trompet Masjarakat (Surabaya)	12,000	Leftist.	Goei Poo-an (*Ed.*)
Perdamaian (Surabaya)	6,000	Communist (PKI).	Tjia Tik Sing (*Ed.*)
Suara Rakjat (Surabaya)	10,000	Independent.	Moh. Sofwandhi (*Ed.*)
Weekly Merdeka	10,000	Political magazine; independent.	Gusti Majur (*Ed.*)
Siasat (weekly)	12,500	General news (PSI).	Sanjoto (*Ed.*)

IRAN

Capital: Tehran
Area: 628,000 square miles
Population: 20,081,510 (1956 estimate)

Ruler
MOHAMED REZA SHAH PAHLEVI
Assumed throne on September 17, 1941

Cabinet
Appointed April 4, 1957

Premier
MANUCHEHR EQBAL

PARLIAMENT

UPPER CHAMBER	LOWER CHAMBER
(Senate)	(Majlis)
Half of the members are appointed by the Shah.	
President: MOHSEN SADR	Speaker: REZA HEKMAT
Number of members 60	Number of members 236

PARTY PROGRAMS AND LEADERS

There are two major political parties in Iran, both of which are still in the early formative stages. The majority Melliyun (Nationalist) Party is led by Manuchehr Eqbal. The opposition Mardom (People's) Party is led by Asadollah Alam. The Communist Tudeh (Masses) Party has been outlawed by the Government.

THE CABINET

The members of the present Cabinet are: Manuchehr Eqbal (Prime Minister), Ali Asqar Hekmat (Foreign Minister), Ali Asqar Naser (Minister of Finance), Abas Qoli Neisari (Minister of Commerce), Jafar Sharif-Emami (Minister of Mines and Industries), Lieutenant General Nader Batmanqelich (Minister of Interior), Major General Hasan Akhavi (Minister of Agriculture), Dr. Jamshid Amuzegar (Minister of Labor), Dr. Mohamad Ali Hedayati (Minister of Justice), Major General Vali Ansari (Minister of Roads and Communications), Dr. Abdol Hosein Raji (Minister of Health), Dr. Mahmud Mehran (Minister of Education), Lieutenant General Ahmad Vosuq (Minister of War), Amir Qasem Eshraqi (Minister of Posts, Telephones and Telegraphs), Major General Ali Akbar Zarqam (Minister of Customs and Monopolies), Khalil Taleqani (Minister Without Portfolio), Dr. Nosratollah Kasemi (Minister Without Portfolio).

PRESS

All papers listed are published in Tehran.

Name of Paper	Character	Proprietor, Editor, etc.
Dad	Morning daily.	Deputy Abol Hasan Amidi-Nuri
Etela'at	Evening daily.	Senator Abbas Masudi
Farman	Morning daily.	Abbas Shahandeh
Kayhan	Evening daily.	Prof. Mostafa Mesbahzadeh
Post-e-Tehran	Evening daily.	Deputy Mohammed Ali Masudi
Bamshad	Morning daily.	Ismail Porvali
Tehran Journal	English daily.	Senator Abbas Masudi
Journal de Tehran	French daily.	Senator Abbas Masudi

IRAQ

Capital: Baghdad
Area: 168,118 square miles
Population: 6,538,109 (1957 census)

Council of Sovereignty
GENERAL NAJIB AL-RUBAI (President)
SAYYID MOHAMMED MAHDI KUBBA
SAYYID KHALID NAQSHBENDI

Prime Minister
BRIGADIER ABDUL KARIM QASSIM
Assumed power on July 14, 1958, as result of a military coup d'état.

PARLIAMENT

The Parliament of the previous régime was prorogued at the time of the *coup d'état*. The present Government is operating under a temporary Constitution promulgated on July 27, 1958, under which the Council of Ministers (Cabinet) has legislative powers with the consent of the Council of Sovereignty.

POLITICAL PARTIES

Political parties are at present banned under the State of Martial Law proclaimed on July 14, 1958. The four most important parties were: the National Democratic Party; the Istiqlal (Independence) Party; the Ba'ath (the National Resurrection Party); and the Communist Party of Iraq. The new regime has promised that normal political life will be resumed as soon as possible.

THE CABINET

The members of the Council of Ministers are: Abdul Karim Qassim (Prime Minister and Acting Minister of Defense), Brig. Ahmed Yahya (Minister of Interior), Dr. Abdul Jabbar Jomard (Foreign Affairs), Mohammed Hadid (Finance and Development), Mustafa Ali (Justice), Ibrahim Kubba (Economics), Brigadier Naji Talib (Social Affairs), Baba Ali (Communications and Works), Salih Mahmoud (Health), Hdaib Haj Hmoud (Agriculture and Education), and Saddiq Shanshal (Guidance).

PRESS

Unless otherwise noted, papers are published in Baghdad.

Name of Paper	Political Affiliation, etc.
al-Bilad	Semi-official.
al-Zaman	Pro-Government.
al-Yaqdha	Pro-United Arab Republic.
al-Hurriyah	Pro-Government.
The Iraq Times (in English)	Independent; conservative.

Name of Paper	Proprietor, Editor, etc.
Quarandel (weekly)	Independent; satirical.
al-Dustoor (Basra)	Independent.
al-Manar (Basra)	Independent.
al-Thaghar (Basra)	Independent.
al-Akhbar al Tijariya (Mosul)	Independent; commercial weekly.
Fata al-Iraq (Mosul)	Independent; weekly.
Sawt al Umma (Mosul)	Independent; weekly.

IRELAND

Capital: Dublin
Area: 26,600 square miles (exclusive of rivers and lakes)
Population: 2,898,264 (1956 Census)

President
SEÁN T. O'KELLY
Elected June 14, 1945; re-elected unopposed, May 16, 1952
Assumed office June 25, 1945

Cabinet
Fianna Fáil
Appointed March 20, 1957

Prime Minister
ÉAMON DE VALÉRA
Elected by Dáil Eireann on March 20, 1957

PARLIAMENT
(Oireachtas)

FIRST CHAMBER
(Dáil Eireann)

Last general election, March 5, 1957 (five-year term)

Speaker:* PATRICK HOGAN (Labor)

Parties	Representation
Fianna Fáil	78
Fine Gael	40
Labor	12
Sinn Fein	4
Clann na Talmhan	3
National Progressive Democrats	2
Clann na Poblachta	1
Independent	7
Total	147

* The Speaker is not required to vacate his seat at a general election.

SECOND CHAMBER
(Seanad Eireann)
Election of May 1957

Chairman: LIAM O BUACHALLA
(Fianna Fáil)

Number of members 60

Forty-three members are elected on a vocational basis, six are elected by the National and Dublin Universities; the remaining eleven are nominated by the Prime Minister.

PARTY PROGRAMS AND LEADERS

FIANNA FÁIL: In office from 1932 to 1948 and again from June 1951 to June 1954, and from March 1957. Voted substantial majority in the general election of March 5, 1957. Advocates the independence of all Ireland under a Republican form of Government; the peaceful ending of Partition imposed on Ireland by the British Act of 1920; advocates State investments to promote agricultural development and manufacturing adequate for full employment; stands for the revival and extension of Irish industry and the decentralization of the siting of factories in order to provide an alternative to emigration for those leaving the farms. Fianna Fáil also includes in its program the restoration of Irish as the national language, and the encouragement of tillage to provide the country's primary needs in food. It advocates that the country maintain sufficient forces to defend its territory in time of war, and prevent its use as a base of attack upon Britain; the party extended electricity and health services; development of turf fuel production; expansion of air and shipping services and development of ship-building industry; increased efficiency in all forms of transport; adjustment of wages by free negotiations; improved social services; adequate state aid for housing activities. Advocates and executes suppression of the Irish Republican Army (I.R.A.), illegal para-military organization.

Leaders: Éamon de Valéra (President); Dr. James Ryan, T.D., Gerald Boland, T.D., Senator Margaret Pearse, Sean MacEntee, T.D. (Vice-Presidents); Kevin Boland, T.D., Seosamh Groome (Honorary Secretaries); Sean O'Donovan, Neil Blaney T.D. (Honorary Treasurers).

FINE GAEL (United Ireland Party): Largest element in coalition which governed Ireland 1954–57. Advocates cooperation between political parties, promotion of friendly relations with Northern Ireland leading towards political unity of Ireland; urges Irish language and culture; assistance to home industry by tariffs and otherwise; full development of agriculture including marketing of Irish products; development of natural resources.

Leaders: General R. Mulcahy, T.D. (President of Party), John A. Costello (Leader of the Opposition in the Dáil), General Seán MacEoin, T.D., James M. Dillon, T.D., Daniel Morrissey, T.D., Liam Cosgrave, T.D. (Vice-Presidents); Senator Michael Hayes and Gerard Sweetman, T.D., (Hon. Secretaries).

LABOR PARTY: The policy of the Labor Party follows closely the social and economic policy of the recent Labor movement in New Zealand, especially in regard to its financial and monetary aspects, social security, agricultural development and full employment. Essentially democratic in its approach to parliamentary government, the Labor Party is based on the orthodox trade union movement and the cooperative aspect of rural development.

Leaders: William Norton, T.D. (Leader of Labor Party); Dan Desmond, T.D. (Deputy Leader of Party); Brendan Corish, T.D. (Vice Chairman of Administrative Council of Party).

CLANN NA TALMHAN (Farmer's Party): Advocates the achievement and safeguarding of the unity and independence of the nation; a Christian and National Social Order based on a minimum economic income for all citizens with adequate provision for the aged and infirm; the subsidization of tillage; the protecting of the agricultural industry against unfair outside competition; a planned national development; reduction of taxation and the cost-of-living; development of native industries; and extension of social services, particularly in ways beneficial to the rural community.

Leaders: Joseph Blowick, T.D.; Ml. Donnellan, T.D.; John Finan.

CLANN NA POBLACHTA (Republican): Ultra-nationalist. Formed in 1946. Advocates more independent financial policy and bolder development projects by limiting investments abroad and utilizing capital resources at home in order to stem emigration and rural depopulation; ending of Partition especially by a further improvement of social conditions; extensive health services; decentralization of industry and government and zoning of agriculture.

IRELAND

Leader: Seán MacBride, S.C.

SINN FEIN (Ultra-nationalist Republican): Reactivated in autumn of 1956; advocates ending of Partition by force. Committed to policy of abstention from the Dáil until it obtains majority of seats.

Leaders: Patrick McLogan, President; Secretaries, Michael Traynor and Maire Nic Gabhann; Vice-Presidents, Tomas O Dubhghaill and Mrs. Margaret Buckley; Treasurers, Paddy O'Hagan and Eamonn Thomas.

NATIONAL PROGRESSIVE DEMOCRATS: Formed in May 1958. Advocates State enterprises and economic development. Opposes teaching of Irish language and expenditures for presidential and ambassadorial establishments, and maintenance of army.

Leaders: Dr. Noel Brown, T.D., and Jack McQuillan, T.D.

THE CABINET

The members of the Cabinet are: Éamon de Valéra, Taoiseach or Head of the Government (Fianna Fáil); Seán Lemass, Tanaiste and Minister for Industry and Commerce; Patrick Smith, Agriculture; Kevin Boland, Defense; John Lynch, Education; Frank Aiken, External Affairs; Dr. James Ryan, Finance; Seán MacEntee, Health; Oscar Traynor, Justice; Erskine Childers, Lands; Neil Blaney, Local Government; John Ormonde, Posts and Telegraphs; Michael Moran, Gaeltacht.

PRESS

Unless otherwise noted, papers are published in capital city.

Name of Paper	Political Affiliation	Proprietor, Editor, etc.
Evening Herald	Independent; nationalist.	Pearse Kelly (*Ed.*)
Evening Mail	Independent; conservative.	Joseph Anderson (*Ed.*)
Evening Press	Independent; pro-Fianna Fáil.	Douglas Gageby (*Ed.*)
Irish Independent	Pro-Coalition.	Frank Geary (*Ed.*)
Irish Times	Conservative; formerly Unionist.	Alec Newman (*Ed.*)
The Irish Press	Fianna Fáil.	Francis Carty (*Ed.*)
Cork Examiner (Cork)	Independent; pro-Fine Gael.	P. J. Dorgan (*Ed.*)
Evening Echo (Cork)	Pro-Fine Gael.	W. D. O'Connell (*Ed.*)
Irish Weekly Independent and Sunday Independent	Pro-Coalition.	Hector C. Legge (*Ed.*)
The Times Pictorial (weekly)	Independent; Unionist background.	Peadar Ward (*Ed.*)
The Leader (weekly)	Nationalist and protectionist.	Miss N. Moran (*Ed.*)
The Standard (weekly)	Catholic.	Peter Kilroy (*Ed.*)
Sunday Press (weekly)	Fianna Fáil.	Matthew Feehan (*Ed.*)
Sunday Review (weekly)	Independent.	Austin Walsh (*Ed.*)
Comhar (monthly)	Gaelic; political and literary.	Tomas O Floinn (*Ed.*)
An Cosantóir (monthly)	Military; historical.	Published by Army.
The Farming Post (monthly)	Organ of Agricultural Association of Ireland.	Brendan Clarke (*Ed.*)
Irish Industry (monthly)	Business and Economics.	P. L. McEvoy (*Ed.*)
Irish Trade Journal. (quarterly)	Economic and commercial.	Irish Govt. Publication
Studies (quarterly)	Political; economic; literary.	Rev. R. Burke-Savage, S. (*Ed.*)

ISRAEL

Capital: Jerusalem
Area: 8,048 square miles
Population: 2,080,000 (1958 estimate)

President
ITZHAK BEN-ZVI
Elected by the Knesset (Parliament) December 8, 1952;
re-elected October 28, 1957, for five-year term

Cabinet
Coalition: Approved by Parliament November 3, 1955

Premier
DAVID BEN-GURION (Mapai Party)
Approved November 3, 1955

KNESSET
(Parliament)
Elected July 26, 1955, for four-year term
Speaker: YOSEF SPRINZAK

Parties	Representation
Mapai (Israel Labor)	40
Mapai Affiliates (three separate Arab Lists)	5
Herut (Freedom)	15
General Zionists	13
Mizrahi (merged list of Hapoel Hamizrahi and Mizrahi)	11
Ahdut Avoda (Unity of Labor)	10
Mapam (United Workers)	9
Agudists (merged list of Agudat Israel and Poalei Agudat Israel)	6
Maki (Communists)	6
Progressives	5
Total	120

POLITICAL PARTIES

The present Cabinet is a coalition of Mapai, Mapam, Ahdut Avoda, and the Progressive parties, commanding 69 seats of 120 in the Knesset. The other parties are in opposition, with most effective criticism emanating from Herut and the General Zionists.

THE CABINET

The composition of the Cabinet is as follows: David Ben-Gurion, Prime Minister, Minister of Defense; Rabbi Jacob Toledano, Minister of Religious Affairs; Israel Barzilai, Minister of Social Welfare, Posts and of Health

(Mapam); Mrs. Golda Meir, Minister of Foreign Affairs (Mapai); Levi Eshkol, Finance (Mapai); Mordechai Namir, Labor (Mapai); Peretz Naphtali, without Portfolio (Mapai); Behor Shitreet, Police (Mapai); Zalman Aranne, Education and Culture (Mapai); Pinhas Sapir, Commerce and Industry (Mapai); Kadish Luz, Agriculture (Mapai); Pinhas Rosen, Justice (Progressive); Israel Bar-Yehuda, Interior (Ahdut Avoda); Moshe Carmel, Communications (Adhut Avoda); Mordechai Bentov, Development (Mapam).

PRESS

Unless otherwise noted, papers are published in Hebrew and in Tel Aviv. The abbreviation *m.* indicates morning; *e.* evening.

Name of Paper	Political Affiliation	Editor
Davar (m)	General Federation of Labor.	H. Shurer
Haaretz (m)	Independent.	G. Schocken
Haboker (m)	General Zionist.	Dr. P. Bernstein
Al Hamishmar (m)	United Workers Party.	Y. Amit
Herut (m)	Freedom Movement.	A. Remba
Hatzofe (m)	World Mizrahi Organization.	S. Daniel
Kol Haam (m)	Communist.	Z. A. Breitstein
Lamerchav (m)	Ahdut Avoda.	A. Tarshish
L'Information	Mapam; in French.	M. Arielly
Letzte Neies (m)	Independent; in Yiddish.	M. Zanin
Nowiny Israelski (m)	Independent; in Polish.	Dr. H. Abir
Maariv (e)	Independent.	A. Dissentshik
Omer (m)	General Federation of Labor.	D. Pines
Yediot Achronot (e)	Independent.	Dr. H. Rosenblum
Yediot Hadashot (m)	Independent; in German.	Dr. A. Lilienfeld
El Yom (Jaffa) (m)	Federation of Labor; in Arabic.	M. Assaf
Hamodia (Jerusalem) (m)	World Agudat Israel.	P. Levine
Jerusalem Post (Jerusalem) (m)	Independent; in English.	T. Lurie
Shearim (m)	Poalei Agudat Israel.	J. Broner
Uj Kelet (m)	Independent; in Hungarian.	Dr. E. Marton
Yediot Hayom (m)	Independent; in German.	Dr. P. Reichenstein

ITALY

Capital: Rome
Area: 116,372 square miles
Population: 50,000,000 (1958 estimate)

President
GIOVANNI GRONCHI
Elected President of the Republic on April 29, 1955

Cabinet
Christian Democrats—17, Democratic Socialists—4
Approved by Parliament on July 19, 1958

Premier
AMINTORE FANFANI (Christian Democrat)
Appointed July 1, 1958

PARLIAMENT

SENATE
Elections of May 25-26, 1958 (Six-year term)
President: CESARE MERZAGORA
(Independent)

Parties	Representation
Christian Democrat	123
Communist	59
Left-Wing Socialist	36
Italian Social (neo-Fascist)	8
Popular Monarchist	5
Right-Wing Socialist	5
Liberal	4
Volkspartei (Tyrol)	2
National Monarchist	2
Leftist Independent	1
Val d'Aosta Union	1
Senators for life	7
Total	253

CHAMBER OF DEPUTIES
Elections of May 25-26, 1958 (Five-year term)
President: GIOVANNI LEONE
(Christian Democrat)

Parties	Representation
Christian Democrat	273
Communist	140
Left-Wing Socialist	84
Italian Social	24
Right-Wing Socialist	22
Liberal	17
Popular Monarchist	14
National Monarchist	11
Republican	6
Volkspartei (Tyrol)	3
Val d'Aosta Union	1
Comunita	1
Total	596

RECENT POLITICAL EVENTS

On September 25, 1945, a Consultative Assembly was set up which included such well known leaders as Orlando, Nitti, Bonomi and Benedetto Croce. Count Carlo Sforza was elected President. Elections were held in June 1946 for a Constituent Assembly and at the same time to vote on the Monarchy. The results were 6 to 5 against the King and the Italian Republic was proclaimed. The royal family went into exile in Portugal shortly thereafter.

ITALY

On December 22, 1947, the Constituent Assembly approved a new Constitution by a vote of 453 to 62. It came into force on New Year's Day, 1948. It provides two houses of Parliament of equal powers, which in joint session elect the President of the Republic.

The first national elections under the new Constitution were held on April 18 and 19, 1948. The campaign battle cry of the conservatives, the center parties and the moderate leftist parties was that the Communist Party was a tool of Soviet Russia and should not be permitted to govern. The extreme left, consisting of the Communists and left-wing Socialists, sought the support of both the proletariat and middle class groups by means of a "Popular Democratic Front." Ninety-two per cent of the electorate voted. The result was a Christian Democrat victory which far exceeded all expectations. The Christian Democrats won 48.5 per cent of the seats in the Chamber of Deputies, and 48 per cent of those in the Senate. The Popular Front won 31 per cent of the seats in the Chamber and 30.8 per cent in the Senate.

In the elections of June 1953, the Center Party coalition lost its former substantial majority. In the Senate it won only 50.2 per cent of the popular vote, giving it a margin of only 14 seats. In the Chamber it received 48.5 per cent giving it a margin of only 16 seats.

In April 1955, Giovanni Gronchi was elected President of the Republic, and in July 1955, Antonio Segni became Prime Minister. He was succeeded in May, 1957 by Adone Zoli who formed a Christian Democratic Cabinet.

After the elections of May 25–26, 1958, which marked a slight increase for Center Left-wing parties, a Left-Center Government headed by Amintore Fanfani was formed by the Christian Democrats and Democratic Socialists who together had a slight majority in Parliament.

PARTY PROGRAMS AND LEADERS

CHRISTIAN DEMOCRATS (Democrazia Cristiana): Is successor to the pre-Fascist Popular Party. The party, which has since 1948 formed the backbone of the Government, occupies a center position, and its program supports the defense of democratic liberties against attacks by both Communist and Neo-Fascist extremist forces.

Leaders: Amintore Fanfani (Secretary), Mario Scelba, Antonio Segni, Giuseppe Pella, Attilio Piccioni, Guilio Andreotti, Guido Gonella.

COMMUNIST PARTY: Advocates sweeping industrial nationalization, labor and social reforms, and land redistribution; general electoral appeal is to the workers or "proletariat" but also attempts to win the support of lower middle-class and intellectual groups. In domestic affairs it is in constant opposition to the Government, and constantly preaches the doctrine of class warfare. In foreign policy it ostensibly favors cooperation with all democratic countries but is openly pro-Soviet and violently denunciatory of the Western Powers, particularly the United States.

Leaders: Palmiro Togliatti (Secretary General), Luigi Longo (Vice-Secretary), Mauro Scoccimarro, Edoardo d'Onofrio, Giancarlo Pajetta, Pietro Secchia, Agostino Novella (National Secretary of left-wing Trade Unions —CGIL), Giorgio Amendola.

ITALIAN SOCIALIST PARTY: Aligned with Communists by a "Unity of Action" pact dating from October 1946. In October 1957 the pact was repealed. In January 1947, the Party split into two groups over this question.

One retained the name of "Partito Socialista Italiano" and based its political conduct on close understanding with the Communists; the other named itself "Partito Socialista dei Lavoratori Italiani" (Socialist Party of Italian Workers) and declared its independence from the Communists and its firm adherence to the principles of Western political democracy. A second split in the old Socialist Party in December 1947, resulted in the formation of the very small Union of Socialists Party led by Ignazio Silone. In May 1949, a third split occurred under Giuseppe Romita, who opposed unity of action with the Communists.

Electoral appeal of the party is to manual and white-collar workers. Advocates nationalization of industrial and commercial monopolies and land reforms. In foreign policy it generally follows the Communist Party line.

Leaders: Pietro Nenni (Party Secretary), Alessandro Pertini, Oreste Lizzadri, Riccardo Lombardi.

DEMOCRATIC SOCIALIST PARTY (Formerly Italian Section of the Socialist International, PS—SIIS): Is the new party resulting from the amalgamation in 1951 of the Italian Workers' Socialist Party with the various Socialist Unity groups headed by Giuseppe Romita and Ignazio Silone, the Unitary Socialist Party and others. The party declares its complete independence from the Communist Party and from the Socialist Party of Pietro Nenni. Although occasionally expressing dissatisfaction with the speed with which moderate reforms are put into effect, it took part in all De Gasperi Governments from May 1947, until 1951, and in the Scelba and Segni Governments.

Leaders: Giuseppe Saragat (Party Secretary), Alberto Simonini, Mario Tanassi, Matteo Matteotti, Paolo Rossi.

REPUBLICANS: A small, moderate leftist group, of Mazzinian inspiration, which supports democratic governments.

Leaders: Oronzo Reale (Secretary), Ugo la Malfa and Randolfo Pacciardi.

LIBERALS: A small conservative party with modern and laicist views. Took part in all De Gasperi Governments from May 1947, until 1951.

Leaders: Raffaele de Caro (President), Giovanni Malagodi (Secretary) and Gaetano Martino.

MONARCHIST PARTY: Although this party has polled only a small fraction of the votes in recent elections, it hopes to capitalize on the attachment to the monarchy as an institution which is still prevalent, particularly in the South. The party generally supports the foreign policy of the Government, although maintaining that not enough has been done to assert Italy's position in the international field. The party split in 1954 into two groups: one led by Achille Lauro, called Partito Monarchico Popolare; the other led by Alfredo Covelli retained the old party name.

SOCIAL MOVEMENT: A small group known as the MSI, which is faithful to the traditions of Fascism and to the memory of Mussolini. Advocates advanced social reforms and has opposed the Government on most issues.

Leaders: Arturo Michelini (Secretary), Augusto De Marsanich, Giorgio Almirante.

ITALY

THE CABINET

The members of the Cabinet are: Amintore Fanfani (Premier and Minister of Foreign Affairs); Antonio Segni (Deputy-Premier and Minister of Defense); Giulio Pastore (without portfolio); Camillo Giardina (without portfolio); Rinaldo Del Bo (without portfolio); Fernando Tambroni (Minister of Interior); Guido Gonella (Justice); Giuseppe Medici (Budget); Luigi Preti (Democratic Socialist, Finance); Giulio Andreotti (Treasury); Aldo Moro (Education); Giuseppe Togni (Public Works); Mario Ferrari-Aggradi (Agriculture); Armando Angelini (Transport); Alberto Simonini (Democratic Socialist, Post); Giorgio Bo (Industry); Ezio Vigorelli (Democratic Socialist, Labor); Emilio Colombo (Foreign Trade); Giuseppe Spataro (Merchant Marine); Edgardo Lami-Startuniti (Democratic Socialist), State Participations; Vincenzo Monaldi (Public Health).

PRESS

Unless otherwise noted, papers are published in Rome.

Name of Paper	Character	Proprietor, Editor, etc.
Avanti	Socialist Party organ.	Tullio Vecchietti (*Dir.*)
Il Giornale d'Italia	Independent, rightist.	Santi Savarino (*Dir.*)
Il Globo	Economic and financial.	Italo Zingarelli (*Dir.*)
Il Messaggero	Independent.	Sandro Perrone (*Dir.*)
Il Momento-Sera	Independent, center.	Antonio Sergio (*Ed.*)
Il Paese	Pro-Communist.	Mario Melloni (*Dir.*)
Il Popolo	Christian Democrat Party organ.	Ettore Bernabei (*Dir.*)
Il Quotidiano	Catholic Action.	Nino Badano (*Dir.*)
Il Secolo d'Italia	MSI, left-wing.	Franz Turchi (*Ed.*)
Il Tempo	Conservative, right.	Renato Angiolillo (*Dir.*)
La Giustizia	PSDI Party organ.	Flavio Orlandi (*Dir.*)
L'Unità	Communist Party organ.	Pietro Ingrao (*Dir.*)
Resto del Carlino (Bologna)	Right-center.	Giovanni Spadolini (*Dir.*)
Unione Sarda (Cagliari)	Right-center.	Fabio M. Crivelli (*Dir.*)
Il Giornale di Sicilia (Palermo)	Right-center.	Girolamo Ardizzone (*Dir.*)
Il Lavoro Nuovo (Genoa)	Left-wing Socialist.	Sandro Pertini (*Dir.*)
Il Secolo XIX (Genoa)	Independent, conservative.	Umberto Cavassa (*Dir.*)
Il Corriere della Sera (Milan)	Independent.	Mario Missiroli (*Dir.*)
Il Giorno (Milan)	Center.	Gaetano Baldacci (*Dir.*)
Roma (Naples)	Monarchist (PMP).	Alfredo Signoretti (*Ed.*)
La Voce Repubblicana	Republican Party organ.	Cino Macrelli (*Dir.*)
La Nazione Italiana (Florence)	Independent, liberal.	Alfio Russo (*Dir.*)
Gazzetta del Popolo (Turin)	Christian Democrat.	Riccardo Forte (*Dir.*)
La Stampa (Turin)	Independent.	Giulio de Benedetti (*Dir.*)
Gazzettino (Venice)	Independent, center.	Attillio Tommasini (*Dir.*)
Corrispondenza Socialista (weekly)	Anti-Communist.	Michele Pellicani (*Ed.*)
Tempo (weekly) (Milan)	Independent, right.	Arturo Tofanelli (*Dir.*)
Oggi (weekly) (Milan)	Independent, right.	Emilio Radius (*Ed.*)
Relazioni Internazionali (weekly) (Milan)	Foreign affairs.	Giovanni Lovisetti (*Dir.*)
Civitas (monthly)	Christian Democrat.	Paolo Emilio Taviani (*Dir.*)
Mondo Operaio (fortnightly)	PSI Party Organ.	Pietro Nenni (*Dir.*)
Rinascita (monthly)	Communist.	Palmiro Togliatti (*Dir.*)

JAPAN

Capital: Tokyo
Area: 142,727 square miles (Japan proper—Honshu, Shikoku, Kyushu and Hokkaido)
Population: 91,760,000 (1958 estimate)

Monarch
EMPEROR HIROHITO
Born in 1901; ascended throne December 25, 1926

Cabinet
Liberal-Democratic Party
Installed June 12, 1958

Prime Minister
NOBUSUKE KISHI (Liberal-Democrat)

PARLIAMENT
(Kokkai)

UPPER CHAMBER
(House of Councillors)
(Sangi-in)
Election of July 1956 (Six-year term; renewed by half every three years).
President: TSURUHEI MATSUNO (Liberal-Democrat)

Parties	Representation
Liberal-Democratic Party	131
Socialists	78
Green Breeze Society (*Ryokufukai*)	25
Communist Party	2
Independents	12
Vacancies	2
Total	250

LOWER CHAMBER
(House of Representatives)
(Shugi-in)
Election of May 22, 1958 (for four years)
Speaker: RYOGORO KATO (Liberal-Democrat)

Parties	Representation
Liberal-Democratic Party	298
Socialists	167
Communist Party	1
Vacancies	1
Total	467

THE CONSTITUTION

A new Constitution was promulgated on November 3, 1946, and became effective on May 3, 1947. This instrument provided for drastic changes in Japan's political system. Sovereign power was placed in the hands of the people and the Emperor was deprived of his supreme authority and given only ceremonial functions. All property of the Imperial Household became the property of the State. War and the threat or use of force were forever renounced as sovereign rights of the nation. The peerage was specifically abolished. The Diet, consisting of a House of Representatives and House of Councillors, became the sole law-making authority with ultimate power residing in the House of Representatives. A bill passed by the House of Representatives and rejected by the House of Councillors becomes law when passed a second time by the House of Representatives by a two-thirds majority of the members present. Members of the House of Councillors are elected for six-year terms with half of the members elected every three years. Members of the House of Representatives are elected for a term of four years unless the House is dissolved within that period. Executive power is vested in a Cabinet, headed by a Prime Minister and collectively responsible to the Diet. The Prime Minister and a majority of the Cabinet members are chosen from among members of the Diet. All Cabinet members must be civilians and serve at the pleasure of the Prime Minister. On a vote of non-confidence by the House of Representatives, the Cabinet must resign or dissolve the House of Representatives. Judicial power is vested in a Supreme Court and in lower courts established by additional legislation. The appointment of Supreme Court judges is reviewed by the electorate at ten-year intervals in the general elections. State finances are administered by the Diet, which has sole power to levy taxes and make appropriations. A bill of rights contains such basic guarantees as universal adult suffrage, secret ballot, freedom of thought, religion and assembly, right of peaceful petition, impartial public trials and due process of law; it also provides for compulsory education, the right to minimum standards of living, and non-discrimination on the basis of social status, sex, race, or religion. Amendments to the Constitution must be initiated by a two-thirds majority of all members of each House of the Diet and must be ratified by a majority vote in a subsequent popular referendum.

RECENT POLITICAL EVENTS

Japan's first post-war cabinets were those of Prince Naruhiko Higashikuni (August 17, 1945, to October 6, 1945) and Baron Kijuro Shidehara (October 9, 1945, to April 22, 1946). General elections which were held on April 10, 1946, resulted in no overwhelming vote for any single party. The Liberals, Progressives and Socialists, in that order, became the major parties, and the Liberal leader, Shigeru Yoshida, formed a cabinet composed of Liberals, Progressives and Independents, which was installed on May 22, 1946.

In the general elections of April 1947 the Socialist Party gained the largest number of Diet seats and as a result Socialist leader Tetsu Katayama became Prime Minister on May 30, 1947. Mr. Katayama resigned February 9, 1948, and on February 21 the Diet elected Hitoshi Ashida as Prime Minister. Mr. Ashida's Democratic-Socialist-People's Cooperative Cabinet, formed on March 9, 1948, resigned on October 7, 1948.

On October 14, 1948, the Diet elected as Ashida's successor Shigeru Yoshida who was the leader of the conservative Democratic Liberal Party which had been formed in March 1948 by the merger of the conservative parties.

General elections for the House of Representatives were held on January 23, 1949, in which the Democratic Liberals won a decisive victory. The Communists gained while the Socialists lost heavily. Mr. Yoshida was re-elected Prime Minister and on February 16, 1949, formed his third Cabinet.

On September 8, 1951, 48 nations signed a treaty of peace with Japan at San Francisco, restoring Japan's sovereign status in the community of nations. On the same day representatives of the United States and the Japanese Governments signed a bi-lateral Security Treaty, under which the United States obtained the right to maintain armed forces in post-treaty Japan. Both these treaties came into effect on April 28, 1952.

Following general elections for the House of Representatives in October 1952, the lower house was again dissolved in March 1953 after a series of events which included the abstention of a group of conservatives led by Ichiro Hatoyama from voting, permitting the passage of a non-confidence motion against the Yoshida Government. In the ensuing elections in April, within a week after the regular triennial House of Councillors election, the Liberals won only 201 seats in the House of Representatives, the Progressives dropped to 76, the newly-formed Hatoyama group won 34, and the Left and Right Socialists gained 71 and 66 seats, respectively. Despite the lack of a Liberal majority, Shigeru Yoshida was again elected Prime Minister and formed his fifth Liberal Cabinet. He resigned on December 7, 1954, and was succeeded by Ichiro Hatoyama.

The Hatoyama forces were victorious in the general elections of February 27, 1955, and Hatoyama formed his second cabinet on March 18, 1955. On October 13, 1955, the Left and Right Socialist Parties united to form a new Socialist Party of Japan. On November 15, 1955, the two Conservative parties—Liberals and Democrats—merged to form the Liberal-Democratic Party.

In the triennial House of Councillors election of July 8, 1956, the Socialist Party increased its representation from 68 to 81 seats, while the strength of the Liberal-Democratic Party remained about as before (123).

In December 1956, Mr. Hatoyama resigned as Prime Minister and was succeeded by Tanzan Ishibashi. The latter, in turn, resigned on February 25, 1957, because of illness, and Nobusuke Kishi was elected his successor on the same day. Mr. Kishi carried out a major reorganization of his Liberal-Democratic Cabinet on July 10, 1957.

Mr. Kishi dissolved the House of Representatives on April 25, 1958, and general elections were held on May 22, 1958. As a result of these elections the Liberal-Democratic Party secured 298 seats and the Socialists 168. The second Kishi Cabinet was formed June 12, 1958.

PARTY PROGRAMS AND LEADERS

LIBERAL-DEMOCRATIC PARTY: Diet Membership—Councillors, 131, Representatives, 298. Formed in 1955 by merger of Liberal and Japan Democratic Parties. Advocates cooperation with Free World, free enterprise, balanced national finances, build-up of national defense, tax reductions, increased social security benefits, aid to small business and foreign trade.

Leaders: Nobusuke Kishi (Premier, President of Party), Ichiro Kono (Chairman, Executive Board), Takeo Fukuda (Chairman, Policy Board), Shojiro Kawashima (Secretary General).

SOCIALIST PARTY: Diet Membership—Councillors, 78; Representatives, 167. Formed in 1955 by the merger of the Right-wing and Left-wing Socialist Parties. Advocates change of capitalistic structure of society into a socialist structure by peaceful means, but states that its policy is not compatible with Communism. Stresses effort to recover "complete independence" for Japan. Advocates eventual nationalization of key industries, no rearmament, tax exemptions for workers, price controls, loans and reduced taxes for small business, encouragement of cooperatives, diplomatic recognition of Communist China, abolition of US-Japan Security Treaty, nonagression pact among U.S., USSR, Communist China and Japan.

JAPAN

Leaders: Mosaburo Suzuki (Chairman), Inejiro Asanuma (Secretary General), Ushiro Ito (Finance Chairman), Mitsu Kono (Diet Policy Chairman), Kozo Sasaki (Election Policy Committee Chairman), Kozo Inomata (Control Committee Chairman), Seiichi Katsumata (Policy Board Chairman).

GREEN BREEZE SOCIETY (RYOKUFUKAI): Diet Membership—Councillors, 25. Organized as a political society following the April 1947 elections and registered as a political party on December 9, 1947. (Is not a political party in the commonly accepted definition of the term, since it claims no constituent membership, no organizational structure and no party finances). The group, which is principally composed of conservative elements but with no specific platform announced, has proved to be an influential body in the House of Councillors through utilization of its independent status. Its seats were reduced from 47 to 29 in the 1956 election, however. The group generally cooperates with the Conservatives.

Leaders: Giichi Murakami (President), Fumio Goto (Chairman, Executive Board), Bunkichi Tamura (Chairman, Political Affairs Research Committee).

COMMUNIST PARTY: Diet Membership—Councillors, 2; Representatives 1. Advocates policies and ideologies of international Communism; endorses the foreign policies of the USSR; and opposes the continuation of the Emperor system in Japan.

Leaders: Sanzo Nozaka (Chairman) and Kenji Miyamoto (Secretary General). There is a Central Executive Committee of 9 members.

THE CABINET

The members of the Cabinet are: Nobusuke Kishi (Premier), Aiichiro Fujiyama (Foreign Affairs), Eisaku Sato (Finance), Tatsunosuke Takasaki (Economic Planning, and International Trade and Industry), Kunio Miura (Agriculture and Forestry), Kiichi Aichi (Justice), Ryugo Hashimoto (Education, and Health and Welfare), Masashi Aoki (Local Autonomy), Saburo Endo (Construction), Mamoru Nagano (Transportation), Tadao Kuraishi (Labor), Yutaka Terao (Postal Services), Gizen Sato (Defense), Kikuichiro Yamaguchi (Administrative Management and Hokkaido (Development).

PRESS

Unless otherwise noted, papers are published in the capital city.

Name of Paper	Circulation	Character	Proprietor, Editor, etc.
Asahi Shimbun	4,400,000	Japan's leading paper: independent; published in Tokyo, Osaka, Nagoya, and Kyushu editions.	Nagataka Murayama (*Pres.*) Tomoo Hirooka (Tokyo) Jiro Shindo (Osaka) Hitoshi Wada (Nagoya) Toshiro Masuda (Kokura)
Mainichi Shimbun	4,150,000	Asahi's closest competitor; independent; published in Tokyo, Osaka, Nagoya, and Kyushu editions.	Chikao Honda (*Pres.*) Tameo Hara (*Dir. Gen.*) Toshi Sumimoto (Tokyo) Goroku Urakami (Osaka) Chikao Kano (Nagoya)
Mainichi (English edition)	83,000		Tatsuo Shibata (*Ed.* Tokyo) Iwao Matsunaga (*Ed.* Osaka)
Yomiuri Shimbun	2,813,000	Independent.	Yusai Takahashi (*Ch. of Bd.*) Mitsuo Mutai (*Dir. Gen.*)
Tokyo Shimbun	743,000	Independent.	Kyosuke Fukuda (*Pres.*) Masami Hijikata (*Ed.*)

Name of Paper	Circulation	Character	Proprietor, Editor, etc.
Nihon Keizai Shimbun	922,000	Leading economic journal.	Naoji Yorozu (*Pres.*) Hakuei Ogiwara (*Ed.*)
Sankei Shimbun	1,100,000	Independent; published in Tokyo and Osaka.	Hisakichi Maeda (*Pres.*) Kiichiro Sato (*Ed.*)
Chubu Nippon (Nagoya)	1,030,000	Independent.	Aichi Yora (*Pres.*) Takeshi Suzuki (*Ed.*)
Nishi Nippon Shimbun (Fukuoka)	726,000	Independent.	Denji Hironaka (*Pres.*) Toshimitsu Fukuda (*Ed.*)
Osaka Shimbun (Osaka)	657,000	Conservative.	Yoshio Sawamura (*Pres.*) Shiro Dobashi (*Ed.*)
Hokkaido Shimbun (Sapporo and other Hokkaido editions)	706,000	Independent.	Isao Nakano (*Pres.*) Naganori Sakurai (*Ed.*)
Chugoku Shimbun (Hiroshima)	373,000	Independent.	Masafusa Yamamoto (*Pres.*) Naritatsu Itokawa (*Ed.*)
Japan Times	79,000	English Language.	Shintaro Fukushima (*Pres.*) Masaro Ogawa (*Mg. Ed.*)

NEWS AGENCIES

Kyodo News Agency	Cooperative press association. Founded Nov. 1945, to replace Domei News Agency, official organ since 1936.	Hideo Nomura (*Ch. of Bd.*) Masayoshi Arai (*Ed.*)
Jiji News Agency	Established Nov. 1945, by former employees of Domei who did not join Kyodo. Primarily services government offices and corporations.	Saiji Hasegawa (*Pres.*) Tsurutaro Adachi (*Ed.*)

PRESS ASSOCIATION

Japan Newspaper Publishers and Editors Association	Corporation of Japanese papers, founded July 23, 1946.	Chikao Honda (*Pres.*) Minoru Yokota (*Dir.*)

JORDAN
(Hashimite Kingdom of Jordan)

Capital: Amman
Area: 37,000 square miles
Population: 1,595,000 (1958 estimate)

Ruler
KING HUSSEIN IBN TALAL

Born November 14, 1935
Ascended throne May 2, 1953

Cabinet
Reorganized August 1958

Premier
SAMIR AL-RIFA'I

PARLIAMENT

COUNCIL OF NOTABLES	COUNCIL OF REPRESENTATIVES
Appointed by the King.	Elected October 21, 1956.
President: SA'ID AL-MUFTI	Speaker: DR. MUSTAFA KHALIFAH
Number of members 20	Number of members 40

RECENT POLITICAL EVENTS

On February 14, 1958, Jordan and Iraq formed a federal union, the *Ittihad al-'Arabi*. The head of the Union was the King of Iraq, Faysal II. After the Iraqi revolution of July 14 and the assassination of Faysal, Hussein formally dissolved the Union and reestablished Jordanian rule on August 2, 1958. British troops sent to protect Jordan's independence after these events were withdrawn as of October 29.

THE CABINET

Samir al-Rifa'i (Prime Minister, Minister of Defense, Minister of Foreign Affairs), Fallah Madadha (Interior), Akif al-Faiz (Agriculture and Construction), Dr. Jamil Tutunji (Health and Social Welfare), Salim Bakhit (Public Works), Muhammad Jabari (Justice and Education), Anistas Hananiya (Finance), Dr. Sami Jawdah (Communications), Hazza Majali (Court).

PRESS

Name of Paper	Circulation	Editor
Al-Difa'a (Jerusalem)	7,000	Ibrahim al-Shanti (*Ed.*)
Falastin (Jerusalem)	2,500	Daud al-'Isa (*Ed.*)
Al-Jihad (Amman)	2,500	Muhammad al-Sharif (*Ed.*)
Al-Urdunn (Amman)	2,500	Anis Nasr (*Ed.*)

LEBANON

Capital: Beirut
Area: 3,977 square miles
Population: 1,416,570 (1956 estimate)

President
GENERAL FUAD CHEHAB
Elected by Parliament July 31, 1958;
assumed office September 23, 1958

Premier
RASHID KARAMI
Appointed October 14, 1958

CHAMBER OF DEPUTIES
Elected June 1957, four-year term
President: ADEL OSSEIRAN

Number of members. 66

Elected by universal suffrage according to the following proportional division amongst religious communities: Maronite Christian 20; Sunni Moslem 14; Shia Moslem 12; Greek Orthodox 7; Druze 4; Greek Catholic 4; Armenian Orthodox 3; Armenian Catholic 1; Minorities 1.

RECENT POLITICAL EVENTS

General elections were held in June 1957, at which time members of Parliament were elected to a four-year term of office to serve in a chamber which had been expanded from 44 to 66 seats.

On November 12, 1958, following five months of increasing lawlessness, the Parliament voted emergency powers to Premier Rashid Karami's Government, permitting it to rule by decree for a period of six months in order to disarm the civilian population and bolster the economy.

THE CABINET

The members of the Cabinet are: Rashid Karami (Premier, Finance, National Economy, Defense, and Information), Hussein Uwayni (Foreign Affairs, Justice, and Planning), Raymond Eddé (Interior, Labor and Social Affairs, and Communications), Pierre Gemayel (Public Works, Education, Agriculture, and Health).

PRESS

Name of Paper	Circulation	Political Affiliation	Proprietor, Editor, etc.
Al Amal	3,000	Phalange Party paper.	Pierre Gemayel (*Prop.*)
Al Bina	5,000	Social Nationalist (PPS).	Al Hashim (*Ed.*)
Al Hayat	9,000	Independent.	Kamel Mrowa (*Prop. & Ed.*)
Al Jarida	5,000	Independent.	Geo. Naccache (*Prop. & Ed.*)
Al Kifeh	3,000	Extreme Arab Nationalist.	Riad Taha (*Prop. & Ed.*)
An Nahar	4,000	Independent.	Ghassan Tweini (*Prop. & Ed.*)
As Siyasah	3,000	Arab Nationalist.	Abdullah Yafi (*Prop.*)
L'Orient	4,000	Independent.	Geo Naccache (*Prop. & Ed.*)
Telegraph	4,000	Pro-Communist.	Tufic Metni (*Prop. & Ed.*)

LIBERIA

Capital: Monrovia
Area: 43,000 square miles
Population: 2,750,000 (1953 estimate)

President
WILLIAM V. S. TUBMAN (True Whig)
Re-elected May 3, 1955, for four-year term

Cabinet
True Whig

PARLIAMENT
(Legislature)

UPPER CHAMBER (Senate)	LOWER CHAMBER (House of Representatives)
President: WILLIAM R. TOLBERT (True Whig)	*Speaker:* RICHARD A. HENRIES (True Whig)
Number of members* 10	Number of members* 36

* All of True Whig Party.

PARTY PROGRAMS AND LEADERS

TRUE WHIG PARTY: Organized in 1869, it has been in power continuously since 1878. Composed of the descendants of the first settlers of American and West Indian origin and civilized aborigines. Supports the United Nations in its policy to resist aggression and to attain collective security. Supports, on equal reciprocal basis, commercial opportunities for all nations. Is carrying out a Nine-Year Program for economic development.

Leaders: William V. S. Tubman (President of Liberia), William R. Tolbert (Vice-President of Liberia), Edwin Morgan (Chairman of Party) and McKinley A. DeShield (General Secretary).

The Reformation and Independent True Whig parties were declared illegal by Parliament in July, 1955, and their newspaper, *The Independent*, was banned.

THE CABINET

The members of the Cabinet are: Momolu Dukuly (Secretary of State), Charles Sherman (Treasurer), Joseph Garber (Attorney General), McKinley A. DeShield (Posts), Ernest C. B. Jones (Defense), Harrison Grigsby (Interior), Nathaniel V. Massaquoi (Education), Thomas E. Buchanan (Public Works), John W. Cooper (Agriculture and Commerce), Joseph N. Togba (Public Health).

PRESS
All papers listed are published in the capital city.

Name of Paper	Political Affiliation	Proprietor, Editor, etc.
The Listener (daily)	True Whig Party.	Charles C. Dennis (*Prop.*)
Liberian Age (bi-weekly) . . .	True Whig Party.	Alston King (*Act. Ed.*)

LIBYA

Capitals: Tripoli and Benghazi
Area: 424,710 square miles
Population: 1,091,830 (1954 census)

Ruler
KING INDRIS I

Premier
ABDEL MAJID KUBAR
Assumed office April 12, 1956

PARLIAMENT

UPPER CHAMBER (Senate)	LOWER CHAMBER (Chamber of Deputies)
President: MAHMOUD BU HEDMA	Speaker: SALEM AL-QUADI
Number of members* 24	Number of members 55

* One-third appointed by the King. The Deputies are all elected.

THE CONSTITUTION

The Constitution, adopted by the National Assembly on October 7, 1951, describes Libya as a State "having a hereditary monarchy, federal form and a representative system of government." The King exercises control over the machinery of government, appoints the Governors of the three provinces, and the Cabinet. There are no political parties in Libya.

THE CABINET

The members of the Cabinet as reconstituted on October 12, 1958, are: Abdel Majid Kubar (Prime Minister and Foreign Minister), Ibrahim ben Sha'ban (Defense), Ismail Ben Lamin (Finance), Muftah Orayqib (Communications), Abu Bakr Ahmad (Health), Wahbi al-Buri (Minister of State), Rajab ben Katu (National Economy), Abu Bakr Naama (Education), Abu al-Hamid Daybani (Justice).

PRESS

Name of Paper	Character	Proprietor, Editor, etc.
Tarablus al-Gharb (Tripoli)	Arabic daily.	Muhammad Fakhr a-Diin (*Ed.*)
Corriere di Tripoli (Tripoli)	Italian daily.	Gianni Massa (*Ed.*)
Al-Raa'id (Tripoli)	Arabic weekly.	Bashiir Yuusuf a-Twaybi (*Ed.*)
L'Ora di Tripoli (Tripoli)	Italian weekly.	Giovanni Gacciola (*Ed.*)
Sunday Ghibli (Tripoli)	English weekly.	Cedric H. Johnston (*Ed.*)
Tarablus al-Gharb (Tripoli)	Arabic monthly magazine.	Muhammad a-Shawish (*Ed.*)
Al-Zaman (Benghazi)	Arabic weekly.	Umar al-Ashhab (*Ed.*)
Cyrenaica Weekly News (Benghazi)	English weekly.	Abd al-Mawla Lenghi and Muhammad ben Swayyid (*Props.*)
Fezzan (Sebha)	Arabic weekly.	Muhammad Umar a-Tishaani (*Ed.*)

LUXEMBOURG

Capital: Luxembourg
Area: 999 square miles
Population: 315,000 (1957 estimate)

Ruler
GRAND DUCHESS CHARLOTTE
Born in 1896; ascended the throne January 9, 1919

Cabinet
Coalition (Christian Social Party and Socialist Party)
Appointed June 29, 1954

This Cabinet resigned on December 10, 1958, but continues as Caretaker Government pending elections on February 1, 1959

Premier
PIERRE FRIEDEN (Christian Social Party)

PARLIAMENT

UPPER CHAMBER
(Conseil d'État)

Chosen by the Sovereign. Acts as a senate. The Conseil d'État enjoys the right of advice and amendment of bills and a temporary suspensive veto.

Number of members 15

LOWER CHAMBER
(Chambre des Députés)

Election of May 30, 1954 (for five-year term)
President: EMILE REUTER (Christian Social Party)

Parties	Representation
Christian Social	26
Socialist	17
Democratic	6
Communist	3
Total	52

PARTY PROGRAMS AND LEADERS

CHRISTIAN SOCIAL PARTY: A Catholic party which supports defense of the present regulations concerning Church and schools, progressive labor legislation, protection for agriculture and for small trade craftsmen.

Leaders: Pierre Frieden (Prime Minister), Emile Reuter (President of the Chamber of Deputies, formerly Prime Minister) and Nicolas Margue (Party leader in the Chamber of Deputies).

SOCIALIST PARTY: Advocates progressive labor legislation, assistance to the injured and aged workmen, and further improvement and extension of labor and social insurance.

Leaders: Antoine Krier (Secretary of CGT Trade Union), Victor Bodson (Minister of Justice and Transport), Nicolas Biever (Minister of Labor), and Paul Wilwertz (Minister of Economic Affairs).

DEMOCRATIC PARTY: Succeeded old Radical Liberal Party and includes resistance elements. Advocates adherence to the existing state institutions, progressive development of liberal and lay institutions, and progress of labor legislation.

Leaders: Eugène Schaus (President of Party), Emile Hamilius (Burgomaster of Luxembourg) and Alphonse Osch.

COMMUNIST PARTY: Advocates usual Communist program.

Leaders: Dominique Urbany and Arthur Useldinger.

THE CABINET

The members of the Caretaker Cabinet are: Pierre Frieden (Prime Minister, Minister of Education, and of Interior); Joseph Bech (Minister of Foreign Affairs and Foreign Trade); Victor Bodson (Minister of Justice, Public Works, and Transport); Nicolas Biever (Minister of Labor, Mines and Social Welfare); Paul Wilwertz (Minister of Economic Affairs, and Tourism); Pierre Werner (Minister of Finance, and National Defense); Emile Colling (Minister of Public Health, and Agriculture); Henry Cravatte (General Commissioner of Economic Affairs).

PRESS

After the invasion in May, 1940, all Luxembourg papers were suppressed and replaced by German Nazi-owned papers.

On the day of liberation the two chief newspapers, the *Luxemburger Wort* (Catholic) and the *Escher Tageblatt* (Organ of Socialist Party) reappeared in their old guise. Since then, the *d'Union* (Organ of Resistance Movement), *Zeitung vum Letzeburger Vollek* (Organ of Communist Party), *La Meuse* (Belgo-Luxembourg, in French) and *Obermosel Zeitung* (in German) have made their appearance. In 1948 *d'Union* and *Obermosel Zeitung* were merged and given the name of *Letzeburger Journal*.

MEXICO

Capital: Mexico City
Area: 763,944 square miles
Population: 31,426,190 (1957 estimate)

President
ADOLFO LOPEZ MATEOS
Elected July 6, 1958; assumed office December 1, 1958, for six-year term

Cabinet
Appointed December 1, 1958

PARLIAMENT
(Congreso)

UPPER CHAMBER
(Cámara de Senadores)
Under Constitutional Amendment of April 29, 1933 (the entire Senate is renewed every six years)
Speaker: Changes each month.
Number of members 60

LOWER CHAMBER
(Cámara de Diputados)
Election of July 6, 1958 (for three-year term)
Speaker: Changes each month.

Parties	Representation
PRI (Government Party)	145
Opposition	8
Vacancies	9
Total	162

PARTY PROGRAMS AND LEADERS

At the opening of Congress in 1928, President Calles announced that he would not run for re-election and asked for the formation of a political party. Thus the National Revolutionary Party was organized. It was in substance the consolidation of many local state groups into a national party. It controlled the Congress and the Government, there being no opposition party. President Cárdenas, in December 1937, proposed that the National Revolutionary Party be superseded by a more popular party to include workers, farmers and soldiers. As a result, the Partido de la Revolución Mexicana was organized in 1938. The Party is now called Partido Revolucionario Institucional (PRI), and its President is Alfonso Corona del Rosal. Its candidate for President won in the 1958 elections, and it is now the party in power, holding all seats in the Senate and all but 17 in the Chamber of Deputies.

The opposition includes four registered parties, as follows (with their 1958 presidential nominees given parenthetically):

The Partido Acción Nacional (Luis H. Alvarez), a rightist, pro-Catholic and conservative party led by Alfonso Iduarte Servín, which was founded during the régime of President Cárdenas; the Partido Popular, a leftist group founded in 1948 by Vicente Lombardo Toledano; and the right-of-center, Catholic-oriented Partido Nacionalista de Mexico, founded in 1949 and led by Salvador Rivero y Martínez. On July 6, 1957, the Government granted registration to the Partido Auténtico de la Revolución Mexicana. Jacinto Blas Treviño Gonzalez is President of PARM.

MEXICO

THE CABINET

The members of the Cabinet are: Gustavo Díaz Ordaz (Interior), Manuel Tello (Foreign Affairs), General Augustín Olachea (National Defense), Antonio Ortiz Mena (Finance), Julián Rodríguez Adame (Agriculture), Jaime Torres Bodet (Education), Salomón Gonzáles Blanco (Labor), Dr. José Alvarez Amézquita (Public Health & Welfare), Javier Barros Sierra (Communications & Public Works), Raúl Salinas (Economy), Alfredo del Mazo (Hydraulic Resources), Eduardo Bustamante (National Property), Vice-Admiral Manuel Zermeño Araico (Navy), Ernesto P. Uruchurtu (Chief of the Department of the Federal District), Roberto Barrios (Chief of the Agrarian Department), Pascual Guitiérrez Roldán (Chief, Mexican Oil Department), Benito Coquet (Chief of the Social Security Department), Fernando López Arias (Attorney General), Fernando Román Lugo (Attorney of the Federal District), Benjamin Méndez (Chief of the National Railways), Donato Mirando (Secretary of the Presidency), Humberto Romero (Private Secretary).

PRESS

Unless otherwise noted, papers are published in the capital city.

Name of Paper	Circulation	Character	Proprietor, Editor, etc.
Boletín Financiero	10,800	Financial.	J. A. Pérez de L. (*Dir.*)
Excelsior	110,000	Independent; conservative.	Rodrigo de Llano (*Dir.*)
El Nacional	50,000	Pro-Government.	Guillermo Ibarra (*Dir.*)
Novedades	76,000	Independent.	Rómulo O'Farrill (*Dir.*)
The News	9,000	English language daily.	Rómulo O'Farrill (*Dir.*)
El Popular	12,000	Supports Lombardo Toledano and Partido Popular.	Manuel O. Padrés (*Dir.*)
La Prensa	87,580	Independent; tabloid.	Mariano D. Urdanivia (*Dir.*)
Últimas Noticias	77,193	Independent.	Rodrigo de Llano (*Dir.*)
El Universal	71,211	Independent; conservative.	Miguel Lanz Duret (*Prop.*)
El Universal Gráfico	29,098	Independent; tabloid.	Santiago G. Garcia (*Dir.*)
La Voz de México	4,500	Communist Party organ.	Manuel Terrazas (*Dir.*)
El Informador (Guadalajara)	31,500	Independent; conservative tendency.	Jesús Alvarez del Castillo (*Dir.*)
El Occidental (Guadalajara)	40,000	Independent; conservative tendency.	Ernesto Corona R. (*Dir.*)
Diario de Yucatán (Mérida)	30,513	Independent; conservative tendency.	Carlos R. Menéndez (*Dir.*)
Diario del Sureste (Mérida)	23,000	Organ of State Government.	Wilberto Canton (*Dir.*)
El Norte (Monterrey)	50,000	Independent; conservative tendency.	Augustin Basave (*Dir.*)
El Porvenir (Monterrey)	42,000	Independent; large circulation along border.	Federico Gómez Z. (*Dir.*)
El Sol (Monterrey)	38,000	Independent; conservative.	R. Junco de la Vega (*Dir.*)
El Tiempo (Monterrey)	18,000	Independent.	Federico Gómez and Oscar F. Castillón (*Dirs.*)
La Opinión (Torreón)	22,000	Independent; conservative.	F. L. Rodriguez (*Dir.*)
El Siglo (Torreón)	31,000	Independent; conservative.	A. de Juambelz (*Dir.*)
El Dictamen (Veracruz)	30,000	Conservative.	Juan Malpica Silva (*Dir.*)
Hoy (weekly)	18,000	Popular weekly magazine.	Rafael Lebrija (*Dir.*)
Mañana (weekly)	16,000	Popular weekly magazine.	Daniel Morales (*Dir.*)
Nuevo Mundo	15,000	Popular monthly.	José Audifred (*Dir.*)
Revista de Revistas	18,000	Popular weekly magazine.	Carlos Denegri (*Dir.*)
Siempre (weekly)	16,000	Popular weekly magazine.	José Pages Llergo (*Pub.*)
Tiempo (weekly)	20,000	News magazine; liberal.	M. L. Guzmán (*Dir.*)
Todo (weekly)	30,000	Anti-Communist.	Enrique S. Ledesma (*Dir.*)

NETHERLANDS

Capital: Amsterdam
Seat of Government: The Hague
Area: 12,850 square miles (excluding water)
Population (not including overseas territories): 11,173,000 (1958 estimate)

Ruler
QUEEN JULIANA
Born April 30, 1909; inaugurated September 6, 1948

Cabinet
Coalition: Catholic People's Party—6;
Anti-Revolutionary Party—2; Christian Historical Union—2;
Appointed December 22, 1958

Minister-President
LOUIS BEAL (Catholic)

PARLIAMENT
(Staten-General)

FIRST CHAMBER
(Eerste Kamer)

Last election October 11, 1956 (six-year term; renewed by halves every three years)

President: J. A. JONKMAN (Labor Party)

Parties	Representation*
Catholic	25
Labor	22
Anti-Revolutionary	8
Christian Historical	8
Liberal (Freedom and Democracy)	7
Communist	4
Political Reformed	1
Total	75

*Constitutional revision in 1956 increased number of members from 50 to 75; chosen by Provincial States.

SECOND CHAMBER
(Tweede Kamer)

Last election June 13, 1956 (four-year term)

President: L. G. KORTENHORST (Catholic)

Parties	Representation*
Labor	50
Catholic	49
Anti-Revolutionary	15
Christian Historical	13
Liberal (Freedom and Democracy)	13
Communist	7
Political Reformed	3
Total	150

*Constitutional revision in 1956 increased number of members from 100 to 150; elected by the people.

PARTY PROGRAMS AND LEADERS

CATHOLIC PEOPLE'S PARTY: Includes most of the Roman Catholic part of the population; favors democratic government and middle-of-the-road social policy, holding religion, family and property to be the foundations of society, and following the principles of the Church's teaching. Favors corporative organizations, small property, limited state control in economic life and strengthening of the moral and spiritual forces of the community. *In foreign policy:* favors United Nations and Western cooperation.

Leaders: H. W. van Doorn, Chairman of the Party's Executive; J. Gielen, member of the Executive; P. Alberts, Treasurer; L. A. H. Albering, Secretary; C. P. M. Romme, Party leader in Second Chamber; G. C. J. D. Kropman, leader in First Chamber.

LABOR PARTY: A moderate constitutional socialist party of democratic principles, accepting personal responsibility and refuting any form of state absolutism. Aims at a non-capitalistic organization of economic life, planning for production and distribution; favors nationalization or other means of regulating monopolistic enterprises, guarding against bureaucracy through decentralization. *In foreign policy:* advocates an active policy, leading to the strengthening of the United Nations and democratic international organization and increasing integration of Western Europe.

Leaders: E. Vermeer, Chairman of Party; H. Vos, Vice-Chairman; J. J. A. Berger, Jr., Political Secretary; E. Meester, Secretary-Treasurer; J. A. W. Burger, Leader in Second Chamber; J. in 't Veldt, Leader in First Chamber.

ANTI-REVOLUTIONARY PARTY: A party of Calvinist religious principles; conservative with democratic tendency in social questions; urges maintenance of a strong Army and Navy; opposes nationalization, planned economy by State organisms; favors Christian state policy, strong defense of morality, strict observance of Sunday rest; stresses rights of Parliament; supports United Nations and Western European economic and military cooperation.

Leaders: T. W. P. Berghuis, Chairman of Party; J. Smallenbroek and A. B. Roosjen, Vice-Chairmen; J. A. M. J. S. Bruins Slot, leader in Second Chamber; Anne Anema, leader in First Chamber; H. van Riessen, Secretary.

CHRISTIAN HISTORICAL UNION: A center group party advocating from the Protestant religious point of view a program generally similar to that of the Anti-Revolutionary Party.

Leaders: H. K. J. Beernink, Chairman of Party; H. W. Tilanus, leader in Second Chamber; G. Kolff, leader in First Chamber; J. W. van Gelder, Secretary.

COMMUNIST PARTY: A Marxist party, currently split into factions, accepting the dialectic materialism of Marx and Lenin as a revolutionary method, but moving within legal actuality. Aims at abolition of capitalism and formation of a Communist society. *In foreign policy:* opposed to NATO and European integration.

Leaders: P. de Groot, Secretary-General, and M. Bakker (De Groot faction); H. Gortzak, B. Brandsen and G. Wagenaar (Gortzak faction).

LIBERAL (PEOPLE'S PARTY FOR FREEDOM AND DEMOCRACY): Stands for individual liberty and free competition; while not opposing social legislation, combats nationalization and restriction of free enterprise. *In foreign policy:* favors Western European Union, North Atlantic Pact.

Leaders: P. J. Oud, Party Chairman and Leader in Second Chamber; A. N. Molenaar, First Chamber Leader; H. van Riel, Vice-Chairman.

POLITICAL REFORMED PARTY: Stands for strict Calvinist principles in political life and legislation.

Leader: Dr. P. Zandt, Chairman of Party and Leader in Second Chamber.

NETHERLANDS

THE CABINET

Louis Beal, Premier, General Affairs, Social Affairs and Public Health (Catholic); A. A. M. Struycken, Vice-Premier, Home Affairs, Industrial Organization, Property Formation and Justice (Catholic); J. M. A. H. Luns, Foreign Affairs (Catholic); J. M. L. T. Cals, Education, Arts and Sciences (Catholic); C. Staf, National Defense, Agriculture, Fisheries and Food (Christian-Historical); H. B. J. Witte, Construction and Housing (Catholic); J. van Aartsen, Transport and Waterways (Anti-Revolutionary); J. Zijlstra, Economic Affairs and Finance (Anti-Revolutionary); Miss M. A. M. Klompe, Social Welfare (Catholic); C. G. Helders, Overseas Affairs (Christian-Historical).

PRESS

Name of Paper	Political Affiliation	Editors
NATIONAL DAILIES		
Nieuwe Rotterdamse Courant (Rotterdam)	Liberal.	A. Stempels
Algemeen Handelsblad (Amsterdam)	Liberal.	C. A. Steketee
De Tijd (Amsterdam)	Catholic; conservative.	W. A. M. van der Kallen
De Maasbode (Rotterdam)	Catholic; conservative.	C. B. M. Wüst
Het Parool (Amsterdam)	Independent Labor.	P. J. Koets
Trouw (Amsterdam)	Calvinist.	Dr. J. A. M. J. S. Bruins Slot
De Volkskrant (Amsterdam)	Catholic.	J. M. Lücker
Het Vrije Volk (Amsterdam)	Labor.	K. Voskuil
Algemeen Dagblad (Rotterdam)	Independent.	A. C. W. van der Vet
De Telegraaf (Amsterdam)	Independent; conservative.	J. J. Stokvis and C. J. Brandt
De Waarheid (Amsterdam)	Communist Party organ.	Editorial Board
WEEKLIES		
De Linie (Amsterdam)	Catholic; conservative.	Dr. S. Maas, S. J.
Haagse Post (The Hague)	Independent.	G. B. J. Hiltermann
Elsevier's Weekblad (Amsterdam)	Independent; conservative.	W. G. N. de Keizer and K. D. Bosch
Vrij Nederland (Amsterdam)	Independent Labor.	M. Smedts
De Groene Amsterdammer (Amsterdam)	Independent; radical.	Editorial Board
NEWS AGENCY		
Algemeen Nederlandsch Persbureau (ANP) (The Hague and Amsterdam)	Independent; operated on cooperative basis by all Dutch newspapers.	H. H. J. van de Pol (*Pres.*) G. A. Knepflé (*Gen. Ed.*)

NEW ZEALAND

Capital: Wellington
Area: 103,939 square miles (including island territories, but excluding Western Samoa)
Population: 2,259,404, including Maoris and residents of annexed islands but excluding Western Samoa (1958 estimate)

Sovereign
QUEEN ELIZABETH II

Governor-General
VISCOUNT COBHAM
Assumed office September 5, 1957

Cabinet
Labor
Took office December 12, 1957

Prime Minister
WALTER NASH (Labor)
Took office December 11, 1957

PARLIAMENT
(House of Representatives)
Election of November 30, 1957 (for three years)
Speaker: R. M. MACFARLANE (Labor)

Parties	Representation
Labor	41
National	39
Total	80

PARTY PROGRAMS AND LEADERS

LABOR PARTY: The Labor Party, which was returned to power at the 1957 elections after eight years in opposition, governed the country from 1935 to 1949. During this tenure of office it inaugurated a vigorous public works policy, a comprehensive social security system, and an ambitious housing program. In the field of labor, the Government introduced compulsory unionism, the forty-hour week, compulsory insurance of all workers by employers, two weeks' paid holiday, a National Employment Service, minimum wages, safety legislation, secret ballots before strikes and lock-outs, an Industrial Advisory Council, restored the full powers of the Arbitration Court and revised the Factories Act. Agricultural legislation included a guaranteed "fair" price to dairy farmers, a Meat Act to control quality, and establishment of the Wool Board.

At the 1957 election the party campaigned on the continuation and extension of the existing social legislation. Its financial policy included the promise of a reduction in interest rates and the adoption of measures to ensure that

NEW ZEALAND

trading banks retain none of the profits on loans from bank-created credit. The party proclaimed its opposition to overseas borrowing and to New Zealand membership in the International Monetary Fund and the World Bank. Labor's foreign policy affirmed New Zealand's closest cooperation with Britain and the British Commonwealth and support for New Zealand's obligations to the United Nations Organization. It promised abolition of compulsory military training and support of the prohibition by international agreement of the use of nuclear and all other weapons of mass slaughter and destruction and promotion of the peaceful uses of atomic energy.

Leaders: Walter Nash (Prime Minister), Michael Moohan (President of Party), A. J. MacDonald (National Secretary).

NATIONAL PARTY: The National Party was in power from 1949 until 1957. Its former leader, Sir Sidney Holland, retired prior to the 1957 election campaign and his successor, Mr. Keith J. Holyoake, led the National Party to the polls. The party campaigned on its claim of progressive, competent government fostering a property-owning democracy. It promised the maintenance of current social legislation with extensions where practicable and necessary. Its policy included protection for New Zealand industry mainly through tariffs, but by quantitative restrictions where this was required, and the encouragement of new, heavy industries. The party promised continuation of the guaranteed price for dairy products and of floor prices for meat and wool. The National Party's foreign policy aimed at the advancement of New Zealand's interests as a sovereign state in every field.

Leaders: Keith J. Holyoake (Leader of the Opposition), Alex. McKenzie (President of Party), T. Hills (Secretary).

SOCIAL CREDIT PARTY: The Social Credit Political League, under the leadership of Mr. Wilfred Owen, made its second appearance at the polls in 1957. The League campaigned mainly on its financial platform promising abolition of the social security tax, increased exemptions for income tax and increased social security benefits. The League has captured no seats in Parliament; in the election of 1954 its candidates received 11.2 per cent of the total popular vote, while this figure declined to 7.4 per cent in the election of 1957.

Leaders: Wilfred Owen (Leader), J. Colechin (National Secretary).

THE CABINET

The Cabinet is composed as follows: W. Nash (Prime Minister, Minister of External Affairs, Minister of Maori Affairs), C. F. Skinner (Deputy Prime Minister, Minister of Agriculture, Minister of Lands), A. H. Nordmeyer (Minister of Finance), H. G. R. Mason (Attorney-General, Minister of Justice, Minister of Health), F. Hackett (Minister of Labour, Minister of Mines, Minister of Immigration), W. A. Fox (Minister of Marine, Minister of Housing), H. Watt (Minister of Works), E. T. Tirikatene (Minister of Forests), P. G. Connolly (Minister of Defense), M. Moohan (Minister of Railways, Postmaster-General), P. N. Holloway (Minister of Industries and Commerce), P. O. S. Skoglund (Minister of Education), Miss M. B. Howard (Minister of Social Security), J. Mathison (Minister of Transport, Minister of Island Territories), R. Boord (Minister of Customs), W. T. Anderton (Minister of Internal Affairs).

NEW ZEALAND

PRESS

Unless otherwise noted, papers are published in the capital city.

Name of Paper	Circulation	Political Sympathies	Proprietor, Editor, etc.
Dominion (morning)	75,000	National.	C. T. C. Watson (*Ed.*)
Evening Post (evening)	73,000	National; established 1865.	G. Freeman (*Ed.*)
Auckland Star (Auckland) (evening)	110,000	National; established 1870.	G. J. Upton (*Ed.*)
New Zealand Herald (Auckland) (morning)	170,000	National; leading New Zealand daily; established 1863.	H. G. Bell (*Ed.*)
Christchurch Star (Christchurch) (evening)	55,000	National.	George Burns (*Ed.*)
Press (morning) (Christchurch)	50,000	National.	A. R. Cant (*Ed.*)
Evening Star (Dunedin) (evening)	26,000	National.	W. J. Noble (*Ed.*)
Otago Daily Times (Dunedin) (morning)	35,000	National.	J. Moffett (*Ed.*)
Waikato Times (Hamilton) (evening)	17,000	National.	A. E. Manning (*Mg. Dir.*)
Southland Times (Invercargill) (morning)	16,000	National.	J. L. Grimaldi (*Ed.*)
Taranaki Daily News (New Plymouth) (morning)	16,000	National.	D. F. C. Saxton (*Ed.*)
Timaru Herald (Timaru) (morning)	12,000	National.	W. Smith (*Ed.*)
Freedom (weekly)	30,000	National.	Ian J. Main (*Ed.*)
Standard (weekly)	33,400	Labor.	S. B. Pickering (*Ed.*)

PRESS ASSOCIATION

New Zealand Press Association	Independent; composed of newspapers of New Zealand.	T. M. Hinkley (*Mgr.*)

NICARAGUA

Capital: Managua
Area: 57,143 square miles
Population: 1,355,570 (1957 estimate)

President
Luis Somoza-Debayle (Nationalist Liberal)
Elected on February 3, 1957,
for six-year term beginning May 1, 1957

Cabinet
Nationalist Liberal

PARLIAMENT

The Senate consists of 12 Nationalist Liberal members and 4 Conservatives, plus the defeated Presidential candidate (Conservative) and two life-time Senators (Conservatives) by virtue of their being ex-Presidents of the Republic. The Chamber of Deputies is made up of the 42 remaining Constituent Assemblymen, 28 Nationalist Liberals and 14 Conservatives.

The Traditional Conservative Party at its Plenary Meeting of May 29, 1955, decided that Party members should withdraw from participation in the National Congress and in the Government. There has been a division in the Conservative Party over this decision, but some of the minority members of Congress and of the Senate have not withdrawn.

PARTY PROGRAMS AND LEADERS

NATIONALIST LIBERAL PARTY: Has historically advocated separation of Church and State, freedom of worship, school system under domination of the laity, democratic principles of government, and social legislation.

Leaders: Luis Somoza-Debayle (President of the Republic), Dr. Luis Manuel Debayle, General José María Zelaya, Gen. Camilo López-Irías, Dr. Leonardo Somarriba, Dr. Oscar Sevilla Sacasa.

TRADITIONALIST CONSERVATIVE PARTY: Has historically advocated co-operation of Government with Catholic Church, with freedom of other sects to exercise their teachings, compulsory primary education under lay teachers in addition to state-encouraged Catholic schools. Favors less government interference in private business, and private control of banks and other financial institutions.

Leaders: Edmundo Amador (Presidential Candidate), Dr. Eduardo Conrada Vado, Dr. Edgardo Buitrago.

INDEPENDENT LIBERAL PARTY: Advocates the restoration of civil and political freedom and the historic principles of the Liberal party. The younger element advocates more effective protection of the working classes and other modern social and economic reforms. Did not take part in last elections.

NICARAGUA

Leaders: Dr. Enoc Aguado, Dr. Alejo Icaza, Dr. Antonio Flores Vega, Dr. Salvador Buitrago Aja and Dr. Roberto González Durón.

THE CABINET

The members of the Cabinet are: Dr. Julio Quintana (Government), Dr. Alejandro Montiel Argüello (Foreign Affairs), Enrique Delgado (Economy), Dr. Carlos Hueck (Finance), Dr. René Schick (Education), Modesto Armijo Mejía (Development and Public Works), Col. Alfonso Mejía Chamorro (War, Navy and Aviation), Dr. Enrique Chamorro (Agriculture), Dr. Rafael Antonio Díaz (Labor), Dr. Doroteo Castillo (Health).

PRESS

Unless otherwise noted, papers are published in the capital city.

Name of Paper	Circulation	Political Affiliation	Proprietor, Editor, etc.
Flecha	7,500	Independent Liberal.	Orlando Barret Argüello (*Gen. Mgr.*)
La Hora	4,000	Pro-Government.	Federico Schneegan (*Dir.*)
La Noticia	7,000	Independent Liberal.	Juan Ramón Alivéz (*Ed.*)
Novedades	22,000	Virtually official.	Alejandro Ortega (*Dir.*)
La Prensa	23,000	Conservative.	Pablo Antonio Cuadra (*Dir.*)
El Gran Diario	2,500	Independent.	Dr. Adán Selva (*Ed.*)
El Centro-Americano. (León)	2,500	Independent Liberal.	Dr. Rodolfo Abaunza (*Ed.*)

NORWAY

Capital: Oslo
Area: 125,064 square miles
Population: 3,500,000 (1958 estimate)

Ruler

KING OLAV V
Born on July 2, 1903
Ascended the throne September 21, 1957

Cabinet

Labor
Reorganized January 22, 1955

Premier

EINAR GERHARDSEN (Labor)

PARLIAMENT
(Storting)

Elected October 7, 1957, for four-year term
President: NILS LANGHELLE (Labor)
President of Upper Section* (Lagting)
BENT RØISELAND (Liberal)
President of Lower Section* (Odelsting)
ALV KJØS (Conservative)

Parties	Representation
Labor	78
Conservative	29
Liberal	15
Agrarian	15
Christian People's	12
Communist	1
Total	150

* After the Storting has been properly constituted, 38 members are elected as members of the Lagting, while the remainder forms the Odelsting. All matters relating to new laws or to the amendment of existing laws are taken up first by the Odelsting and then by the Lagting, and, failing agreement by those two bodies separately, by the Storting sitting as a whole. Matters in which the resulting decisions do not take the form of law because they do not affect the legal status of the subjects of Norwegian law, such as the budget and all other money bills, are treated by the whole Storting. The King's veto power may be overridden by the subsequent passage of an act by three successively elected Stortings. Constitutional amendments must be adopted by a two-thirds majority of a newly-elected Storting after having been considered by the previous one. The Lagting, together with the Supreme Court, comprises the National Court for the trial of members of the Cabinet, Supreme Court, and the Storting.

RECENT POLITICAL EVENTS

After the return of King Haakon VII and the Government from their wartime stay in London, a "caretaker" National government was formed which ruled until a general election was held on October 8, 1945, resulting in a clear Labor majority, and a Labor Government was established on November 5, 1945.

NORWAY

Parliamentary elections held on October 10, 1949, resulted in an overwhelming victory for the Prime Minister, Einar Gerhardsen, and his Labor Party. The Communists lost their 11 seats in the previous parliament.

In the general election of October 12, 1953, Labor polled more votes than in 1949, but a new system of allocating seats reduced their representation from 85 to 77. Communists polled 15 per cent less votes but secured 3 seats.

In the 1957 general election Labor won an additional seat, and the Communists lost 2, retaining only one seat.

PARTY PROGRAMS AND LEADERS

LABOR PARTY: Has radical history including association from 1919 to 1923 with Third International, but is now basically Reformist, its program differing only slightly from other Scandinavian Social Democratic Parties; advocates State planning and State ownership of certain industries, but its present program does not propose any new nationalization measures; strongly supports rearmament and NATO.

Leaders: Einar Gerhardsen (Premier and Party Chairman), Trygve Bratteli (Vice-Chairman), Haakon Lie (Party Secretary), Konrad Nordahl (Chairman, Norwegian Federation of Trade Unions), Halvard M. Lange (Minister of Foreign Affairs), Erik Brofoss (Director of the Bank of Norway) and Nils Langhelle (President of Storting).

CONSERVATIVE PARTY: Strongly supports free enterprise, armaments, NATO.

Leaders: Alv Kjøs (Party Chairman), Bernt Ingvaldsen and Håkon Kyllingmark (Vice-Chairmen), Rolf Stranger (Chairman of Oslo City Council) and Holger Ursin (Party Secretary).

LIBERAL PARTY: Has become heterogeneous in recent years; includes Bergen group strongly favoring free enterprise and free trade, Ny Norsk language groups, religious and fishing factions as well as an economic left-wing group supporting state planning and cultural radicalism, also NATO.

Leaders: Bent Røiseland (Party Chairman), Paul Ingebretsen (Member of Storting), and Helge Seip (Member of Storting).

AGRARIAN PARTY: Supports farmers' and rural interests. Conservative; strongly supports NATO.

Leaders: Per Borten (Party Chairman), L. Elisaeus Vatnaland (Party Vice-Chairman), Hans Holten (Editor *Nationen*) and Jon Leirfall (Member of Storting).

CHRISTIAN PEOPLE'S PARTY: Strives to incorporate principles of Christianity into political life; supports social legislation. Strongly supports NATO and Norway's defense program.

Leaders: Einar Hareide (Party Chairman), Kjell Bondevik (Vice-Chairman), Erling Wikborg (Party Leader in Storting).

COMMUNIST PARTY: Anti-NATO; in all respects follows Soviet line.

Leaders: Emil Løvlien (Party Chairman), Just Lippe (Party Vice-Chairman and Political Secretary), Henry Hoff (Organizational Secretary).

NORWAY

THE CABINET

The members of the Cabinet are: Einar Gerhardsen (Prime Minister), Halvard Lange (Foreign Affairs), Gustav Sjaastad (Industry and Handicraft), Harald Löbak (Agriculture), Gudmund Harlem (Social Affairs), Kolbjørn Varmann (Communications), Jens Haugland (Justice and Police), Arne Skaug (Commerce and Shipping), Nils Lysø (Fisheries), Nils K. Handal (Defense), Trygve Bratteli (Finance and Customs), Birger Bergersen (Education and Ecclesiastical Affairs), Andreas Cappelen (Municipal and Labor Affairs), Gunnar Braathen (Prices and Wages), Mrs. Aase Bjerkholt (Consumer, Home and Family Affairs).

PRESS

Unless otherwise noted, papers are published in capital city.

Name of Paper	Political Affiliation	Proprietor, Editor, etc.
Aftenposten	Conservative.	Herman Smitt Ingebretsen, H. J. S. Huitfeldt and Einar Diesen (*Eds.*)
Arbeiderbladet	Labor.	Olav Larssen, Rolf Gerhardsen, Per Monsen (*Eds.*)
Dagbladet	Liberal.	Helge Seip (*Ed.*)
Friheten	Communist.	Reidar Larsen (*Ed.*)
Morgenbladet	Conservative.	Birger Kildal (*Ed.*)
Morgenposten	Independent.	Asbjørn Engen (*Ed.*)
Nationen	Agrarian.	Hans Holten and Erling Johnsen (*Eds.*)
Norges Handels—og Sjöfartstidende	Independent; commercial news.	Eivind Thon (*Ed.*)
Vaart Land	Christian People's.	Bjarne Höye (*Ed.*)
Verdens Gang	Independent.	Chr. A. R. Christensen and Oskar Hasselknippe (*Eds*).
Bergens Tidende (Bergen)	Liberal.	Ingem. Faenn (*Ed.*)
Morgenavisen (Bergen)	Conservative.	Erling Lauhn (*Ed.*)
Drammens Tidende (Drammen)	Conservative.	Torolv Kandahl (*Ed.*)
Fremtiden (Drammen)	Labor.	Jon Vraa (*Ed.*)
Fredrikstad Blad (Fredrikstad)	Conservative.	Ragnar Henriksen and R. Henry Haugen (*Eds.*)
Hamar Arbeiderblad (Hamar)	Labor.	E. O. Solbakken (*Ed.*)
Faedrelandsvennen (Kristiansand S.)	Liberal.	Johannes Seland (*Ed.*)
Rogalands Avis (Stavanger)	Labor.	Peder Naesheim and Harald Riis (*Eds.*)
Stavanger Aftenblad (Stavanger)	Liberal.	Per Thomsen, Fr. Lund, Jon Arnöy (*Eds.*)
Lofotposten (Svolvaer)	Independent.	M. C. Amundsen (*Ed.*)
Tönsberg Blad (Tönsberg)	Conservative.	Realph Norland and Sverre Mitsem (*Eds.*)
Adresseavisen (Trondheim)	Conservative.	Harald Torp, Sverre J. Herstad and Reidar Stavseth (*Eds.*)
Farmand (weekly)	Economic and financial.	Trygve J. B. Hoff (*Ed.*)

PRESS ASSOCIATIONS AND AGENCIES

Arbeidernes Pressekontor	Labor.	Olav Brunvand (*Ed.*)
Bondepartiets Pressekontor	Agrarian.	Odd Bye (*Ed.*)
Venstres Pressekontor	Liberal.	H. Kongshaug (*Ed.*)
Høires Pressekontor	Conservative.	R. Halle (*Ed.*)
Norsk Presseforbund	Norwegian press association.	Chr. A. R. Christensen (*Ch.*)
Norsk Telegrambyraa	News agency.	B. Knudsen (*Mg. Dir.*)

PAKISTAN*

Capital: Karachi
Area: 364,737 square miles
Population: 80,167,000 (1954 estimate)

President

GENERAL MOHAMMAD AYUB KHAN
Assumed office as Chief Martial Law Administrator
on October 7, 1958

Assumed Presidency on October 27, 1958, on resignation of
President Iskander Mirza

Cabinet
Appointed October 24, 1958

RECENT POLITICAL EVENTS

President Iskander Mirza declared martial law throughout Pakistan on October 7, 1958, abolished the Constitution and dissolved the National and Provincial Assemblies. He dismissed the Government of Prime Minister Malik Firoz Khan Noon and the Provincial Governments and dissolved all political parties. He appointed Gen. Mohammad Ayub Khan as Supreme Commander of the Armed Forces and Chief Martial Law Administrator. On October 27, 1958, he in turn resigned under pressure of the military and turned over his office to Gen. Ayub Khan.

THE CABINET

The members of the Cabinet are: General Mohammad Ayub Khan (President, Supreme Commander of the Armed Forces, Chief Martial Law Administrator, Cabinet-Secretariat, Defense, Kashmir Affairs), Manzoor Qadir (Foreign Affairs), Lt. Gen. Mohammad Azam Khan (Rehabilitation), F. M. Khan (Communications), Lt. Gen. W. A. Burki (Health and Social Welfare), Habibur Rahman (Education, Information and Broadcasting), Lt. Gen. K. M. Sheikh (Interior), Abul Kasim Khan (Industries, Irrigation, Works and Power), Hafizur Rahman (Food and Agriculture), Zulfiqar Ali Khan Bhutto (Commerce), Mohammad Shoaib (Finance), Maulvi Mohammad Ibrahim (Law).

* The Indian Independence Act, passed by the British Parliament in July 1947, came into effect on August 15, 1947, with the establishment of the two independent dominions of India and of Pakistan. Under the terms of the Indian Independence Act, full self-government was granted these two Dominions, and British control came to an end. The Dominion of India, although containing over 35 million Muslims, is predominantly Hindu while Pakistan is predominantly Muslim. The Indian Princely States have entered into agreements of close affiliation with one or the other of the two countries, and have merged into their respective provinces.

PAKISTAN

PRESS

ENGLISH LANGUAGE PUBLICATIONS

Name of Paper	Former Political Affiliation	Proprietor, Editor, etc.
Dawn (Karachi)	Pro-Muslim League.	Altaf Husain (*Ed.*)
Times of Karachi (Karachi)	Pro-Republican.	Z. A. Suleri (*Ed.*)
Civil & Military Gazette (Lahore)	Independent.	Mohammad Yaqub Khan (*Ed.*)
Pakistan Observer (Dacca)	Pro-Krishak Sramik.	Abdus Salam (*Ed.*)
Khyber Mail (Peshawar)		S. Sanaullah (*Ed.*)
Evening Star (Karachi)	Pro-Muslim League.	M. A. Zuberi (*Ed.*)
Morning News (Dacca and Karachi)	Independent.	Syed Mohsin Ali (*Ed.*)
Pakistan Times (Lahore)	Pro-Communist.	Mazhar Ali Khan (*Ed.*)
Pakistan Quarterly (Karachi)	Cultural.	Government (*Pub.*)
Comment (Karachi)	Independent.	H. M. Abbasi (*Ed.*)

NEWS AGENCIES

Associated Press of Pakistan.
Pakistan Press Association.
United Press of Pakistan.

PANAMA

Capital: Panama City
Area: 28,754 square miles (excluding Canal Zone)
Population: 1,000,000, excluding Canal Zone (1958 estimate)

President
ERNESTO DE LA GUARDIA, JR.
Elected May 13, 1956
Assumed office on October 1, 1956, for four-year term

Cabinet
Reorganized May 30, 1958

PARLIAMENT
(Asamblea Nacional)

Elected May 11, 1956; took office October 1, 1956; four-year term

Parties	Representation
National Patriotic Coalition	37
National Liberal	10
Independents	6
Total	53

RECENT POLITICAL EVENTS

The spectacular Remón assassination trial, which ended December 6, 1957, with the acquittal of all seven defendants, overshadowed National Assembly activity. However, the legislative session (October 1, 1957–January 30, 1958) produced several valuable laws, including a new Electoral Code.

An outburst of student violence in Panamá and Colón from May 16–19, 1958, left an estimated 9 dead and several score injured. The riots, which had begun with protests against deficiencies in the educational system, were settled with an Administration-student "pact" by which the Government agreed to introduce legislation in the 1958–59 session of the National Assembly providing (1) educational reforms and (2) restrictions upon the terms of office and extra-official activities of the National Guard.

THE CABINET

The members of the present Cabinet are: Max Heurtematte (Minister of Government and Justice), Miguel J. Moreno, Jr. (Minister of Foreign Relations), Fernando Eleta (Minister of Finance and Treasury), Carlos Sucre C. (Minister of Education), Roberto López Fábrega (Minister of Public Works), Alberto A. Boyd (Minister of Agriculture, Commerce and Industries), Heraclio Barletta (Minister of Labor, Social Welfare and Public Health), Inocencio Galindo (Assistant to the President), Mario Cal (Minister of the Presidency), and Roberto Heurtematte (Comptroller General).

PANAMA

PRESS

Unless otherwise noted, papers are published in the capital city.

Name of Paper	Circulation	Political Affiliation	Proprietor, Editor, etc.
Estrella de Panamá	11,000	Independent.	Tomás Gabriel Duque (*Pres. and Dir.*)
Star and Herald	10,000	English section of *Estrella de Panamá*.	T. Gabriel Duque (*Pub.*)
The Panamá American	11,000	Independent; English counterpart of *El Panamá-América*.	Dr. Harmodio Arias (*Ed.*)
El Panamá-América	10,000	Independent.	Dr. Harmodio Arias (*Dir.*)
La Nación	9,000	National Liberation Movement.	Manuel M. Valdés (*Dir.*)
El Dia	6,000	Nationalistic.	Fabián Velarde, Jr. (*Dir.*)
La Hora	10,000	Controlled by Harmodio Arias; independent; nationalistic.	Arquimedes Fernández (*Dir.*)
El País	4,000	National Patriotic Coalition.	Heliodoro Patiño (*Dir.*)
The Panamá Tribune (weekly)	6,500	West Indian Negro publication; in English.	Sidney A. Young (*Pub. and Ed.*)
Atlántico (Colon) (weekly)	4,000	Independent; English-Spanish edition.	Mario Julio (*Pub.*)
Ecos del Valle (David, Chiriqui Province)	1,000	Independent; hinterland viewpoint.	Miguel Angel Brenes (*Dir.*)

PARAGUAY

Capital: Asunción
Area: 157,000 square miles
Population: 1,565,000 (1955 estimate)

President
GENERAL ALFREDO STROESSNER
Re-elected on February 9, 1958, for five-year term
Took office August 15, 1958

Cabinet
Appointed August 15, 1958

PARLIAMENT
(Congreso)

President Felipe Molas López dissolved the House of Representatives on March 5, 1949. In accordance with the Constitution, elections for a new House were held and on April 17, a new House of 40 members was elected. It assembled for the first time on May 3, and was composed exclusively of Colorados whose names appeared on the single slate offered to the voters by the Government. Uncontested general elections were again held on July 16, 1950, and on February 9, 1958. There are presently 60 deputies and 20 alternates, all Colorados.

There is no Senate under the present Constitution (of 1940), but the Council of State acts somewhat as a second chamber.

RECENT POLITICAL EVENTS

On January 13, 1947, the Febreristas resigned from the coalition Cabinet, leaving only the Colorado Party supporting President Morínigo. On March 7, an attack on the police station in Asunción, sponsored principally by Febreristas with some Communist help, precipitated a civil war which lasted for five months. Upon the conclusion of the war late in August, with the defeat of the combined rebel troops, the Colorado Party remained the sole political party in Paraguay.

In 1948 the Colorado Party split and the extreme element forced the resignation of President Morínigo. He was followed by Provisional President Juan Manuel Frutos, who served until J. Natalicio González, who had been elected during the Morínigo régime, took office.

Following the overthrow of President González on January 30, 1949, the National Assembly met and elected General Rolón as Provisional President.

General Rolón was overthrown by a "civil and military movement" on February 26, 1949, and was succeeded by Dr. Felipe Molas López. On April 17, he was elected President with the support of the democratic wing of the Colorado Party. On September 10 he resigned, after losing support of the Party; and the following day Federico Cháves was named Provisional President by Congress. Cháves was elected President on a one-party ballot in 1950 and re-elected in 1953. On May 5, 1954, the Army deposed Cháves. The leader of the revolt, General Stroessner, was later nominated by the Colorado Party and elected President.

PARAGUAY

PARTY PROGRAMS AND LEADERS

NATIONAL REPUBLICAN (COLORADO) PARTY: Has been the ruling Party in Paraguay since 1947. This Party, like the Liberal Party, is conservative. It and the Liberals are the two great traditional parties. In November 1947 a convention of the Party was held to nominate candidates for the February 1948 elections. A split took place which kept the Party in a state of turmoil until 1956, when relative unification of the factions was achieved.

Leaders: General Alfredo Stroessner (President of Paraguay), Tomás Romero Pereira (President of Party), Dr. J. Bernardino Gorostiaga (Vice President of Party), Crispin Insaurralde, J. Eulogio Estigarribia.

LIBERAL PARTY: This Party governed Paraguay from 1904 to 1936, and from 1937 to 1940. Its program is conservative.

Leaders: Dr. Alejandro Arce (President of Party), Justo P. Benitez, Jr. (First Secretary), Efraím Cardozo, Justo P. Prieto.

FEBRERISTA PARTY: Formerly known as the Franquista Party. Followers of Colonel Rafael Franco, who became Provisional President in 1936 through a military *coup d'état* and was himself overthrown 18 months later. His brief régime was characterized by social legislation, some of an advanced order, and suppression of political liberties. Leaders are principally former Liberals and other dissidents. Party is leftist, directing its appeal to underprivileged, but it is not permitted to operate openly.

Leaders: Colonel Rafael Franco, Elpidio Yegros, Dr. Juan Stefanich, Dr. Arnaldo Valdovinos.

COMMUNIST PARTY (Outlawed): Followed orthodox Communist line.

Leaders: Oscar Creydt, Obdulio Barthe, Antonio Maidana and Augusto Canete.

THE CABINET

The members of the Cabinet are: Dr. Edgar Insfrán, Interior; Tomás Romero Pereira, without Portfolio; Dr. Raúl Sapena Pastor, Foreign Affairs; Gen. César Barrientos, Finance; Dr. Raúl Peña, Health; Gen. Mario Coscia T., Public Works and Communications; J. Bernardino Gorostiaga, Education; Gen. Marcial Samaniego, Defense; Dr. Ezequiel Gonzalez Alsina, Agriculture; Dr. César Garay, Justice and Labor; Dr. Fabio da Silva, Industry and Commerce.

PRESS

Papers are published in the capital city.

Name of Paper	Circulation	Proprietor, Editor, etc.
El País (official Government organ)	10,000	Leopoldo Ramos Giménez (*Dir.*)
La Tribuna	30,000	Arturo Schaerer (*Dir.*)
Patria	10,000	Dr. Ezequiel González Alsina (*Dir.*)

PERU

Capital: Lima
Area: 482,258 square miles
Population: 9,396,000 (1955 estimate)

President
Dr. Manuel Prado y Ugarteche
Elected June 17, 1956
Assumed office July 28, 1956, for six-year term

Cabinet
Appointed July 2, 1956
Reorganized September 22, 1957

PARLIAMENT
(Congreso)

UPPER CHAMBER (Senado)	
Election of June, 1956 (Six-year term)	
President: Dr. Rodrigo Franco	
Parties	*Representation*
Democrático Peruano	24
Unificacion Nacional	8
Acción Popular	4
Demócrata-Cristiano	4
Independents and others	12
Total	52

LOWER CHAMBER (Cámara de Diputados)	
Election of June, 1956 (Six-year term)	
President: Dr. Javier Ortiz de Zevallos	
Parties	*Representation*
Democrático Peruano	75
Unificacion Nacional	29
Acción Popular	16
Demócrata-Christiano	14
Independents and others	48
Total	182

RECENT POLITICAL EVENTS

Dr. José Luis Bustamante y Rivero was elected President in the 1945 general elections for the 1945–1951 term, as the candidate of the National Democratic Front (FDN). He viewed his administration as one of "transition to democracy" and attempted to follow a middle-of-the-road policy of conciliation of the opposing political factions. Even before the end of 1945, opposition to Apra, or the People's Party—legalized shortly before the elections—had split the FDN itself. In the two succeeding years the cleavage between the Aprista forces and their opponents became deeper and the rivalry more acute. Following the assassination of the director of the conservative newspaper *La Prensa*, Francisco Graña Garland, early in 1947, the various anti-Aprista groups were able to join forces in a series of coalitions, of which the most important was the Alianza Nacional. Following the abortive Navy revolt in Callao on October 3, 1948, which the Government stated had been planned by Apra and had had its support, Apra was again outlawed.

Three weeks later, Army groups headed by General Manuel A. Odría successfully raised the standard of revolution in Arequipa. General Odría's proclamation attacked President Bustamante for being too lenient with Apra

PERU

and for opposing and dividing the Armed Forces. President Bustamante was deposed and departed for Argentina, and a new Military Board of Government headed by Odría assumed office on October 27, 1948. Both Apra and the Communist Party were thereupon outlawed under Article 53 of the Constitution, which prohibits international parties. Victor Raúl Haya de la Torre, the Apra leader, was expelled in 1954 after five years in asylum at the Colombian Embassy in Lima.

General Odría continued as President of the Military Junta of Government until June 1, 1950, on which date he surrendered office to General Zenón Noriega in order to become presidential candidate in the elections of July 2. In an election in which no opposition presidential candidate was qualified, General Odría won the Presidency. No Odríista party was formally created, but an overwhelmingly pro-Odría Congress was elected.

In the elections of 1956, the first really free elections since 1945, there were three candidates: Hernando de Lavalle, chosen for the succession by President Odría; Fernando Belaunde Terry; and Dr. Manuel Prado, who was President, 1939–1945. The latter won. His first act was to restore political freedom in Peru and to legalize again the left-wing Apra.

PARTY PROGRAMS AND LEADERS

PARTIDO DEMOCRÁTICO PERUANO: Party of President Prado. Moderate.

Leaders: Manuel Prado, Manuel Cisneros, Rodrigo Franco.

ACCIÓN POPULAR: New left-wing party claiming its main strength in young middle class.

Leaders: Fernando Belaunde, Celso Pastor de la Torre, Miguel Dammert.

PARTIDO COMUNISTO PERUANO: Peruvian Communist Party.

Leaders: Raúl Acosta Salas, Genaro Carnero Checa, Jorge del Prado.

PARTIDO DEMÓCRATA-CRISTIANO: Moderate and seeks to solve political, social and economic problems by Christian principles.

Leaders: Javier Correa Elias, Mario Polar Ugarteche, José Barreda Moller, Héctor Cornejo Chávez.

PARTIDO DEL PUEBLO (Apra): Left-wing party; anti-Communist and anti-imperialist with strength in labor movement.

Leaders: V. R. Haya de la Torre, Manuel Seoane, Ramiro Prialé.

THE CABINET

The members of the Cabinet are: Luis Gallo Porras (Premier and Finance and Commerce), Dr. Raúl Porras Barrenechea (Foreign Affairs), Dr. Carlos Carrillo Smith (Government and Police), Gen. Alejandro Cuadra Ravines (War), Rear Admiral Guillermo Tirado Lamb (Navy), Gen. Manuel P. García (Air), Emilio Romero Padilla (Education), Eduardo Dibós Dammert (Development and Public Works), Dr. Ulises Montoya Manfredi (Justice and Worship), Dr. Francisco Sánchez Moreno (Health and Social Assistance), Enrique Labarthe Correa (Agriculture), Dr. Ricardo Elías Aparicio (Labor).

PERU

PRESS

Unless otherwise noted, papers are published in the capital city.

Name of Paper	Circulation	Political Affiliation	Proprietor, Editor, etc.
El Comercio	125,000 (2 Editions)	Conservative; oldest and leading paper in Peru.	Luis Miró Quesada Guerra (Dir.)
La Crónica	80,000 (2 Editions)	Popular; pro-Administration.	Ing. Luis de los Heros (Dir.)
El Peruano	10,000	Official gazette for laws, decrees, etc.	Esteban Pavletich (Dir.)
La Prensa	70,000	Independent; conservative.	Pedro G. Beltrán (Dir.)
La Tribuna	15,000	Apra paper.	Manuel Solano (Dir.)
Última Hora	87,000	Independent evening tabloid.	Luis Miglio Manini (Dir.)
El Deber (Arequipa)	5,000	Catholic, conservative.	Erasmo Hinojosa H. (Dir.)
Noticias (Arequipa)	15,000	Pro-Administration.	Alejandro Arispe (Dir.)
El Pueblo (Arequipa)	10,000	Independent, conservative.	Luis Durand Flores (Dir.)
El Comercio (Cuzco)	7,000	Independent, conservative.	José Antonio Velazco (Dir.)
El Sol (Cuzco)	3,000	Independent, conservative.	José Gabriel Cosio (Dir.)
El Tiempo (Piura)	5,000	Independent, conservative.	Victor M. Helguero Checa (Dir.)
La Industria (Piura)	5,000	Independent, conservative.	Miguel F. Cerro (Dir.)
La Industria (Trujillo)	5,000	Pro-Administration.	Rafael J. Mauricci (Ed.)
La Nación (Trujillo)	5,000	Independent, conservative.	José Angel Miñano (Dir.)
Andean Air Mail and Peruvian Times (weekly)	2,500	Independent; in English.	C. N. Griffis (Ed.)
Rochabus (weekly)	14,000	Political cartoon weekly.	Guido Monteverde (Dir.)
Vanguardia (weekly)	8,000	Conservative weekly.	Eudocio Ravines (Dir.)
Verdades (weekly)	1,000	Catholic.	Luis Solari (Dir.)
Caretas (bi-monthly)	15,000	Literary.	Francisco Igartúa (Dir.)
Cultura Peruana (monthly)	8,000	Literary.	José Flores Araez (Dir.)
Mensajero Agricola (monthly)	500	Farmers' magazine.	Rosa Hermando (Ed.)

PHILIPPINES

Capital: Quezon City (Manila)
Area: 115,600 square miles
Population: 23,000,000 (1958 estimate)

President
CARLOS P. GARCIA (Nacionalista)
Elected President on November 12, 1957, for four-year term

Vice-President
DIOSDADO MACAPAGAL (Liberal)

Cabinet
Nacionalista; appointed in January 1958

PARLIAMENT
(Congress)

UPPER CHAMBER
(Senate)

Election of November 12, 1957 (Six-year term; renewed by thirds every two years)

President: EULOGIO RODRIGUEZ

Parties	Representation
Nacionalistas	20
Nationalist Citizen	2
Liberal	2
Total	24

LOWER CHAMBER
(House of Representatives)

Election of November 12, 1957 (four-year term)

Speaker: DANIEL Z. ROMUALDEZ

Parties	Representation
Nacionalistas	83
Liberals	19
Total	102

RECENT POLITICAL EVENTS

On July 4, 1946, the Republic of the Philippines was inaugurated amid the ruins of Manila. The Bell and Tydings Acts governing relations between the Philippines and the United States were confirmed by a plebiscite in 1947; in 1955 the Bell Act, governing economic relations, was revised by mutual agreement between the two countries. The Philippines, an active member of the Southeast Asia Treaty Organization, was host to the March 1958 SEATO foreign ministers meeting.

President Carlos P. Garcia, who was elected Vice-President November 10, 1953, succeeded the late President Ramon Magsaysay upon the latter's death March 17, 1957, and was continued in office by the elections of November 12, 1957. The Nacionalista administration under Magsaysay was chiefly concerned with defeat of the Communist Hukbalahap rebellion, in which it succeeded, and with programs of social amelioration and rural rehabilitation. Since its inception, the Garcia administration has been primarily concerned with solving various problems arising from an unfavorable balance-of-payments position and with a program to eliminate graft and corruption in the government.

PHILIPPINES

The election of the opposition Liberal Party Vice-Presidential candidate, Diosdado Macapagal, in 1957 was a historically unique occurrence which has presented the administration with many problems involving the Vice-President's membership in various policy-making bodies.

PARTY PROGRAMS AND LEADERS

The majority party in the Philippines, the Nacionalista Party (President, Senator Eulogio Rodriguez), came into power with the defeat of President Elpidio Quirino and the Liberal Party (present President, Representative Cornelio T. Villareal), by Magsaysay in 1953. Two other legal parties are active. The Progressive party, or PPP (President, Manuel Manahan), is composed mainly of younger elements who supported Magsaysay but who seceded from the NP after his death. The PPP failed to elect any of its slate of national candidates in 1957, but remains a potentially significant force in Philippine politics. The Nacionalist-Citizens party, or NCP (President, Senator Claro Recto) is largely a vehicle for the political ambitions and nationalistic views of Senators Recto and Lorenzo Tañada, who were defeated as Presidential and Vice-Presidential candidate, respectively, in 1957.

The Philippine Communist party, or PKP, was outlawed by the Anti-Subversion Act of June, 1957, which also made it a crime to affiliate knowingly with the party. While its attempt to seize power through armed revolt has ended, the PKP is still active and has declared a "legal struggle" phase in its operations which involves penetration of non-communist groups and various forms of subversion. Two important leaders of the PKP are still at large, Dr. Jesus Lava and Castro Alejandrino. Alfredo Saulo was captured in 1958.

THE CABINET

The present members of the Cabinet are: Felixberto M. Serrano (Secretary of Foreign Affairs), Jaime Hernandez (Secretary of Finance), Jesus Barrera (Secretary of Justice), Juan de G. Rodriguez (Secretary of Agriculture and Natural Resources), Pedro Hernaez (Secretary of Commerce and Industry), Elpidio Valencia (Secretary of Health), Manuel Lim (Secretary of Education), Jesus V. Vargas (Secretary of National Defense), Florencio Moreno (Secretary of Public Works and Communications), Angel M. Castaño (Secretary of Labor), Dominador R. Aytona (Commissioner of the Budget), Amparo P. Villamor (Administrator of Social Welfare), Juan C. Pajo (Executive Secretary), José Nable (Press Secretary), Alejandro Almendras (Secretary of General Services), José Locsin (Chairman, National Economic Council), Juan Concon (Administrator of Economic Coordination), Makdi Alonto (Commissioner of National Integration), Paulino Garcia (Chairman, National Science Development Board).

PRESS

All the papers are published in Manila.

Name of Paper	Character	Proprietor, Editor, etc.
Manila Times	Conservative.	Roces Publications (*Pub.*) David Boguslav (*Ed.*)
Manila Chronicle	Nationalist.	Eugenio Lopez (*Pub.*) Ernesto del Rosario (*Ed.*)
Philippines Herald	Conservative.	Philippine Publishers, Inc. (*Pub.*) O. Abad Santos (*Mg. Ed.*)

Name of Paper	Character	Proprietor, Editor, etc.
Manila Daily Bulletin	Conservative.	Hans Menzi (*Pub.*) Ford Wilkins (*Ed.*)
Evening News	Conservative.	Amadeo R. Dacanay (*Ed.*)
Daily Mirror	Nationalist.	Roces Publications (*Pub.*) Manuel V. Villareal (*Ed.*)
Fookien Times	In Chinese; pro-Taiwan.	Go Puan Seng (*Pub.*)
Bagong Buhay	In Tagalog.	Dionisio San Agustin (*Ed.*)
Mabuhay	In Tagalog.	Philippine Publishers, Inc. (*Pub.*) Catalino Flores (*Ed.*)
El Debate	In Spanish.	Philippine Publishers, Inc. (*Pub.*) Antonio L. Serrano (*Ed.*)
Philippines Free Press (weekly)	Independent.	R. McCulloch Dick (*Ed.*)
Kislap Graphic (weekly)	In English and Tagalog.	Roces Publications (*Pub.*)
Liwayway (weekly)	In Tagalog.	Roces Publications (*Pub.*) José Domingo Karasig (*Ed.*)

POLAND

Capital: Warszawa (Warsaw)
Area: 120,347 square miles (1948 estimate)
Population: 28,535,000 (1958 estimate)

Council of State
ALEKSANDER ZAWADZKI (Chairman)

Cabinet
Communist-dominated National Front, primarily
Polish United Worker's Party

Premier
JOSEF CYRANKIEWICZ
Elected by Parliament on February 26, 1957

PARLIAMENT
(Sejm)
Election of January 20, 1957 (four-year term)
Speaker: CZESLAW WYCECH

Name of Party	Representation
Polish United Workers' Party	237
United Peasant Party	119
Democratic Party	39
Catholics	12
Non-Party	51
Total	458

The Polish parliamentary system is based on the Constitution adopted on July 22, 1952. In most respects it follows the pattern set by the USSR Constitution of 1936. The first Parliament under the new Constitution was elected on a one-party ticket, all candidates representing the communist-controlled National Front. The office of President has been abolished and the Council of State is now the highest organ of the Government.

POLITICAL EVENTS SINCE 1944

In July 1944, the USSR recognized a Polish Committee of National Liberation which was organized in Moscow and moved to Lublin, Poland, when the latter place was liberated. On December 31, 1944, this Committee proclaimed itself as the Provisional Government of Poland. After lengthy negotiations, some of the former members of the Polish Government, which was located in London during the war, and the Provisional Government in Poland were united to form the Polish Government of National Unity on June 28, 1945. A Cabinet of 23 members was chosen which included Stanislaw Mikolajczyk, former Premier of the exiled Government in London, as Vice-Premier. Two other former ministers of the exiled Government and two members of the Polish Peasant Party from inside Poland, were also appointed. The other members were all formerly associated with the Provisional Government in Poland. This Cabinet was superseded on February 7, 1947, by a government in which the Socialists and Communists divided the most important posts.

On February 19, 1947, a Constituent Assembly adopted what was called the "Little Constitution" laying down the structure and sphere of activity of the supreme organs of the Polish Republic. This, together with two important decrees, one providing for nationalization and the other aiming at extirpation of opposition to the Government, constituted the basis for the organization of the State.

In December 1948, delegates of the Socialist Party (PPS) and of the Communist or Workers' Party (PPR) met to effect a merger into one consolidated Polish United Workers' Party, thus further consolidating political activities under the Communists.

In the fall of 1951, a Constitutional Committee was set up to draft a new Constitution. It completed its work and the new constitution was adopted on June 22, 1952.

In June 1956, serious riots broke out in Poznan led by workers protesting the hard conditions of life. This led to a reorganization of the Politburo of the Communist party and to the return to power of Wladyslaw Gomulka, after serving three years in prison as a "Titoist." Gomulka, as First Secretary of the Party, succeeded in negotiations with the Russians in winning a degree of freedom for the Polish Communist party from Moscow control. Marshal Konstantin K. Rokossovsky, the former Soviet Army hero, was excluded from the Politburo, dropped as Minister of Defense and returned to the Soviet Union. Under Gomulka's leadership Poland has attempted to find her own "road to socialism" but "independent from Moscow."

PARTY PROGRAMS AND LEADERS

After the adoption of the new Constitution in 1952, the individual political parties, except the United Workers' Party, had little significance. They are listed below primarily as a matter of record.

POLISH UNITED WORKERS' PARTY: Polska Zjednoczona Partia Robotnicza (PZPR): The one political party of importance in Poland which dominates and controls the National Front and all political activities in the country. The mass political organization of the Communists, known, prior to absorption of the Socialist Party in 1948, as the Polish Workers' Party (PPR). The PZPR claims direct descent from Rosa Luxemburg's "Social Democracy of the Kingdom of Poland and Lithuania" (1893–1918), which changed its name to "Communist Workers' Party of Poland" after the first World War and later changed it again to "Communist Party of Poland, Section of the Communist International." Prohibited from 1919 onward, it went underground and was eventually dissolved by the Comintern in 1938 because of alleged Trotskyism and infiltration by police agents. In January, 1942, the Communists' organization was revived in German-occupied Poland under the name, "Polish Workers' Party," of which Wladyslaw Gomulka became Secretary-General (1943–1948). In September, 1948, Gomulka was ousted from leadership for "rightest-nationalist deviationism," but he regained power in 1956. Domestically, the ultimate aim of the PZPR is full socialism based on the Soviet model. The nationalization of trade and industry is already achieved, and the collectivization of agriculture is officially promoted. *In foreign policy:* it follows the line taken by the Soviet Union. It held its Second Congress March 10-17, 1954. Since October 1956 it strives to achieve a measure of independence within the framework of the Soviet-Polish Alliance.

Leaders: Members of the Politburo: Wladyslaw Gomulka (First Secretary); Edward Ochab, Jerzy Morawski, Aleksander Zawadzki, Josef Cyrankiewicz, Roman Zambrowski, Adam Rapacki, Stefan Jedrychowski and Ignacy Loga-Sowinski.

Members of the Secretariat: Wladyslaw Gomulka, Jerzy Albrecht, Edward Gierek, Witold Jarosinski, Wladyslaw Matwin, Roman Zambrowski, Zenon Kliszko, Jerzy Morawski.

POLISH SOCIALIST PARTY: Polska Partia Socjalistyczna (PPS): This party has ceased to exist as a legal political organization, in consequence of the action of its left-wing leadership, by which it was merged with the Polish United Workers' Party in December 1948.

UNITED PEASANT PARTY: Zjednoczone Stronnictwo Ludowe (ZSL): Originally established in 1895 in the Austrian part of partitioned Poland, the Peasant Party up to the second World War was a strong movement under the leadership of Wincenty Witos, whose program included land reform. During the war its record, both in the underground resistance at home and abroad, was outstanding. After the war its exile leader, Stanislaw Mikolajczyk, returned to Poland and reorganized the majority of the party's adherents into the Polish Peasant Party (PSL), which attempted to promote the traditional aims of the former Peasant Party (SL). Mikolajczyk, however, was forced to flee in 1947 because of government persecution, and the PSL no longer exists as a legal political entity in Poland. A group of former Party members collaborate with the Communists under the name of the United Peasant Party (ZSL), which is in the National Front.

Leaders: (Pro-Government): Stefan Ignar (Chairman of Party and Vice-Premier); Jozef Ozga-Michalski, Boleslaw Podedworny, Czeslaw Wycech (Vice-Chairmen); Kazimierz Banach, Bronislaw Drzewiecki, Wladyslaw Jagusztyn, Ludomir Stasiak (Secretaries).

DEMOCRATIC PARTY: Stronnictwo Demokratyczne (SD); A numerically insignificant representation of intellectuals, white-collar workers and handicrafts. In July, 1950, it absorbed the Labor Party (Stronnictwo Pracy). It follows the political line of the Government.

Leaders: (Pro-Government): Stanislaw Kulczynski (Chairman); Jerzy Jodlowski, Wlodzimierz Lechowicz and Jan Karol Wende (Vice-Chairmen); Leon Chajn (Secretary-General); Ryszard Burchacki, Boleslaw Szlasak, and Kazimierz Zawadski (Deputy Secretaries General).

THE CABINET

The members of the Cabinet are: Jozef Cyrankiewicz, Chairman of the Council of Ministers (Workers); Stefan Ignar, Vice-Premier (Peasant); Piotr Jaroszewicz, Vice-Premier (Workers); Zenon Nowak, Vice-Premier (Workers); Stefan Jedrychowski, Chairman of the Planning Commission (Workers); Marian Spychalski, National Defense (Workers); Adam Rapacki, Foreign Affairs (Workers); Witold Trampczynski, Foreign Trade (Workers); Wladyslaw Wicha, Internal Affairs (Workers); Franciszek Waniolka, Mining

Industry and Power Industry (Workers); Kiejstut Zemajtis, Heavy Industry (Workers); Antoni Radlinski, Chemical Industry (Workers); Eugeniusz Stawinski, Light Industry (Workers); Edward Ochab, Agriculture (Workers); Jan Dab-Kociol, Forestry and Wood Industry (Peasant); Feliks Pisula, Food and Agriculture Industry (Peasant); Stefan Pietrusiewicz, Construction and Construction Materials Industry (Workers); Ryszard Strzelecki, Railways (Workers); Stanislaw Darski, Shipping (non-party); Mieczyslaw Lesz, Internal Trade (Workers); Tadeusz Dietrich, Finance (Workers); Wladyslaw Bienkowski, Education (Workers); Stefan Zolkiewski, Schools of Higher Learning (Workers); Tadeusz Galinski, Culture and Art (Workers); Stanislaw Zawadzki, Labor and Social Welfare (Workers); Marian Rybicki, Justice (Workers); Rajmund Baranski, Health (non-party); Zygmunt Moskwa, Communication (Democratic); Jerzy Sztachelski, without Portfolio, Chairman of the Office for Religious Affairs (Workers); Stanislaw Sroka (Workers), in charge of Communal Economy. The last ministry is in liquidation.

PRESS

Name of Paper	Representation
Trybuna Ludu (daily, Warsaw)	United Workers' Party
Zycie Warszawy (daily, Warsaw)	Government
Glos Pracy (daily, Warsaw)	Trade Unions
Zolnierz Wolnosci (daily, Warsaw)	Polish Army
Dziennik Baltycki (daily, Gdansk)	Government
Dziennik Polski (daily, Krakow)	Government
Dziennik Ludowy (daily, Warsaw)	United Peasant Party
Glos Wielkopolski (daily, Poznan)	Government
Dziennik Zachodni (daily, Katowice)	Government
Kurier Polski (daily, Warsaw)	Democratic Party
Kurier Szczecinski (daily, Szczecin)	Government
Gazeta Robotnicza (daily, Wroclaw)	United Workers' Party
Slowo Powszechne (daily, Warsaw)	Catholic-Social
Kierunki (weekly, Warsaw)	Catholic-Social
Tygodnik Demokratyczny (weekly, Warsaw)	Democratic Party
Chlopska Droga (weekly, Warsaw)	United Workers' Party
Polityka (weekly, Warsaw)	Government
Rolnik Polski (thrice weekly, Warsaw)	Government
Zielony Sztandar (weekly, Warsaw)	United Peasant Party
Szpilki (weekly, Warsaw)	Communist, satirical
Nowa Kultura (weekly, Warsaw)	Communist, literary
Nowe Drogi (monthly, Warsaw)	United Workers' Party
Ekonomista (quarterly, Warsaw)	Government
Gospodarka Planowa (monthly, Warsaw)	Government
Prawo i Zycie (twice weekly, Warsaw)	Government, legal
Tygodnik Powszechny (weekly, Cracow)	Catholic
Tworczosc (monthly, Cracow)	Communist, literary

PORTUGAL

Capital: Lisbon
Area: 35,490 square miles
Population: 8,765,000 (1955 estimate)

President
REAR ADMIRAL AMÉRICO DEUS RODRIGUES THOMAZ
Elected June 8, 1958; assumed office August 9, 1958,
for seven-year term

Cabinet
Non-partisan
Reorganized August 14, 1958

Premier
DR. ANTÓNIO DE OLIVEIRA SALAZAR

PARLIAMENT

CORPORATIVE CHAMBER	NATIONAL ASSEMBLY
President: LUIS SUPICO PINTO	*Election of November 3, 1957 (four-year term)*
Members are appointed representing the various economic, administrative, moral, and cultural associations making up the Portuguese Corporative System.	*President:* DR. ALBINO SOARES PINTO DOS REIS, JR.
	Members are elected by the citizen electors.
Number of members varies.	Number of members 120

RECENT POLITICAL EVENTS

Portugal is a unitary corporative republic. Its constitution, adopted on March 19, 1933, and revised on June 11, 1951, provides for the popular election of a President for a term of seven years, and of a National Assembly of 120 members for a term of four years. In addition, a Corporative Chamber, composed of a variable number of members representing the various economic, administrative, moral and cultural associations, acts in an advisory capacity to the National Assembly.

A Council of State, constituted on April 11, 1933, consists of the following ex-officio members: the Premier; the Presidents of the National Assembly, Corporative Chamber, and Supreme Court; and the Attorney General of the Republic. In addition, provision is made for ten life members, appointed by the President. The Council renders opinions to the Supreme Court on the political eligibility of presidential candidates, advises the President in connection with certain of his powers relating to the National Assembly, determines the physical fitness of the President when especially convoked to do so, and issues opinions whenever this is considered necessary by the President. It may also postpone elections following the dissolution of the National Assembly. The President appoints the Premier, who in turn selects the Cabinet. The Cabinet is not responsible to the Assembly.

PORTUGAL

Following the death on April 18, 1951, of Marshal Carmona, who had occupied the Presidency since 1926, presidential elections were held on July 22, 1951. In these elections the National Union and the Administration backed General Francisco Higino Craveiro Lopes, of the Army Air Force. At the November 1953, elections for the National Assembly the National Union was opposed in three election districts by democratic candidates with no formal party organization. All the National Union candidates, however, were elected, as they were again in 1957.

The Government was reorganized by decree-law on August 1, 1950, at which time a Ministry of Defense was created for defense planning, a Ministry of the Presidency was established to function immediately under the Premier, and a new Ministry of Corporations and Social Security was set up.

The first step was taken on August 26, 1956, to complete the corporative character of the régime with the passage of a government bill establishing the statutes of the "corporations" to cover the fields of Agriculture, Industry, Commerce, Transport and Tourism, Banking and Insurance, and Fishing and Canning.

In the 1958 Presidential elections, the Government candidate, Admiral Thomaz, was elected. Upon taking office he requested Dr. Salazar to continue as President of the Council of Ministers. The Cabinet was reorganized on August 13–14, 1958.

PARTY PROGRAMS AND LEADERS

Since the military revolution of 1926 and the dissolution of the old Parliament, the party system in the ordinary sense has ceased to exist. Pro-Government political forces have in general adhered to the National Union (see below) while remnants of some of the old parties have from time to time contributed to the formation of opposition coalitions, such as the Movement of Democratic Unity (M.U.D.), formed in 1945 but outlawed in 1948 as a Communist front, and the more recent National Democratic Movement (M.N.D.), which is now also outlawed.

NATIONAL UNION (União Nacional): A semi-official political association formed to work for the progress of Portugal and drawn from all classes of society, regardless of previous political affiliations or religious beliefs.

Leaders: Dr. António de Oliveira Salazar, President of Central Committee; Dr. Albino Soares Pinto dos Reis, Jr., Vice-President of Central Committee; and Dr. João Pinto da Costa Leite, President of Executive Committee. The Central Committee consists of 11 members and the Executive Committee, which was reorganized July 4, 1957, of 5 members.

THE CABINET

The members of the Cabinet are: Dr. Antonio de Oliveira Salazar (Premier), Dr. Pedro Theotonio Pereira (Presidency), General Julio Carlos Alves Dias Botelho Moniz (Defense), Lt. Col. Arnaldo Schulz (Interior), Dr. João Antunes Varela (Justice), Dr. António Manuel Pinto Barbosa (Finance), Colonel Afonso Magalhaes de Almeida Fernandes (Army), Commodore Fernando Quintanilha de Mendonça Dias (Navy), Dr. Marcelo Gonçalves Nunes Duarte Matias (Foreign Affairs), Engineer Eduardo de Arantes e Oliveira (Public Works), Commodore Vasco Lopes Alves (Overseas Territories), Professor Francisco Leite Pinto (Education), Engineer José Nascimento Ferreira Dias, Jr. (Economy), Engineer Carlos Gomes da Silva Ribeiro (Communications), Dr. Henrique Veiga de Macedo (Corporations), Dr. Henrique de Miranda Vasconcellos Martins de Carvalho (Health).

PRESS

Unless otherwise noted, papers are published in the capital city.
(*m.* morning; *e.* evening)

Name of Paper	Character	Proprietor, Editor, etc.
Diario de Lisboa (*e.*)	Liberal republican.	Renascença Gráfica (*Prop.*) Norberto Lopes (*Dir.*)
Diario da Manhã (*m.*)	Organ of National Union; semi-official Government paper.	Companhia Nacional Editora (*Prop.*) José Manuel da Costa (*Dir.*)
Diario de Noticias (*m.*)	Conservative; long-established paper, with foreign news service; large circulation.	Empreza Nacional de Publicidade (*Prop.*) Augusto de Castro (*Dir.*)
Diario do Governo	Government gazette.	Imprensa Nacional (*Prop.*)
Diario Ilustrado	Independent.	Manuel Nunes Correa (*Dir.*)
Diario Popular (*e.*)	Conservative; foreign news service.	Martinho Nobre de Melo (*Dir.*)
Jornal do Comércio (*m.*)	Independent; conservative; long-established paper; influential in commercial and industrial circles.	Fausto Lopo de Carvalho (*Dir.*)
Novidades (*m.*)	Organ of Catholic Church.	Rev. Avelino Gonçalves (*Dir.*)
Republica (*e.*)	Republican; left tendency.	Carvalhão Duarte (*Dir.*)
O Século (*m.*)	Independent; progressive republican; foreign news service.	Sociedade Nacional de Tipografia (*Prop.*) J. Pereira da Rosa (*Dir.*)
A Voz (*m.*)	Conservative Catholic; monarchistic.	Empreza A Voz (*Prop.*) Pedro Correia Marques (*Dir.*)
Anglo-Portuguese News (weekly)	British weekly, includes articles in Portuguese.	Luís Marques (*Dir.*)

PROVINCIAL DAILY PAPERS

O Correio do Minho (Braga)	Organ of National Union.	Manuel Araújo (*Dir.*)
Diario do Minho (Braga)	Catholic.	A. Luis Vaz (*Dir.*)
Diario de Coimbra (Coimbra)	Independent.	Alvaro dos Santos Madeira (*Dir.*)
Diario do Alentejo (Beja)	Independent.	M. A. Engana (*Dir.*)
Democracia do Sul (Evora)	Republican; liberal.	João da Silva (*Dir.*)
Noticias de Evora (Evora)	Conservative.	Joaquim dos Santos Reis (*Dir.*)
Diario do Norte (*e.*) (Oporto)	Independent; popular.	Dr. António Cruz (*Dir.*)
Primeiro de Janeiro (*m.*) (Oporto)	Liberal Republican.	M. Pinto de Azevedo, Jr. (*Dir.*)
O Comércio do Porto (*m.*) (Oporto)	Organ of commerce and industry in the North.	Fortunato Seara Cardoso (*Prop.*)
Jornal de Noticias (*m.*) (Oporto)	Progressive; popular.	M. Pacheco de Miranda (*Dir.*)

RUMANIA

Capital: Bucharest
Area: 92,000 square miles (1947 estimate)
Population: 17,489,794 (1956 estimate)

Praesidium of the Grand National Assembly (19 members)
ION GHEORGHE MAURER (President)
Elected by the Assembly on January 11, 1958

Cabinet

All ministers are members of the Rumanian Workers' (Communist) Party or are non-Party technical experts selected by the Party.

Premier
CHIVU STOICA
Proclaimed by the National Assembly on October 3, 1955

PARLIAMENT
(Grand National Assembly)
Election of February 3, 1957 (four-year term)

All 437 Deputies were the candidates of the Front of the People's Democracy. No opposition candidates were presented in any election district. The Front is officially a roof organization for the Rumanian Workers' Party (created by a merger of the Communists and a part of the Socialist Party in January, 1948), mass organizations and the general public. Parliament has only nominal functions.

POLITICAL EVENTS SINCE 1944

In consequence of the invasion of Rumania by the Soviet Army in August 1944, King Michael directed a *coup d'état* which overthrew the Antonescu Government. Rumania ceased hostilities and accepted armistice terms (September 12) signed in Moscow by Marshal R. Y. Malinovsky, acting on behalf of Great Britain and the United States as well as the USSR. Premier Antonescu was arrested and the King called upon General Constantin Sanatescu to form a new Government, which he did with himself as Premier. He was replaced on December 7, 1944, by General Nicolae Radescu.

At the Potsdam Conference (July 17–August 2, 1945), the three principal Allied Powers expressed their intention to conclude a treaty of peace with a recognized Rumanian Government which should be "broadly representative of all democratic elements of the population."

At the Moscow Conference of Foreign Ministers in December 1945, the question of recognition was discussed. Britain and the United States agreed to recognize the Rumanian Government when satisfied that two truly representative members of two important political parties not then represented had been brought into the Government, and when satisfactory assurances had been given regarding free elections and freedom of speech, press, religion and association.

On January 8, 1946, the Groza Government was broadened by the inclusion of two Ministers without Portfolio, members of the National Peasant and Liberal Parties, and gave assurances of fundamental public freedoms and agreed to hold early "free and unfettered elections." The British and American Governments later permitted the naming of Rumanian Political Representatives at London and at Washington. Opposing the Government coalition in the elections of November 19, 1946, were Dr. I. Maniu's National Peasant, C. Bratianu's National Liberal and Petrescu's Independent Socialist Parties. Results were decried by this opposition as completely fraudulent, the two Ministers without Portfolio resigned, and public statements of the American and British Governments characterized the elections as failing to comply with the assurances given by the Rumanian Government in conformity with the Moscow Agreement.

The principal opposition leader, Dr. Maniu, was tried and sentenced to life imprisonment on November 11, 1947, on charges of high treason. On December 30, 1947, King Michael was forced to abdicate and later left the country. The Government proclaimed the "People's Republic," and vested supreme authority in a five-member Praesidium headed by Mihail Sadoveanu, the then President of Parliament, pending the adoption of a new Constitution. Systematic measures were taken by the Groza Government to suppress all organized opposition. The new Constitution was adopted on April 13, 1948.

During 1948 and 1949, Government leaders concentrated on consolidating their position under the new Constitution broadly modeled on that of the Soviet Union. The principal economic enterprises were nationalized, educational and religious laws revised, the State's administrative apparatus reorganized to provide "People's Councils" or local Soviets, and the first collective farms were introduced. In 1950 the process of nationalization and collectivization was carried still further. In December 1950 a one-party election was held to "consolidate the dictatorship of the proletariat" and to approve 80,000 candidates of the People's Democratic Front for People's Councils. In 1952 a number of leaders were removed from the Politburo of the Workers' Party (Teohari Georgescu, Vasile Luca, Ana Pauker, among others). A new Constitution was voted on September 24, 1952. In December 1953, new elections for the "People's Councils" were held.

In March 1957 the Central Committee reduced the number of Cabinet ministries from thirty to sixteen, the office of First Deputy Premier was abolished and five Deputy Premiers named. A sixth was named in 1957 and a seventh in 1958.

PARTY PROGRAMS AND LEADERS

Rumanian Workers' Party: The only Party now permitted to exist in Rumania. It has a doctrinaire Communist program. In *foreign policy:* follows the USSR.

Leaders: The members of the Politburo of the Workers' Party are: Gheorghe Gheorghiu-Dej (First Secretary), Gheorghe Apostol, Emil Bodnăras, Petre Borilă, Nicolae Ceausescu, Chivu Stoica, Alexandru Drăghici, Alexandru Moghioros, Constantin Pîrvulescu (Chairman of the Party Control Commission).

COUNCIL OF MINISTERS

Premier—Chivu Stoica
Deputy Premiers: Emil Bodnăras
                 Petre Borilă
                 Alexandru Moghioros

RUMANIA 167

Stefan Voitec
Alexandru Bîrlădeanu
Gherasim Popa
Atanase Joja

Ministers

Agriculture: Ion Cozma
Trade: Marcel Popescu
Construction and Building Materials: Mihai Suder
Consumer Goods Industry: Stefan Voitec
Heavy Industry: Gherasim Popa
Oil and Chemical Industry: Mihail Florescu
Education and Culture: Atanase Joja
Transport and Communications: Emil Bodnăras
Affairs of Local Organs and State Administration: Petre Costache
Foreign Affairs: Avram Bunaciu
Internal Affairs: Col. Gen. Alexandru Drăghici
Armed Forces: Col. Gen. Leontin Sălăjan
Justice: Gheorghe Diaconescu
Health and Social Welfare: Dr. Voinea Marinescu
Finance: Aurel Vijoli
State Planning Commission: Gheorghe Gaston Marin
State Control Commission: Dumitru Coliu

PRESS

Only papers controlled by or affiliated with the Government exist in Rumania at present.

Name of Paper	Affiliation	Editor
Scinteia	Official Organ of Communist Party.	Sorin Toma
Rominia Libera	Organ of the People's Councils.	Mircea Rădulescu
Steagul Rosu	Organ of People's Councils of Bucharest.	Bucur Brănisteanu
Scînteia Tineretului	Official Organ of Working Youth.	Dumitru Popescu
Munca	Trade Union Council Organ.	Al. Bondoc

NEWS AGENCY

Agerpres	Official telegraph agency.	Teodor Marinescu (Dir. Gen.)

EL SALVADOR

Capital: San Salvador
Area: Approximately 8,260 square miles
Population: 2,350,201 (1957 estimate)

President
Lt. Col. José María Lemus
Elected March 4, 1956; assumed office September 14, 1956, for six-year term

PARLIAMENT
(Asamblea Legislativa)
President: Dr. Victor Manuel Esquivel
Number of Members 54

In November 1945, the 1886 Constitution was restored by the Assembly; but on December 14, 1948, a revolutionary Junta deposed President Salvador Castaneda Castro. Elections for a Constitutional Assembly were held in 1950 and a new Constitution became effective on September 14, 1950.

POLITICAL PARTIES
The five leading political parties in El Salvador are: Partido Revolucionario Unificación Democrática (PRUD), Partido Acción Renovadora (PAR), Partido Independiente Democrático (PID), Partido Auténtico Constitucional (PAC), and the Partido Acción Nacional (PAN).

THE CABINET
Members of the Cabinet are: Dr. Alfredo Ortiz Mancía (Foreign Affairs); Dr. Luis Rivas Palacios (Interior); Dr. Alfonso Rochac (Economy); Dr. Mauricio Guzmán (Education); Dr. Humberto Costa (Finance); General Adán Parada (Defense); Dr. Ramón Avila Agacio (Labor); Federico Garcia Prieto (Agriculture); Dr. Humberto Escapini (Public Health and Social Welfare); Roberto A. Parker (Public Works); Dr. Rafael Antonio Carballo (Justice).

PRESS
Unless otherwise noted, papers are published in the capital city.

Name of Paper	Circulation	Proprietor, Editor, etc.
El Diario de Hoy (morning)	35,000	N. Viera Altamirano (Prop.)
Diario Latino (evening)	10,000	Miguel Pinto (Ed.)
Diario Oficial	2,000	J. Edgardo Salgado (Dir.)
La Prensa Gráfica (morning & Sunday)	44,000	Dutriz Hermanos (Prop.)
Tribuna Libre (morning)	10,000	F. J. Siero y Rojas (Dir.)
Diario de Occidente (Santa Ana)	1,500	Alfredo Parada (Dir.)
El Heraldo de Sonsonate (Sonsonate)	1,000	Fernando Garzona (Prop.)
Diario de Oriente (San Miguel)	1,000	C. Augusto Osegueda (Prop.)
Tiempos Nuevos (weekly)	3,000	Francisco Siero y Rojas (Dir.)

SOUTH AFRICA

Capital: Pretoria (seat of administration)
Cape Town (seat of legislature)
Population: 14,418,000 (1958 estimate) of which 3,011,000 are White

Sovereign
QUEEN ELIZABETH II

Governor-General
DR. ERNEST GEORGE JANSEN
Assumed office January 1, 1951

Cabinet
National Party
Appointed October 24, 1958

Prime Minister
DR. H. F. VERWOERD
Assumed office September 2, 1958

PARLIAMENT

UPPER CHAMBER (Senate)
Election of November 25, 1955 (for ten years)
President: C. A. VAN NIEKERK (National)

Parties	Representation
National	77
United	8
Representatives of the Natives	4*
Total	89

*Two are Liberal Party members, two independent.

LOWER CHAMBER (House of Assembly)
Election of April 16, 1958 (for five years)
Speaker: J. H. CONRADIE (National)

Parties	Representation
National	103
United	53
Representatives of the Natives	3*
Representatives of the Coloreds	4†
Total	163

*Two are Liberal Party members, one independent.
† One United Party, three independent.

PARTY PROGRAMS AND LEADERS

NATIONAL PARTY: On June 23, 1951, Prime Minister D. F. Malan and N. C. Havenga, Minister of Finance, issued a joint statement, as leaders of the National and Afrikaner Parties, recommending a merger of the two parties to form a united National front. The basic aims of this merged party were: furthering the welfare of South Africa and its people, and the development of an effective sense of national self-sufficiency based on undivided loyalty to South Africa and the acknowledgement of the equal rights of Afrikaans- and English-speaking South Africans. The National Party favors *apartheid* (racial separation), a republic separated from the British Crown, but created only by the broad will of the people, through a special mandate. It favors White immigration of "desirable people" with "due regard" to the interests of "the established population." Equal language rights of the Afrikaans and English-speaking sections of the country are guaranteed. Education is to give proper consideration to the Christian National basis of the State. The need for economic advancement is recognized through promoting self-sufficiency and expanding trade relations; on the financial side, confidence in the economic future of South Africa is to be maintained by protecting its monetary system and capital resources. The civilized worker is to be protected against displacement by uncivilized labor, and his position and living standards would be likewise protected.

On October 22, 1951, the two parties formally merged. This merger was an important development as it meant a united political front composed of the majority of the Afrikaans-speaking people.

In the 1951 session of Parliament there was passed by simple majority the Separate Representation of Voters Act, removing Colored voters from the common roll. This Act was invalidated by the Appellate Court (the highest Court of the Union). The Government accepted the decision but announced that it would go to the country with the Colored voters on the common roll and bid for re-election on the removal of the Colored voters to a separate roll, and the "sovereignty of Parliament." In the 1953 election the National Party won, increasing its seats in the House from 86 to 94. In 1956 the Appellate Court validated Government legislation providing separate Colored voters rolls and direct representation for this group in Parliament.

On November 30, 1954, Dr. D. F. Malan retired as Prime Minister and National Party leader and was succeeded by J. G. Strijdom, Transvaal National leader and previously Minister of Lands and Irrigation. N. C. Havenga, Deputy Prime Minister, announced his retirement from public life on Strijdom's election as National Party leader.

In the general election of April 16, 1958, the National Party increased both its parliamentary majority and its popular majority. For the first time in the Union's history the White electorate is represented by only two parties.

Mr. Strijdom died on August 24, 1958. On September 2, Dr. H. F. Verwoerd was elected Leader of the National Party.

Leaders: Dr. H. F. Verwoerd (Transvaal), C. R. Swart (Orange Free State), Dr. T. E. Dönges (Cape Province), W. A. Maree (Natal), and other members of the Cabinet.

UNITED PARTY: In the 1943 general election, which was fought largely on the war issue (see previous editions of the *Political Handbook of the World*), the United Party, led by the late Field Marshal Smuts, won a clear-cut victory and emerged with a substantial majority in Parliament. In October and November 1945, the South African Labor Party and the Dominion Party, respectively, withdrew from the coalition which formed the wartime Government.

The United Party, according to its 1958 campaign, stands for furtherance of national unity by upholding the Act of Union of 1910, the equality of the Afrikaans-speaking and English-speaking sections, and cooperation with other countries in international affairs. It maintains that sovereign independence is fully consonant with membership in, and cooperation with, the Commonwealth. It advocates a progressive social welfare and labor policy but rejects socialism and "cradle-to-grave" State responsibility. It recognizes the right of White workers to protection against unequal competition from non-White labor. Its agricultural policy is based on collective bargaining and soil conservation. Main principles of the United Party's Native policy (restated at the Party's 1954 congress) are: (1) European leadership with justice, (2) economic integration, (3) social and residential segregation, which recognizes the permanence of non-White settlement in urban areas, and (4) political development, including additional parliamentary representation (by Whites). The United Party also stresses the creation of a climate in which private enterprise can develop to its full potential.

The Party was defeated in the 1948, 1953, and 1958 general elections. Although winning about half the popular vote (allowing for uncontested seats), it now has only 53 out of 163 seats in the lower house.

Leader: Sir de Villiers Graaff.

THE SOUTH AFRICAN LABOR PARTY: With the end of the pact with the Nationalist Party made in 1924 and continued in 1929, and the split in the party, the South African Labor Party lost practically all of its former strength and importance. It continued to win seats in Parliament, however. In 1953 it formed an electoral pact with the United Party, but after the election both parties decided to end the pact. The Labor Party's two members of Parliament were defeated in the 1958 election. The Party is virtually extinct today.

Leader: Alex Hepple (Parliamentary Leader).

LIBERAL PARTY: Formed after 1953 general election. Seeks to build a common society with common citizenship irrespective of race. It aims at a system of universal adult franchise. It opposes all laws which impose disabilities on citizens by reasons of their race or color. It recognizes private enterprise as the basis of the South African economy; however, it supports the right and duty of the State to intervene to prevent exploitation and to redress gross maldistribution of wealth. It sees its principal task at present as the maintenance of contact and goodwill between the different racial groups in South Africa. No party members have been elected to Parliament, but two Native Representatives in the House and two in the Senate are Party members.

Leader: Alan Paton (National Chairman).

THE CABINET

A new Cabinet entered office on October 24, 1958. It was enlarged from 14 to 16 ministers, and ministerial functions were re-organized. Members of the Cabinet are: Dr. H. F. Verwoerd (Prime Minister), C. R. Swart (Justice), P. O. Sauer (Lands, Forestry, and Public Works), E. H. Louw (External Affairs), Dr. T. E. Donges (Finance), F. C. Erasmus (Defense), B. J. Schoeman (Transport), J. F. Naude (Interior), J. J. Serfontein (Education, Arts and Science, Social Welfare and Pensions), J. de Klerk (Labor and Mines), M. D. C. de Wet Nel (Bantu Administration and Development), P. M. K. le Roux (Agricultural Technical Services and Water Affairs), W. A. Maree (Bantu Education), Dr. N. Diederichs (Economic Affairs), Dr. J. A. M. Hertzog (Posts and Telegraphs and Health), D. C. H. Uys (Agricultural Economics and Marketing).

PRESS

Name of Paper	Political Orientation	Proprietor, Editor, etc.
Cape Argus (Cape Town) (evening)	United Party; Argus group.	M. Broughton (*Ed.*)
Cape Times (Cape Town)	United Party.	Victor Norton (*Ed.*)

SOUTH AFRICA

Name of Paper	Political Orientation	Proprietor, Editor, etc.
Die Burger (Cape Town)	National Party; in Afrikaans.	P. J. Cillie (*Ed.*)
The Friend (Bloemfontein)	United Party; Argus group.	W. W. McKenzie (*Ed.*)
Die Volksblad (Bloemfontein) (evening)	Official organ of National Party in Orange Free State; in Afrikaans.	H. H. Dreyer (*Ed.*)
Natal Daily News (Durban) (evening)	United Party; Argus group.	J. S. M. Simpson (*Ed.*)
Natal Mercury (Durban)	Independent.	John Robinson (*Ed.*)
Sunday Tribune (Durban)	United Party; Argus group.	G. Makepeace (*Ed.*)
Daily Dispatch (East London)	Independent.	V. A. Barber (*Ed.*)
Dagbreek en Sondagnuus (Johannesburg) (weekly)	National Party; in Afrikaans.	W. van Heerden (*Ed.*)
Die Vaderland (Johannesburg) (evening)	National Party; in Afrikaans.	J. Wilcocks (*Ed.*)
Golden City Post (Johannesburg) (weekly)	Independent.	C. L. Eprile (*Ed.*)
World (Johannesburg) (twice-weekly)	Independent.	B. Legwate (*Act. Ed.*)
Rand Daily Mail (Johannesburg)	United Party.	L. O. V. Gander (*Ed.*)
Sunday Express (Johannesburg)	United Party.	H. Huxham (*Ed.*)
Sunday Times (Johannesburg)	United Paper.	Joel Mervis (*Ed.*)
The Star (Johannesburg) (evening)	United Party; Argus group.	Horace Flather (*Ed.*)
Die Transvaler (Johannesburg)	Transvaal National Party; in Afrikaans.	J. J. Kruger (*Ed.*)
Diamond Fields Advertiser (Kimberley)	United Party; Argus group.	D. Brechin (*Ed.*)
Natal Witness (Pietermaritzburg)	Independent.	E. R. Bridges (*Ed.*)
Die Oosterlig (Port Elizabeth)	National Party.	D. C. de Villiers (*Ed.*)
Eastern Province Herald (Port Elizabeth)	United Party.	A. M. Pollock (*Ed.*)
Evening Post (Port Elizabeth)	United Party.	J. G. Sutherland (*Ed.*)
Pretoria News (Pretoria) (evening)	United Party; Argus group.	Jack Pattern (*Ed.*)
Die Landstem (Cape Town) (weekly)	Independent; in Afrikaans.	P. J. Beukes (*Ed.*)
Drum (Johannesburg) (monthly)	Independent.	T. H. Hopkinson (*Ed.*)
New Age (Cape Town and Johannesburg) (weekly)	Communist.	Brian Bunting (*Ed.*)
Die Stem (Johannesburg) (weekly)	United Party.	A. A. van der Merwe (*Ed.*)
Contact (Cape Town) (fortnightly)	Liberal.	Patrick Duncan (*Ed.*)
The Graphic (Durban) (weekly)	Independent.	H. M. Pillay (*Ed.*)

NEWS AGENCY

South African Press Association	Independent; owned by South African daily press.	D. Friedman (*Ed.-in-Chief*)

SPAIN

Capital: Madrid
Area: 194,945 square miles
Population: 29,431,000 (1957 estimate)

Chief of State
GENERAL FRANCISCO FRANCO Y BAHAMONDE
Assumed leadership of the Revolution in 1936

Cabinet
Military-Civilian
Reconstructed February 25, 1957

Premier
GENERAL FRANCISCO FRANCO

PARLIAMENT
(Cortes)
President: ESTEBAN BILBAO EGUÍA
Number of members 577

The Cortes is composed of Procuradores, consisting of members who hold office by virtue of some other position, and of certain elected members.

Ex-officio members of the Cortes are the Cabinet Ministers; the Falange National Councilors; Presidents of the State Council, of the Supreme Court, of the Institute of Spain, and of the Supreme Council of Military Justice; Chiefs of the National Syndicates; mayors of the fifty provincial capitals, and of Ceuta and Melilla; and the Rectors of the Universities.

The elective members of the Cortes are representatives of the National Syndicates, other than National Chiefs (the total of syndical representatives may not exceed one-third of the total number of Procuradores); one representative of the municipalities (other than the provincial capitals) for each of the fifty provinces; one representative each of the fifty provincial governments, including the Canary Islands; two representatives each of the Institute of Spain, of the Superior Council for Scientific Investigation, Institute of Civil Engineers, of the Bar Association and of the Medical Association; one representative each of the Associations of Pharmacists, Veterinarians, Architects, Doctors and Bachelors of Science, Philosophy and Arts, Notaries, Property Registrars and Proctors of Courts; and three representatives of the Chambers of Commerce. The Chief of State may appoint no more than fifty Procuradores from the ecclesiastical, military, administrative and social spheres, or because of "eminent services to Spain."

Members of the Cortes must be Spanish, twenty-one years of age, and without political disability. Procuradores so named by virtue of another office lose the post upon losing the other office, those designated by the Chief of State upon revocation by him; the remaining hold office for three years and are eligible for re-election. The Chief of State appoints the President, the Vice-Presidents, and the Secretaries. The President in agreement with the Government appoints Committees.

The Cortes in full or in committee shall be heard for ratification of treaties on matters within its competence. In addition to examining and submitting draft laws of the Government, the committees may submit proposals for law to the President of the Cortes, who will include them in the Order of the Day. There is no provision for the introduction of legislation by individual members of the Cortes, and no law can go into effect without the approval of the Chief of State. The President of the Cortes will return draft laws as approved by the Cortes for submission to the Chief of State's approval. The latter may return laws to the Cortes for new study.

POLITICAL EVENTS SINCE 1936

Following the election of February 16, 1936, when the Left parties won a majority in the Cortes, the political situation became more and more confused, until armed revolt under Army leadership broke out on July 18, 1936. The Republican Government capitulated on March 29, 1939.

In January 1938 the organic laws establishing the Spanish Syndicalist State were promulgated by the Burgos Government. While these laws continue as the basis for the present régime, the Law of Succession signed by General Franco on July 26, 1947, declared Spain to be a kingdom with Franco as Chief of State.

The Law of July 17, 1942, and Decrees of October 15, 1942, and March 9, 1946, established a new Cortes, as "the superior organ of participation of the Spanish people in the tasks of the State," with its principal mission "the preparation and elaboration of the Laws, without prejudice to the sanction pertaining to the Chief of State."

On June 7, 1947, the Cortes passed an act of succession to the headship of the State and this was ratified by a referendum on July 6, 1947, and reaffirmed by General Franco in 1955. The act provides for a Council of Regency and a Council of the Realm who shall, in case the Headship of the State should fall vacant, propose to the Cortes a person of royal descent as King; or, no one of royal descent being qualified, propose one of proper capacities as Regent. The new Head of the State, whether he be King or Regent, must be male, Spanish, and thirty years of age. The act also listed and established the fundamental laws of the Nation.

PARTIES

By decree of General Franco, there exists only one "political entity" in Spain, the Falange Española Tradicionalista y de los JONS (Juntas de Ofensiva Nacional Sindicalista), which is under his control. It is not referred to as a party but as "The National Movement." Various shades of political opinion exist apart from the Falange, but the expression of these opinions through political activity is not permitted.

THE CABINET

The present Cabinet is composed as follows: General Francisco Franco (Premier), Luis Carrero Blanco (Minister Undersecretary of the Presidency), Fernando Maria Castiella y Maíz (Foreign Affairs), Antonio Iturmendi Bañales (Justice), Lt. Gen. Antonio Barroso y Sánchez-Guerra (Army),

SPAIN

Admiral Felipe José Abárzuza y Oliva (Navy), Mariano Navarro Rubio (Finance), Camilo Alonso Vega (Interior), Jorge Vigón Suero-Diaz (Public Works), Jesús Rubio Garcia-Mina (Education), Fermín Sanz Orrio (Labor), Joaquín Planell Riera (Industry), Cirilo Cánovas Garcia (Agriculture), Lt. Gen. José Rodriguez y Diaz de Lecea (Air), José Solis Ruiz (National Movement), Alberto Ullastres Calvo (Commerce), Gabriel Arias-Salgado y de Cubas (Information and Tourism), José Luis de Arrese y Magra (Housing), Pedro Gual Villalbi (Minister Without Portfolio).

PRESS

Unless otherwise noted, the newspapers listed are dailies which are published six times a week; that is, exclusive of Sunday evening or Monday morning. In the large cities there is a paper which comes out only on Monday morning and is called the *Hoja Oficial del Lunes*. It is edited by the press association of the city where it is printed.

The entire press is subject to control by the Ministry of Information and Tourism.

Name of Paper	Character	Proprietor, Editor, etc.
PAPERS PUBLISHED IN MADRID		
A. B. C.	Monarchist.	Luis Calvo (*Dir.*)
Arriba	Falange Organ.	Vicente Cebrián (*Act. Dir.*)
El Alcázar	Traditionalist.	Jesús María Zuloaga (*Dir.*)
Hoja Oficial del Lunes (Mondays only)	Edited by Press Association of Madrid.	Pedro Gómez Aparicio (*Ed.*)
Informaciones	Independent; Catholic.	Ramón Sierra Bustamante (*Dir.*)
Madrid	Independent.	Juan Pujol (*Dir.*)
Pueblo	National Syndicalist Organ.	Emilio Romero (*Dir.*)
Ya	Catholic action.	Aquilino Morcillo (*Dir.*)
PROVINCIAL NEWSPAPERS		
A. B. C. (Seville)	Monarchist.	Antonio Olmedo Delgado (*Dir.*)
Baleares (Palma de Mallorca)	Falange Organ.	Waldo de Mier (*Dir.*)
El Correo Catalán (Barcelona)	Carlist Organ.	Claudio Colomer Marqués (*Dir.*)
Diario de Barcelona (Barcelona)	Monarchist.	Enrique del Castillo Yurrita (*Dir.*)
El Correo Español (Bilbao)	Independent.	Alejandro Echevarría (*Ed.*)
Diario Vasco (San Sebastian)	Independent.	Juan M. Peña Ibañez (*Ed.*)
Faro de Vigo (Vigo)	Independent.	Francisco Leal Insua (*Ed.*)
La Gaceta del Norte (Bilbao)	Catholic.	Antonio Gonzalez (*Ed.*)
Hierro (Bilbao)	Falange Organ.	Bernardo Bureba Muro (*Ed.*)
Levante (Valencia)	Falange Organ.	Sabino Alonso Fueyo (*Dir.*)
Noticiero Universal (Barcelona)	Independent.	Luis G. Manegat (*Ed.*)
Las Provincias (Valencia)	Independent.	Martin Domínguez Barberá (*Ed.*)
El Pueblo Gallego (Vigo)	Falange Organ.	Feliz Moreno Perez (*Ed.*)
Solidaridad Nacional (Barcelona)	Falange Organ.	Luis Santamarina (*Ed.*)
Sur (Málaga)	Falange Organ.	Francisco Sanz Cagigas (*Dir.*)
La Vanguardia Española (Barcelona)	Independent.	Luis de Galinsoga (*Ed.*) Carlos Godo y Vals (*Pub.*)
Hoy (Badajoz)	Catholic.	Gregorio Hermino Penilla (*Dir.*)
El Heraldo de Aragon (Zaragoza)	Independent.	Antonio Bruned Mompeon (*Dir.*)
El Correo de Andalucia (Seville)	Catholic.	José Montoto (*Dir.*)
El Ideal de Granáda (Granáda)		Candido Ortiz (*Dir.*)
La Voz de España (San Sebastian)	Falange Organ.	Jesús Revuelta Imaz (*Ed.*)
NEWS AGENCIES		
EFE	Official news agency.	Manuel Aznar (*Dir.*)
CIFRA	Local news agency; domestic branch of EFE.	Manuel Aznar (*Dir.*)
MENCHETA	Independent local news agency.	Luis Peris Mencheta (*Dir.*)
LOGOS	Local and foreign; Catholic action.	Manuel Jiménez Quilez (*Dir.*)

SWEDEN

Capital: Stockholm
Area: 173,569 square miles
Population: 7,395,000 (1958 estimate)

Ruler
KING GUSTAF VI ADOLF
Born in 1882; ascended throne October 29, 1950

Cabinet
Social Democratic
Appointed October 31, 1957

Premier
TAGE ERLANDER (Social Democrat)

PARLIAMENT
(Riksdag)

UPPER CHAMBER*
(Första Kammaren)

Speaker: JOHN BERGWALL (Liberal)

Parties	Representation
Social Democratic	79
Liberal	33
Center	22
Conservative	15
Communist	2
Total	151

* One-eighth elected annually by provincial and city councils, *for eight-year terms.*

LOWER CHAMBER
(Andra Kammaren)

Election of June 1, 1958 (for term ending September 1960)

Speaker: S. PATRIK SWENSSON (Social Democrat)

Parties	Representation
Social Democratic	111
Conservative	45
Liberal	38
Center	32
Communist	5
Total	231

PARTY PROGRAMS AND LEADERS

SOCIAL DEMOCRATIC PARTY: A moderate, constitutional, socialist labor party. In *foreign policy:* the Party firmly adheres to the traditional Swedish policy of neutrality, aloof from Great Power alliances, but favors universal cooperation among all peace-loving nations within the framework of the United Nations, and the Nordic Council. Endorses Sweden's participation in European economic cooperation but refuses to extend this cooperation also to the distinctly politico-military field. Favors a strong defense organization as a means of ensuring a policy of "armed neutrality." In *domestic policy:* advocates democracy in management of industry, a certain amount of Government supervision of industry and trade, collective forms of enterprise where this may be suitable, a reasonable redistribution of wealth, and an extensive social insurance system and other public welfare services.

Leaders: Tage Erlander (Premier, President of Party), Gunnar Sträng (Minister of Finance), Torsten Nilsson (Minister for Social Welfare), Sven

SWEDEN

Andersson (Minister of Defense), Sven Aspling (Secretary of Party) and Arne Geijer (President, Trade Union Confederation).

CENTER PARTY: A middle way party, working for a synthesis of liberty and safety. In *foreign policy:* follows the same policy as the Social Democratic Party. In *domestic policy:* favors protection for domestic agriculture, handicraft, trade and industry, particularly small enterprises, reduction of estate and enterprise taxation, farm and industry credit facilities, increase of local self-government and protection of private ownership.

Leaders: Gunnar Hedlund (former Minister of Interior), Lars Eliasson, Nils Hansson and Torsten Bengtson.

LIBERAL PARTY: Consists of people of all social classes and derives large vote from temperance and free-church movements in rural districts, but also includes intellectuals. In *foreign policy:* follows mainly the same policy as the Social Democrats but stresses necessity for close ideological ties with the Western democracies. In *domestic policy:* favors promotion of private enterprise, commerce, handicraft and small industry and abolition of many Government controls.

Leaders: Bertil Ohlin, Waldemar Svensson, Sven Wedén.

CONSERVATIVE PARTY. Represents urban as well as rural population. In *foreign policy:* follows mainly the same policy as the Social Democratic Party but advocates closer cooperation with the Western democracies, and favors a still stronger national defense. In *domestic policy:* favors maintenance of existing private system of production and free enterprise, opposes State control of industry and trade, favors social reforms but only on condition that tax burden does not impede sound development of industry, commerce and agriculture; supports Christian creed and ethical education of youth.

Leaders: Jarl Hjalmarson, Leif Cassel, Gunnar Heckscher.

COMMUNIST PARTY: Party with typical Communist program. In *foreign policy:* advocates cooperation with the USSR and the "people's democracies," violently opposed to Sweden's participation in European economic cooperation, and favors reduced armaments. In *domestic policy:* advocates working classes' interests and nationalization of private industry.

Leader: Hilding Hagberg, Helmer Persson.

THE CABINET

The Social Democratic one-party Cabinet which on October 31, 1957, succeeded the Social Democratic-Agrarian Coalition Government (which had been in office since 1951) comprises the following members: Tage Erlander (Premier), Östen Undén (Foreign Affairs), Ingvar Lindell (Justice), Sven Andersson (Defense), Torsten Nilsson (Social Welfare), Rune Johansson (Interior), Gösta Skoglund (Transportation and Communications), Gunnar Sträng (Finance), Ragnar Edenman (Education), Gösta Netzén (Agriculture), Gunnar Lange (Commerce), Sigurd Lindholm (Civil Service), and Mrs. Ulla Lindström, Herman Kling and Sven Geijerstam (Ministers without Portfolio).

SWEDEN

PRESS

Unless otherwise noted, papers are published in the capital city.

Name of Paper	Circulation	Political Affiliation	Proprietor, Editor, etc.
Aftonbladet	184,000	Social Democratic.	Allan Fagerström (Ed.)
Dagens Nyheter	348,000	Liberal.	Herbert Tingsten (Ed.)
Expressen	347,000	Liberal.	Ivar Harrie (Ed.)
Ny Dag	15,000	Communist.	Gustav Johansson (Ed.)
Stockholms-Tidningen	135,000	Social Democratic.	Victor Vinde (Ed.)
Svenska Dagbladet	129,000	Conservative.	Allan Hernelius (Ed.)
Norrländska Social-Demokarten (Boden)	35,000	Social Democratic.	Lars Fagerström (Ed.)
Göteborgs Handels-och Sjöfarstidning (Gothenburg)	48,000	Liberal.	Harald Wigforss (Ed.)
Göteborgs-Posten (Gothenburg)	225,000	Liberal.	Harry Hjörne (Ed.)
Göteborgs-Tidningen (Gothenburg)	67,000	Liberal.	Ferdinand Lärn (Ed.)
Ny Tid (Gothenburg)	49,000	Social Democratic.	Kaj Björk (Ed.)
Nya Wermlands-Tidningen (Karlstad)	63,000	Conservative.	Gustaf Ander (Ed.)
Östgöta Correspondenten (Linköping)	51,000	Conservative.	Ebbe Johnson (Ed.)
Arbetet (Malmö)	58,000	Social Democratic.	Alvar Alsterdal (Ed.)
Kvällsposten (Malmö)	38,000	Conservative.	Sven Olof Berlin (Ed.)
Skånska Dagbladet (Malmö)	42,000	Center.	Lennart Pettersson (Ed.)
Sydsvenska Dagbladet Snällposten (Malmö)	91,000	Conservative.	Christer Wahlgren (Ed.)
Västerbottens-Kuriren (Umeå)	31,000	Liberal.	Stellan Rosén (Ed.)
Vestmanlands Läns Tidning (Västerås)	38,000	Liberal.	Anders Y. Pers (Ed.)
Upsala Nya Tidning (Upsala)	38,000	Liberal.	Sven-Erik Larsson (Ed.)
Tiden (monthly)		Social Democratic.	Olle Svensson (Ed.)
Politisk Tidskrift (m.)		Center.	Gunnar Söder (Ed.)
Svensk Tidskrift (monthly)		Conservative.	Erik Anners (Ed.)
Industria (monthly)		Industry.	Tell Dahllöf (Ed.)
Affärsvärlden (weekly)		Financial.	Arne Nilsson (Ed.)
Finanstidningen (weekly)		Financial.	Hans von Rosen (Ed.)
Vi (weekly)	552,000	Consumers Cooperative.	Nils Thedin (Ed.)
Svensk Export (m.)		Foreign Trade.	T. Winell (Ed.)
Utrikespolitik (every other month)		Foreign Affairs.	L. Hirschfeldt (Ed.)

PRESS ASSOCIATIONS AND AGENCIES

Tidningarnas Telegrambyrå	Central news agency, owned by Swedish press.	Olof Sundell (Mg. Dir.)
Svensk-Amerikanska Nyhetsbyrån	Independent.	Axel Iveroth (Ch.)
Swedish International Press Bureau	Owned by General Export Association.	E. Hummelgren (Ed.)

SWITZERLAND

Federal capital: Berne
Area: 15,944 square miles
Population: 5,117,000 (1958 estimate)

Federal Council

Composed of seven members, chosen by Federal Assembly for term ending December 31, 1959

Dr. Philipp Etter (Catholic Conservative) Interior
Dr. Max Petitpierre (Radical Democratic) Foreign Affairs
Dr. Friedrich T. Wahlen (Peasants, Artisans and Middle Class) Justice and Police
Dr. Hans Streuli (Radical Democratic) Finance and Customs
Dr. Thomas Holenstein (Catholic Conservative) Public Economy
Paul Chaudet (Radical Democratic) Army
Dr. Giuseppe Lepori (Catholic Conservative) Posts and Railroads

President of the Confederation

Paul Chaudet (Radical Democrat)
Elected by Federal Assembly, December 1958; assumed office January 1, 1959, for one-year term

Vice-President of the Federal Council

Giuseppe Lepori (Catholic Conservative)

FEDERAL ASSEMBLY

(Assemblée fédérale; Bundesversammlung; Assemblea federale)

COUNCIL OF STATES
(Conseil des Etats; Ständerat; Consiglio degli Stati)

Chosen by the 22 cantons of the Confederation, 2 for each canton

President: Dr. Lusser (Catholic Conservative)

Parties	Representation
Catholic Conservative	17
Radical Democratic	12
Socialist	5
Peasants, Artisans and Middle Class	3
Liberal Democratic	3
Democratic and Evangelical	2
Non-Party	2
Total	44

NATIONAL COUNCIL
(Conseil National; Nationalrat; Consiglio Nazionale)

Election of October 1955 (for legislative period ending December 1959)

President: Dr. E. Dietschi (Radical Democratic)

Parties	Representation
Socialist	53
Radical Democratic	50
Catholic Conservative	47
Peasants, Artisans and Middle Class	22
Independents' Party	10
Liberal Democratic	5
Communists (Labor)	4
Democratic and Evangelical	5
Total	196

SWITZERLAND

PARTY PROGRAMS AND LEADERS

RADICAL DEMOCRATIC PARTY: A progressive, middle-class party; brought about the revolution of 1847, which definitely impelled the change from a confederation to a federative state; centralist, responsible for the Constitution of 1874, and in large part for assumption of control of railways by the Federal Government. Favors strengthening of national defense; advocates reform legislation including social measures, factory laws, etc., and use of alcohol and tobacco revenues for social welfare.

Leaders: Max Petitpierre, Dr. Hans Streuli, Paul Chaudet (Members of Federal Council), Aleardo Pini (Member of National Council), Eugen Dietschi (President of the Party); Willy Bretscher, Alfred Schaller, Karl Obrecht, Hermann Häberlin (Members of National Council); François Perréard, Ernest Speiser, Jean-Louis Barrelet (Members of Council of States).

SOCIALIST PARTY: A constitutional and trade-union socialist party, with an active radical wing; adherent of the 2nd International. Advocates wider State ownership and control, direct federal taxation and women's suffrage; its parliamentary success dates from the introduction of proportional representation as well as its defense of higher salaries for government employees and workmen.

Leaders: Walter Bringolf (Member of National Council, President of Party); Max Weber, Fritz Grütter, Robert Bratschi, Hans Oprecht, Harald Huber, Pierre Graber, Ernst Herzog, Adolphe Graedel (Members of the National Council); Willy Spühler (Member of Council of States).

CATHOLIC CONSERVATIVE PARTY: A clerical federalist party, dating from opposition to the revolution of 1847. Opposes centralization of national power; advocates freedom for the cantons as to control of religious education; opposes direct taxation and favors alcohol and tobacco taxes; advocates social measures; comprises two factions, one tending to social conservatism and one to Christian socialist principles.

Leaders: Dr. Phillip Etter, Dr. Giuseppe Lepori, Dr. Thomas Holenstein (Members of Federal Council); Jean Bourgknecht (President of the Party); Joseph Condrau, Carl Eder, Theodor Eisenring, Fernand Cottier, Franco Maspoli (Members of National Council); F. Stähli (Member of Council of States).

PEASANTS, ARTISANS AND MIDDLE CLASS PARTY: Seceded from Progressive Democratic Party in 1919; a Governmental party, but more conservative and strongly in favor of agrarian reforms. Advocates laws and tariffs protecting agricultural interest and small industry, and strong national defense.

Leaders: Dr. Friedrich T. Wahlen (Member of Federal Council), Karl Renold (Member of National Council), Rudolf Weber (Member of Council of States, President of the Party); Paul Burgdorfer, Otto Wartmann, Paul Gysler, Rudolf Reichling (Members of National Council); Erich Ullmann, Dewet Buri (Members of Council of States).

LIBERAL DEMOCRATIC PARTY: Similar to Catholic Conservative Party in program, but recruited more in Protestant circles; federalist; opposed to socialism and strong centralist tendencies in government; supported by middle classes of the larger towns. Favors free trade and social insurance measures, and opposes direct federal taxation.

SWITZERLAND

Leaders: Peter Zschokke (President of Party); Olivier Reverdin, Nicolas Jaquet, Louis Guisan (Members of National Council); Sydney de Coulon, Victor Gautier (Members of Council of States).

INDEPENDENTS' PARTY: A progressive, middle-class party representing consumers' interests; favors reduction of cost of living, and anti-trust legislation.

Leaders: A. Stahel (President of Party), Walter Trueb, Gottlieb Duttweiler and Hans Munz (Members of National Council).

DEMOCRATIC PARTY OF SWITZERLAND: Formed in 1941 by the democratic parties of the cantons of Zurich, Grisons and Glarus; its objectives are to unite the left middle-class of the country, so as finally to create an understanding between outdated differences which separate socialism and the middle class; it advocates the realization of social democracy.

Leaders: Philipp Schmid (Member of National Council) and Arno Theuss (Member of Council of States).

SWISS LABOR PARTY (Communist): Extreme left-wing Marxist party, publicly organized in Zurich in October, 1944; has main strength in larger cities among workers dissatisfied with moderate evolutionary policies of Socialist Party; absorbed bulk of membership of dissident Swiss Socialist Federation and Swiss Communist Party after these were prohibited (temporarily) in 1941. Advocates usual Communist program.

Leaders: Jean Vincent, Marino Bodenmann, André Muret (Members of National Council) and Edgar Woog.

PRESS

Unless otherwise noted, papers are published in the capital city.

Name of Paper	Circulation	Political Affiliation	Proprietor, Editor, etc.
Berner Tagblatt	33,600	Independent.	Dr. R. Th. Weiss (*Ed.*) W. Thormann (*For. Ed.*)
Berner Tagwacht	15,200	Socialist.	Alfons Scherrer (*Ed.*)
Der Bund	32,900	Radical Democratic.	Walter Egger (*Ed.*)
Aargauer Tagblatt (Aarau)	11,000	Radical Democratic.	H. Suter (*Ed.*)
Basler Arbeiterzeitung (Basel)	6,000	Socialist.	Max Schärer (*Ed.*)
Basler Nachrichten (Basel)	17,200	Liberal Democratic.	Peter Dürrenmatt (*Ed.*)
Nationalzeitung (Basel)	49,300	Radical Democratic.	F. & M. Hagemann (*Pub.*)
Dovere (Bellinzona)	9,400	Radical Democratic.	Plinio Verda (*Ed.*)
Popolo e Libertà (Bellinzona)	6,100	Catholic Conservative.	C. Darani (*Ed.*)
Thurgauer Zeitung (Frauenfeld)	15,600	Radical Democratic.	Edwin Altwegg (*Ed.*)
Liberté (Fribourg)	15,800	Catholic Conservative.	Roger Pochon (*Ed.*)
Le Courrier (Geneva)	10,200	Catholic Conservative.	René Leyvraz (*Ed.*)
Journal de Genève (Geneva)	10,200	National Democratic.	René Payot (*Dir.*)
La Suisse (Geneva)	34,200	Independent.	Marc Chenevière (*Ed.*)
Tribune de Genève (Geneva)	52,000	Independent.	Gaston Bridel (*Ed.*)
Voix Ouvrière (Geneva)	8,000	Communist.	Etienne Lentillon (*Ed.*)
Feuille d'Avis de Lausanne (Lausanne)	75,100	Independent.	Pierre Cordey (*Ed.*)
Gazette de Lausanne (Lausanne)	17,400	Liberal.	Pierre Béguin (*Ed.*)
Nouvelle Revue de Lausanne (Lausanne)	10,000	Radical Democratic.	Michel Jaccard (*Ed.*)

Name of Paper	Circulation	Political Affiliation	Proprietor, Editor, etc.
Tribune de Lausanne (Lausanne)	25,900	Independent.	Georges Peillex (*Ed.*)
Luzerner Tagblatt (Lucerne)	20,100	Radical Democratic.	Dr. F. Keller (*Ed.*)
Vaterland (Lucerne)	25,000	Catholic Conservative.	K. Wick (*Ed.*)
Corriere del Ticino (Lugano)	9,500	Independent.	Vittore Frigerio (*Ed.*)
Giornale del Popolo (Lugano)	10,300	Catholic Conservative.	Don Alfredo Leber (*Ed.*)
Feuille d'Avis de Neuchâtel (Neuchâtel)	20,600	Independent.	R. Braichet (*Ed.*)
Ostschweiz (St. Gall)	8,600	Catholic Conservative.	Eugen Knecht (*Ed.*)
St. Galler Tagblatt (St. Gall)	19,600	Radical Democratic.	Erwin Burckhardt (*Ed.*)
Landbote (Winterthur)	17,900	Democratic.	Oscar Hürsch (*Ed.*)
Neue Zuercher Nachrichten (Zurich)	14,100	Catholic Conservative.	Hermann Odermatt (*Ed.*)
Neue Zuercher Zeitung (Zurich)	69,700	Radical Democratic.	Willy Bretscher (*Ed.*)
Tages-Anzeiger für Stadt und Kanton Zurich (Zurich)	140,200	Independent.	E. Syfrig (*Ed.*)
Die Tat (Zurich)	31,400	Independents' Party.	Migros Genossenschaftsbund (*Prop.*) Dr. E. Jaeckle (*Ed.*)
Volksrecht (Zurich)	15,400	Socialist.	Paul Schmid-Ammann (*Ed.*)
Die Weltwoche (weekly) (Zurich)	123,000	Independent.	Dr. P. von Schumacher (*Dir.*) Lorenz Stucki (*For. Ed.*)
Vorwärts (weekly) (Basel)	12,000	Communist.	Karl Odermatt (*Ed.*)
Evolution (monthly)	5,000	Liberal Socialist.	F. Schwarz (*Ed.*)
Politische Rundschau (Berne) (monthly)	3,200	Radical Democratic.	H. R. Hilty (*Ed.*)
Rote Revue (Zurich) (monthly)	2,000	Socialist.	Valentin Gitermann (*Ed.*)
Schweizer Rundschau (Einsiedeln) (monthly)	2,200	Catholic.	Dr. Siegfried Streicher (*Ed.*)
Schweizerische Monatshefte für Politik und Kultur (Zurich) (monthly)	2,000	Swiss and European politics.	Dr. Jann von Sprecher (*Ed.*)

NEWS AGENCIES

Swiss Telegraphic Agency		Independent.	Siegfried Frey (*Dir.*)
Swiss Political Correspondence		Independent.	Vischer von Planta (*Pres.*)

THAILAND (SIAM)

Capital: Bangkok
Area: 200,148 square miles
Population: 22,000,000 (1957 estimate)

Ruler
KING PHUMIPHON ADUNDET
Born December 5, 1927; ascended throne on May 5, 1950

Head of Government
FIELD MARSHAL SARIT THANARAT
Seized power in a bloodless coup on October 20, 1958

PARLIAMENT

The 1932 Constitution has been abrogated and the Parliament dissolved. The country is being ruled from army headquarters.

POLITICAL EVENTS SINCE 1941

Field Marshal P. Pibulsonggram was Premier when Japan occupied Thailand on December 8, 1941. A Treaty of Alliance was concluded with the Japanese, and on January 25, 1942, the Thai Government declared war against Great Britain and the United States. The former country recognized the state of war, but the United States considered Thailand's declaration of war to have been made under duress.

Thailand's state of war with Britain was terminated by a treaty concluded on January 1, 1946, and on January 5, 1946, the United States and Britain both announced their formal recognition of the Thai Government.

Since August 1944 there have been ten Governments in office in Thailand under the following Prime Ministers: Khuang Aphaiwong (August 1944–August 1945), Thawi Bunyaket (September, 1945), M. R. Seni Pramoj (September 1945–January 1946), Khuang Aphaiwong (February 1946–March 1946), Pridi Phanomyong (March 1946–August 1946), Rear Admiral Luang Thamrong Nawasawat (August 1946–November 1947), Khuang Aphaiwong (November 1947–April 1948), Field Marshal Pibulsonggram (April 1948–September 1957), Pote Sarasin (September 1957–December 1957), Gen. Thanom Kittikachorn (January 1958–October 1958).

On November 8, 1947, in a bloodless coup, a military group overthrew the Government, appointed a Privy Council, a new Cabinet, and announced a new Constitution which provided for a two-chamber Parliament. Field Marshal Pibulsonggram was reappointed Premier in 1948. In November, 1951, essentially the same group of military leaders dissolved the legislature and overthrew the Cabinet, but restored the Premier to power a few hours later. They also restored the 1932 Constitution with some amendments.

In 1952 the Thai Government passed an Anti-Communist Activities Act which outlawed Communist activity.

The Political Parties Act of 1955 permitted the establishment of political parties for the first time since 1951. A number of political parties have since been created. Field Marshal Pibulsonggram was returned to power by the elections of February 1957. However, another bloodless coup led by the military occurred in September 1957. Pote Sarasin was appointed Premier to preside over a Provisional Government until the December 1957 elections provided the basis for formation of a regular Government. Following the election, General Thanom Kittikachorn became Premier.

On October 20, 1958, the Thanom Government resigned, and power was assumed by the Revolutionary Party under the leadership of Field Marshal Sarit Thanarat, Supreme Commander of the Thai Armed Forces. The National Assembly was dissolved and the Constitution abrogated. The Revolutionary Party has announced that a provisional government will be formed and an interim constitution will be promulgated. A Constituent Assembly will also be appointed to draft a new, permanent Constitution. The Political Parties Act of 1955 has been abrogated.

THE CABINET

The Cabinet of Gen. Thanom Kittikachorn resigned on October 20, 1958. New Ministers have not yet been announced and the country, meanwhile, is being ruled by the military.

PRESS

All publications listed are published in the capital city.

THAI LANGUAGE

Name of Publication	Editor
Kiattisak	Sala Likhitkul
Lak Muang	Prayudh Sittiphan (closed temporarily)
Naewna	Vara Sasingh
Prachathipatai (The Democrat)	Sawai Phrommi
Chao Thai	Chalerm Vudhikosit
Siam Nikorn	Charn Sinsuk
Siam Rath	Prachuab Thong-Urai
Phim Thai	Busya Simasathira
Daily Trade News	Sawasdi Sawasdisaringkarn
Sanseri	Surachit Chandrasakha
Thai Raiwan	Lamool Atiphayak
Krung Dheb	Sanit Chaengkrachang
Thai Rath	Ramphan Pukkachiem
Prachakorn	Udom Pramualvidhya
Ploenchit (weekly)	Samut Sirikai
Sansook (weekly)	Sucharti Phanucharas
Sri Sapdah (weekly)	M. L. Chitti Nopawong
Daily Mail Monday Edition	Manit Srisakorn
Siam Smai (weekly)	Prayoon Chanyawongse
Kiattisak (weekly)	Sala Likhitakul
Bangkok Time (weekly)	Charoon Kuwanon
Sakul Thai (weekly)	Drayaan Sangserm Swasti
Satri Sarn (weekly)	Miss Nilwan Pinthong
Thai Sapdah (weekly)	Lamool Atiphayak
Siam Rath Saphda Wicharn (weekly)	Prayad S. Nakhanant

CHINESE LANGUAGE

Sing Sian Yit Pao	Yang Chien-hsing
Sing Sian Wan Pao	Wu Chung-heng
Shih Chieh Yih Pao (morning)	Yao Ti-hwa
Shih Chieh Wan Pao (evening)	Chang Yen-lieh

THAILAND (SIAM)

ENGLISH LANGUAGE

Name of Publication	Editor
Bangkok Post	Harry Frederick
Bangkok Tribune	Plang Phloyphrom
Standard (weekly)	Ngarmchit Prem Burachat
Siamrat Weekly Review	M. R. Kukrit Pramotj
Bangkok World	Darrell Berrigan
Thai People	G. C. Earde

TURKEY

Capital: Ankara
Area: 296,503 square miles
Population: 24,131,778 (1957 estimate)

President
CELÂL BAYAR (Democratic Party)
Re-elected by the National Assembly on November 1, 1957
Term customarily four years subject to dissolution
of Parliament and new elections

Cabinet
Democratic Party
Cabinet formed November 25, 1957

Premier
ADNAN MENDERES (Democratic Party)

PARLIAMENT
(Grand National Assembly)
(Büyük Millet Meclisi)
Election of October 27, 1957 (four-year term unless dissolved earlier)
President: REFIK KORALTAN (Democratic Party)

Parties	Representation
Democratic	415
Republican People's Party	175
Republican Rural Nation's Party	4
Independents	3
Vacant	13
Total	610

PARTY PROGRAMS AND LEADERS

DEMOCRATIC PARTY: Organized in 1945. Was in opposition to Republican People's Party until 1950, when it won a sweeping victory in the May 14th elections and took over the Government. Gained even larger majority in elections of May 1954 and October 1957. In *foreign policy:* it supports the United Nations and attaches utmost importance to treaty relationship with Britain and France, and friendship with the United States. Considers North Atlantic Treaty, Balkan Alliance and Baghdad Pact as most effective security against aggression. Supports Council of Europe. In *domestic policy:* advocates aid in rapid development of private enterprise; favors conditions under which Turkey may benefit from private foreign capital, enterprise and techniques; would limit state enterprises to specified public services, and would return certain of them to private control.

Leaders: Celâl Bayar (founder of Party, President of the Republic), Adnan Menderes (President of Party, Prime Minister).

REPUBLICAN PEOPLE'S PARTY: Former leading party in Turkey, strongly nationalistic. In *foreign policy:* supports the United Nations, within the framework of which it relies on its treaty relationship with Britain and France, its friendship with the United States, and its friendship with its neighbors. In *domestic policy:* the party advocates the modernization of Turkey, the building of highways and railways for economic and strategic reasons, the separation of Church and State, and the support of the Turkish language and culture to assure unity among the people. In economic matters it supports *étatism*. By a unanimous vote of a special Party Congress in December 1938, the election of General Ismet Inönü as President-General of the Party was rendered valid for life. However, General Inönü, feeling that his position should be ratified by the Party, in 1946 stood for re-election to this position and won by a unanimous vote at the Party Congress held at Ankara on May 10–11, 1946. In the elections of 1950, 1954 and 1957 the party was defeated. The Freedom Party dissolved itself in 1958 and merged with the Republican People's Party.

Leaders: General Ismet Inönü (former President of the Republic and President of the People's Party), Kasim Gülek (Secretary General of the Party), Faik Ahmet Barutçu (Vice-President of Assembly group).

REPUBLICAN RURAL NATION'S PARTY: Founded in 1958 by merger of the Nation Party and the Rural Party.

Leaders: Osman Bölükbaşi (President-General of Party), Tahsin Demiray (Vice-President of Party), Ahmet Bilgin (Secretary-General of Party).

OTHER PARTIES: There are 18 other registered parties in Turkey, but they are ineffective and local in character and lack wide public support.

THE CABINET

The members of the Cabinet are: Adnan Menderes (Premier), Abdullah Aker (Minister of State), Muzaffer Kurbanoğlu (Minister of State), Haluk Şaman (Minister of State), Fatin Rüştü Zorlu (Minister of Foreign Affairs), Etem Menderes (Minister of Defense), Hasan Polatkan (Minister of Finance), Esat Budakoğlu (Justice), Tevfik Ileri (Minister of Public Works), Dr. Namik Gedik (Minister of Interior), Celâl Yardimci (Education), Hayrettin Erkmen (Commerce), Lufti Kirdar (Health), Hadi Hüsman (Customs and Monopolies), Nedim Ökmen (Agriculture), Muzaffer Kurbanoğlu (Acting Communications), Haluk Şaman (Acting Labor), Sebati Ataman (Acting Industry), Server Somuncuoğlu (Information and Tourism), Medeni Berk (Reconstruction), Sebati Ataman (Coordination).

PRESS

Unless otherwise noted, papers are published in Istanbul.

Name of Paper	Character	Proprietor, Edit?r, etc.
Akşam	Independent.	Malik Yolaç (*Prop.*)
Cumhuriyet	Independent.	Nazime Nadi (*Prop., Ed.*)
Dünya	Opposition.	Falih Rifki Atay (*Ed.*)
Havadis	Supports Government.	Atif Benderlioglu (*Ed.*)

TURKEY

Name of Paper	Character	Proprietor, Editor, etc.
Hergün	Independent.	Faruk Gürtunca (*Prop.*)
Hürriyet	Independent.	Haldun Simavi (*Prop.*)
Istanbul	In French.	Jules Compte-Calix (*Prop.*)
Istanbul Ekspres	Supports Government.	Mithat Perin (*Prop.*)
Le Journal D'Orient	In French.	Albert Karasu (*Prop., Ed.*)
Milliyet	Independent.	Ercüment Karacan (*Ed.*)
Son Posta	Supports Government.	Selim Ragip Emeç (*Prop., Ed.*)
Ulus (Ankara)	Republican People's Party Organ.	Kasim Gülek (*Prop.*)
Vakit	Opposition.	Asim Us (*Prop., Ed.*)
Vatan	Independent.	Ahmet Emin Yalman (*Ed.*)
Yeni Istanbul	Independent; liberal.	Habib Edip Törehan (*Prop.*)
Yeni Sabah	Independent.	Safa Kiliçoğlu (*Prop.*)
Ankara Telegraf (Ankara)	Pro-Government.	Fethi Giray (*Prop.*)
Zafer (Ankara)	Democratic Party Organ.	Kâmil Gündeş (*Prop.*)
Resmi Gazete (Ankara)	Laws, decrees and official notices.	Prime Minister's Office (*Pub.*)
Son Havadis (Ankara)	Opposition.	Cemil Sait Barlas (*Prop.*)
Yeni Gun (Ankara)	Freedom Party Organ.	Fethi Celikbaş (*Prop.*)
Democrat Izmir (Izmir)	Opposition.	Adnan Düvenci (*Prop.*)
Yeni Asir (Izmir)	Supports Government.	Şevket Bilgin (*Prop.*)

NEWS AGENCIES

Anadolu News Agency	Semi-official.	Şerif Arzik (*Dir.*)
Şark News Agency	Independent.	Ilhami Ömeroğlu (*Prop.*)
Türk News Agency	Independent.	Kadri Kayabal (*Prop.*)

UNION OF SOVIET SOCIALIST REPUBLICS

(The USSR is a federal state composed of Russian Federative, Ukrainian, Byelorussian, Azerbaijan, Georgian, Armenian, Kazak, Turkmenian, Kirghiz, Tadjik, Uzbek, Estonian, Latvian, Lithuanian and Moldavian Soviet Socialist Republics)

Capital: Moscow
Area: 8,590,000 square miles (1947)
Population: 200,200,000 (1956 estimate)

Chairman of the Praesidium of the Supreme Soviet of the USSR
KLIMENT YEFREMOVICH VOROSHILOV (Communist)
Re-elected by Supreme Soviet on April 21, 1954, and March 27, 1958

Cabinet (Council of Ministers)
Appointed by the Supreme Soviet

Chairman of Council of Ministers
NIKITA SERGEIVITCH KHRUSHCHEV (Communist)
Appointed March 27, 1958

PARLIAMENT
(Supreme Soviet of the USSR)

The Constitution of December 5, 1936, provides that the highest organ in the USSR is the Supreme Soviet consisting of two equal houses; that members thereof shall be chosen on the basis of universal, equal and direct suffrage by secret ballot for a term of 4 years; that regular sessions of each body shall be held twice each year; that there shall be a president of each house; that there shall be a Praesidium of the Supreme Soviet, which shall consist of a president, 15 vice-presidents (one vice-president for each constituent republic of the Union), a secretary and 16 members; that the Praesidium shall act as an executive and directive body between the sessions of the Supreme Soviet.

SOVIET OF THE UNION	SOVIET OF NATIONALITIES
President: P. P. LOBANOV	*President:* YA. V. PEYVE
(Elected at general elections March 16, 1958, for four-year term; one deputy for each 300,000 inhabitants.)	(Elected on March 16, 1958, for four-year term; each constituent republic has 25 deputies; each autonomous republic 11; each autonomous region 5; and each national area one.)
Number of members 738	Number of members 640

SOVIET UNION

POLITICAL DEVELOPMENTS SINCE 1917

In March 1917 the last Tsar, Nicholas II, abdicated under pressure from the Duma. The Provisional Government, of which Prince Lvov and Kerensky were successively Premiers, was forcibly overthrown on November 7, 1917, by a small, well-organized and strictly disciplined radical revolutionary group led by V. I. Lenin and Leon Trotsky, known as the Bolshevik Wing of the Russian Social Democratic Labor Party, and which proclaimed a dictatorship of the proletariat that has been continued to the present time.

All land was declared the property of the State and, through a rapid succession of decrees, all other important means of production, banks, railroads, and means of communication were also nationalized. In June 1918 the first Constitution of the Russian Soviet Federated Socialist Republic was adopted. The civil war which had been in progress since November 1917 ended in 1921 with the absolute victory of the Bolsheviks.

In 1922 four Soviet Socialist Republics formed the Union of Soviet Socialist Republics, and a new Union Constitution was adopted in 1924. There are now 15 Soviet Republics in the Union. In 1924 the founder of the Soviet régime, V. I. Lenin, died. Joseph V. Stalin, General Secretary of the Communist Party since 1922, consolidated his position of power through the purges in the 1930's, and in 1941 also assumed the top governmental post.

Under the First Five Year Plan (1928–1932) a broad heavy industry base was begun, and at the same time collectivization of agriculture was in the main completed. Further consolidation of the national economy was made under the Second Five Year Plan (1933–1937). In 1936 a new Union Constitution was adopted. The Third Five Year Plan (1938–1942) was interrupted by the German invasion of 1941. With the victorious ending of the war, a Fourth Five Year Plan was launched in 1946. A Fifth Plan, for 1951–55, was announced in 1952, and a Sixth Plan, for 1956–60, was announced in 1956. The latter was abandoned in 1957 and a Seven-Year Plan for 1959–65 was to be adopted in January 1959.

J. V. Stalin died in March 1953 and G. M. Malenkov succeeded him as Chairman of the Council of Ministers. Malenkov resigned in February 1955 admitting "lack of experience," and was replaced by N. A. Bulganin. On March 27, 1958, Bulganin was replaced by N. S. Khrushchev.

PARTY PROGRAMS AND LEADERS

COMMUNIST PARTY: The only political party permitted to exist in the Soviet Union is the Communist Party of the Soviet Union, formerly called the All-Union Communist Party of Bolsheviks. The highest organ of the Party is the All-Union Party Congress, of which the last, the 20th Congress, was held in February 1956. The Party Congress elects a Central Committee which functions through : (1) a policy-making body known as the Praesidium (replacing the Politburo) which now has 14 members and 10 candidate members; (2) a Secretariat, which is now composed of 10 members; (3) a Committee of Party Control. The title of General Secretary, which Stalin held, was dropped in October 1952 and N. S. Khrushchev was designated First Secretary of the Party Central Committee in September 1953. An extraordinary Party Congress, the 21st, has been called for January 29, 1959. Its announced purpose will be to discuss the 1959–65 Seven Year Plan.

SOVIET UNION

PRAESIDIUM OF THE CENTRAL COMMITTEE OF THE COMMUNIST PARTY OF THE SOVIET UNION

Full Members

A. B. Aristov—Secretary of Central Committee of CPSU.
N. I. Belyayev—First Secretary of Kazakhstan Communist Party.
L. I. Brezhnev—Secretary of Central Committee of CPSU.
Ye. A. Furtseva—Secretary of Central Committee of CPSU.
N. G. Ignatov—Secretary of Central Committee of CPSU.
A. I. Kirichenko—Secretary of Central Committee of CPSU.
N. S. Khrushchev—First Secretary of Central Committee of CPSU; Chairman of USSR Council of Ministers; Chairman of Bureau for the RSFSR of CPSU Central Committee.
F. R. Kozlov—First Deputy Chairman, USSR Council of Ministers.
O. V. Kuusinen—Secretary of Central Committee of CPSU.
A. I. Mikoyan—First Deputy Chairman, Council of Ministers.
N. A. Mukhitdinov—Secretary of Central Committee of CPSU.
N. M. Shvernik—Chairman, Party Control Committee.
M. A. Suslov—Secretary of Central Committee of CPSU.
K. Ye. Voroshilov—Chairman of the Praesidium of the USSR Supreme Soviet.

Candidate Members

Ya. E. Kalnberzin—First Secretary of Latvian Communist Party.
A. P. Kirilenko—First Secretary of Sverdlovsk *Oblast* Committee of CPSU.
D. S. Korotchenko—Chairman, Ukraine Supreme Soviet.
A. N. Kosygin—Deputy Chairman of USSR Council of Ministers.
K. T. Mazurov—First Secretary of Byelorussian Communist Party.
V. P. Mzhavanadze—First Secretary of Georgian Communist Party.
M. G. Pervukhin—Ambassador to East Germany.
P. N. Pospelov—Secretary of Central Committee of CPSU.
N. V. Podgorny—First Secretary of Ukrainian Communist Party.
D. S. Polyansky—Chairman of Council of Ministers of RSFSR.

Secretariat of Central Committee

First Secretary—N. S. Khrushchev.
Secretaries—A. B. Aristov.
           L. I. Brezhnev.
           Ye. A. Furtseva.
           N. G. Ignatov.
           A. I. Kirichenko
           O. V. Kuusinen.
           N. A. Mukhidinov.
           P. N. Pospelov.
           M. A. Suslov.

COUNCIL OF MINISTERS

Chairman—N. S. Khrushchev.
First Deputy Chairmen—A. I. Mikoyan.
                          F. R. Kozlov.

Deputies—A. N. Kosygin.
  I. I. Kuzmin (also Chairman USSR Gosplan).
  Dmitri F. Ustinov.
  A. F. Zasyadko.

Ministers

P. Ya. Antropov—USSR Minister of Geology and Conservation of Mineral Deposits.
V. G. Bakayev—USSR Minister of the Maritime Fleet.
V. P. Beshchev—USSR Minister of Ways of Communication.
N. P. Dudurov—USSR Minister of Internal Affairs.
A. A. Gromyko—USSR Minister of Foreign Affairs.
M. D. Kovrigina—USSR Minister of Health.
Ye. F. Kozhevnikov—USSR Minister of Transport Construction.
R. Y. Malinovsky—Marshal of the Soviet Union; USSR Minister of Defense.
V. V. Matskevich—USSR Minister of Agriculture.
N. A. Mikhailov—USSR Minister of Culture.
A. S. Pavlenko—USSR Minister of Electric Power Stations.
N. S. Patolichev—USSR Minister of Foreign Trade.
N. D. Psurtsev—USSR Minister of Communications.
Ye. P. Slavskiy—USSR Minister of Medium Machine Building.
V. P. Yelyutin—USSR Minister of Higher Education.
A. G. Zverev—USSR Minister of Finance.

Other Members

A. A. Ishkov—Chief of Section of Gosplan.
M. V. Khrunichev—Deputy Chairman of Gosplan.
A. K. Korovyshkin—Chairman, Board of State Bank.
A. N. Shelepin—Chairman, Committee of State Security.
N. I. Strokin—Deputy Chairman of Gosplan.
A. P. Volkov—Chairman, State Committee for Questions of Labor and Wages.
V. P. Zotov—Deputy Chairman of Gosplan.
V. N. Starovsky—Chief of the Central Statistical Administration.
G. S. Khlamov—Chief of Section of Gosplan.
Ye. S. Novoselov—Chief of Section of Gosplan.
B. Ye. Butoma—Chairman, State Committee for Shipbuilding.
P. V. Dementyev—Chairman, State Committee for Aviation Technology.
V. A. Kucherenko—Chairman, State Committee for Construction Affairs.
K. N. Rudnev—Chairman, State Committee for Defense Technology.
Yu. Maksarev—Chairman, State Scientific-Technical Committee.
V. D. Kalmykov—Chairman, State Committee for Radio-electronics.
S. A. Skachov—Chairman, State Committee for Foreign Economic Relations.
V. C. Federov—Chairman, State Committee for Chemistry.
G. V. Perov—First Deputy Chairman of Gosplan.
M. A. Lesechko—First Deputy Chairman of Gosplan.
I. G. Kabanov—Minister of the USSR.
G. Yenyutin—Chairman of Soviet Control Commission.
L. R. Korniyets—Chairman, State Committee for Grain Products.

Also included in the composition of the USSR Council of Ministers are the 15 Chairmen of the Union Republic Councils of Ministers, *ex officio*.

SOVIET UNION

PRESS

All publications are censored by the Chief Administration for Literary and Publishing Matters attached to the USSR Council of Ministers.

Unless otherwise noted, papers are published in Moscow, and appear daily except Monday.

Name of Paper	Organ of	Editor
Pravda (daily)	Party Central Committee.	Pavel A. Satyukov (*Ed.*)
Izvestiya	Praesidium of USSR Supreme Soviet.	Editorial Board K. A. Gubin (*Ed.*)
Krasnaya Zvezda	USSR Ministry of Defense.	N. I. Makeev (*Ed.*)
Komsomolskaya Pravda	Komsomol Central Committee.	Editorial Board A. I. Adzhubey (*Ed.*)
Trud	Central Council of Trade Unions.	B. S. Burkov (*Ed.*)
Literaturnaya Gazeta (thrice weekly)	Union of Soviet Writers.	V. Druzin (*Act. Ed.*)
Gudok	Ministry of Railways of USSR and Central Committee of Trade Unions of Railway Transport Workers.	B. I. Krasnikov (*Ed.*)
Moskovskaya Pravda	Moscow City and Oblast Party Committee.	A. M. Subbotin (*Ed.*)
Selskoye Khozyaistvo	Ministries of Agriculture and State Farms.	A. M. Sirotin (*Ed.*)
Sovetskaya Kultura (thrice weekly)	USSR Ministry of Culture.	Y. I. Orlov (*Ed.*)
Sovetskaya Torgovlya	USSR Ministry of Trade.	A. G. Kozlov (*Ed.*)
Vedomosti Verkhovnogo Soveta SSSR	USSR Supreme Soviet.	Editorial Board
Uchitelskaya Gazeta (twice weekly)	Union Republic Ministries of Education and Trade Unions of Educational Workers.	N. M. Parfenova (*Ed.*)
Leningradskaya Pravda (Leningrad)	Leningrad City and Oblast Party Committee.	M. C. Kurtynin (*Ed.*)
Pravda Ukrainy (Kiev)	Ukrainian Party Central Committee, Supreme Soviet, and Council of Ministers.	N. K. Belogurov (*Ed.*)
Sovetskaya Belorussiya (Minsk)	Byelorussian Party Central Committee, Supreme Soviet, and Council of Ministers.	Ya. I. Kachan (*Ed.*)
Sovetskaya Estoniya (Tallinn)	Estonian Party Central Committee, Supreme Soviet, and Council of Ministers.	N. Karnaushenko (*Ed.*)
Sovetskaya Latviya (Riga)	Latvian Party Central Committee and Supreme Soviet.	N. P. Saleev (*Ed.*)
Bakinskii Rabochii (Baku)	Azerbaidzhan Party Central and Baku Committees.	A. M. Malyutin (*Ed.*)
Sovetskaya Kirgiziya (Frunze)	Kirgiz Party Central and Frunze Oblast Committees, and Supreme Soviet.	P. S. Denisyuk (*Ed.*)
Sovetskaya Litva (Vilnius)	Lithuanian Party Central Committee, Supreme Soviet, and Council of Ministers.	V. A. Meshcheryakov (*Ed.*)
Sovetskaya Rossiya	Buro of Central Committee of All-Union Communist Party for the RSFSR and of the Council of Ministers of the RSFSR.	Editorial Collegium
Sovetskaya Moldaviya (Kishinev)	Moldavian Party Central Committee and Supreme Soviet.	A. A. Golubitskii (*Ed.*)
Kazakhstanskaya Pravda (Alma-Ata)	Kazakh Party Central Committee.	F. F. Boyarsky (*Ed.*)
Kommunist Tadzhikistana (Stalinabad)	Tadzhik Party Central Committee, Stalinabad Obkom, and Supreme Soviet.	V. V. Sinitsin (*Ed.*)
Turkmenskaya Iskra (Ashkhabad)	Turkmen Party Central Committee, Ashkhabad Gorkom and Obkom, and Supreme Soviet.	A. Makhinin (*Ed.*)

Name of Paper	Organ of	Editor
Kommunist (Yerevan)	Armenian Party Central and Erevan Committees.	Zh. G. Akopyan (*Dep. Ed.*)
Zarya Vostoka (Tbilisi)	Georgian Party Central and Tbilisi Committees and Supreme Soviet.	I. I. Chkhikvishvili (*Ed.*)
Pravda Vostoka (Tashkent)	Uzbek Party Central Committee, Supreme Soviet, and Council of Ministers.	S. S. Chernik (*Ed.*)

MAGAZINES

Kommunist (every 20 days)	Party Central Committee.	F. V. Konstantinov (*Ed.*)
Vneshnyaya Torgovlya (monthly)	Ministry of Foreign Trade.	M. N. Begicheva (*Tech. Ed.*)
Molodoi Kommunist (monthly)	Komsomol Central Committee.	M. I. Khaldeev
Moskovski Propagandist (monthly)	Moscow Communist Party Committee.	Ye. Yakovleva (*Tech. Ed.*)
News (twice monthly)	Publishers of *Trud*.	Ye. Kosminski
Planovoe Khozyaistvo (bi-monthly)	State Planning Committee.	G. V. Perov
Novoe Vremya (weekly)	Publishers of *Trud*.	L. A. Leontyev
Partiinaya Zhizn (semi monthly)	Party Central Committee.	Editorial Board
Voprosy Filosofii (bi-monthly)	Academy of Sciences' Philosophy Institute.	M. D. Kammari
Voprosy Ekonomikii (monthly)	Academy of Sciences' Economics Institute.	L. M. Gatovsky
Voprosy Istorii (monthly)	Academy of Sciences' History Institute.	N. I. Matyushkin (*Dep. Ed.*)
Bloknot Agitatora (two or three times monthly)	Propaganda and Agitation Section of Moscow City and Oblast Party Committees.	K. Ya. Lutovinova
Sovetskoe Gosudarstvo i Pravo (8 times yearly)	Academy of Sciences' Law Institute.	I. V. Pavlov
Sovetskiye Profsoyuzy (monthly)	All-Union Central Council of Trade Unions.	M. T. Skobeev (*Ch. Ed.*)
Economika Selskoe Khozyaistvo (monthly)	USSR Ministry of Agriculture.	N. I. Anisimov
Sobranie Postanovlenii i Rasporyazhenii (irregular)	Council of Ministers.	Editorial Board
Voprosy Istorii KPSS	Party Central Committee.	G. D. Obichkin

NEWS AGENCY

Tass	Official Telegraphic News Agency of the Soviet Union.	N. G. Palgunov

UNITED ARAB REPUBLIC

Capital: Cairo
Area: 452,156 square miles
Population: 28,500,000 (1958 estimate)

President
GAMAL ABDEL NASSER
Elected President on February 21, 1958
for an indefinite term

Cabinet
Appointed October 7, 1958

RECENT POLITICAL EVENTS

On February 1, 1958, the birth of the United Arab Republic was proclaimed by Presidents Nasser of Egypt and Shukri al-Quwwatli of Syria.

On February 21, 1958, a plebiscite was held in which the voters of Egypt and Syria were called upon to decide for or against union and for or against Nasser as President of the new state. Announced results of the plebiscite showed virtual unanimity in favor of both proposals.

On February 22, 1958, the establishment of the United Arab Republic was officially declared. Eleven days later, March 5, 1958, President Nasser at Damascus proclaimed the Provisional Constitution of the United Arab Republic.

On March 6, 1958, Nasser issued a decree at Damascus appointing a new 34 member Cabinet for the United Arab Republic including four Vice-Presidents, two from the Egyptian region and two from the Syrian region, and two Ministers of State. The merged portfolios of the Egyptian and Syrian regions included Foreign Affairs, War, Education, Industry, and National Guidance. Executive Councils were also established for the Egyptian and Syrian regions, but these regional cabinets were without executive authority and purely advisory in character.

On October 7, 1958, Nasser decreed a reorganization of the government of the United Arab Republic. The new governmental set-up consisted of a central government covering all ministries with the President, Vice-Presidents, and UAR ministers all located in Cairo and Executive Councils for each of the two regions to administer local government and carry out policies formulated by the Central Cabinet. He named a new UAR central cabinet composed of 21 ministers, including 3 Vice-Presidents and 7 Syrians; and Egyptian and Syrian Regional Executive Councils made up of 15 and 14 ministers respectively.

THE CONSTITUTION

On March 5, 1958, the Provisional Constitution of the United Arab Republic was proclaimed. Of its 73 articles, the majority of them were taken from the 1956 Egyptian Constitution. It subscribes to democratic institutions and principles, but also grants wide executive powers to the President. The legislative power will be vested in a National Assembly to be chosen by Presidential decree, but at least half the members must also be members of the National Assembly of Egypt and of the Syrian Chamber of Deputies. The intentions of the régime regarding establishment of the National Assembly and holding of elections have not yet been announced.

PARTY PROGRAMS

There are no political parties in the United Arab Republic. In Egypt the only political entity is the National Union which may be described as a government-sponsored organization whose purpose is the mobilization of popular political support. In Syria, by a law issued March 10, 1958, all political parties existing in the region were abolished and the formation of new parties prohibited. The present regime has announced its intention of establishing a National Union in Syria in the near future.

THE CABINET

The Cabinet is composed as follows: Abd al-Latif al-Baghdadi, (Vice-President and Minister for Planning), Field Marshal Abd al-Hakim 'Amer (Vice President and Minister of War), Akram al-Hawrani, Syrian (Vice-President and Minister of Justice), Zakaria Muhyi al-Din (Interior), Hussein al-Shafei (Social Affairs and Labor), Kamal al-Din Hussein, (Education), Mahmoud Fawzi (Foreign Affairs), Hasan Jibara, Syrian (Treasury), Abd al-Moneim al-Qaisuni (Economy and Commerce), Ahmad al-Sharabasi (Public Works), Ahmad Hasan al-Baquri (Wakfs), Fakher El Kayyali, Syrian (Minister of State), Salah al-Din al-Bitar, Syrian (Cultural Affairs and National Guidance), Ali Sabri (Presidential Affairs), Amin al-Nafuri, Syrian (Communications), Bashir al-'Amza, Syrian (Health), Ahmad Abd al-Karim, Syrian (Municipal and Rural Affairs), 'Aziz Sidqi (Industry), Kamal Ramzi Stino (Supply), Sayed Marei (Agriculture and Agrarian Reform), Kamal al-Din Rifaat (Minister of State).

SYRIAN REGION

Capital: Damascus
Area: 66,046 square miles
Population: 4,500,000 (1958 estimate)

SYRIAN REGIONAL EXECUTIVE COUNCIL
Appointed October 7, 1958

The Syrian Regional Executive Council is composed as follows: Nur Al-Din Kahhala (Chairman, Minister of Public Works and Acting Minister of Planning), Abd al-Wahhab Hawmad (Treasury), Khalil al-Kallas (Economy), Abd al-Hamid al-Sarraj (Interior), Mustafa Hamdun (Agrarian Reform), Ahmed al-Hajj Yunes (Agriculture), Tu'ema al-'Awdatallah (Municipal and Rural Affairs), Abd al-Ghani Qanut (Social Affairs and Labor), Riyad al-Malki (Cultural Affairs and National Guidance), Amjad al-Tarabulsi (Education), Muhammad al-'Alem (Communications), Shawkat al-Qanawati (Health), Wajih al-Samman (Industry), Nihad al-Qasem (Justice).

UNITED ARAB REPUBLIC

EGYPTIAN REGION

Capital: Cairo
Total area: 386,110 square miles
Population: 24,000,000 (1958 estimate)

EGYPTIAN REGIONAL EXECUTIVE COUNCIL
Appointed October 7, 1958

The Egyptian Regional Executive Council is composed as follows: Dr. Nur al-Din Tarraf (Chairman), Ahmad Husni (Justice), Muhammad Abu Nuseir (Municipal and Rural Affairs), Mustafa Khalil (Communications), Hasan Abbas Zaki (Economy and Supply), Fathi Rizq (Industry), Tharwat 'Okasha (Cultural Affairs and National Guidance), Tawfiq Abd al-Fattah (Social Affairs and Labor), Abbas Radwan (Interior), Ahmad al-Mahruqi (Agriculture), Hasan Boghdadi (Agrarian Reform), Musa 'Arafa (Public Works), Dr. Muhammad Nassar (Health), Hasan Salah al-Din (Treasury), Ahmad Nagib Hashem (Education).

EGYPTIAN PRESS

Unless otherwise noted, papers are published in Cairo. All newspapers and magazines more or less support the present Government.

Name of Paper	Proprietor, Editor, etc.
Al Ahram (morning)	Heirs of Gabriel Takla (*Props.*)
	Mohamed Hassanein Heikal (*Ed.*)
Al Akhbar (morning)	Mustafa and Ali Amin (*Props.*)
	Mustafa and Ali Amin, Mohamed Zaki Abdel Kader (*Eds.*)
Al Shaab (morning)	Ali Sabri (*Chmn. of Brd.*)
	Hussein Fahmy and Lutfi Wakid (*Eds.*)
Al Gumhouria (morning)	Anwar El Sadat (*Chmn. of Brd.*)
	Galal El Din El Hamamsy (*Ed.*)
Al Masaa (afternoon)	Khaled Mohie El Din (*Prop. and Ed.*)
Al Kahira (afternoon)	Assad Dagher (*Prop.*)
	Hafiz Mahmoud (*Ed.*)
Akhbar El Yom (weekly)	Mustafa and Ali Amin (*Props. and Eds.*)
Al Izaa (weekly)	Egyptian Broadcasting Service (*Props.*)
	Helmi Sallam (*Ed.*)
Rose El Youssef (weekly)	Heirs of Fatima Al Youssef (*Props.*)
	Ihsan Abdel Kuddous (*Ed.*)
Al Mussawar (weekly)	Al Hilal Publishing House (*Props.*)
	Fikri Abaza (*Ed.*)
Akher Saa (weekly)	Mustafa and Ali Amin (*Props.*)
	Mohamed Hassanein Heikal (*Ed.*)
Al Guil (weekly)	Mustafa and Ali Amin (*Props.*)
	Moussa Sabri (*Ed.*)
Sabah El Kheir (weekly)	Heirs of Fatima Al Youssef (*Props.*)
	Ahmed Baha' El Din (*Ed.*)
Al Itnein (weekly)	Al Hilal Publishing House (*Props.*)
	Fahim Naguib (*Ed.*)
Al Tahrir (weekly)	Anwar Sadat (*Chmn. of Brd.*)
	Ahmed Hamroush (*Ed.*)
Al Police (weekly)	Police Officers Club (*Props.*)
	Ahmed El Weteidi (*Ed.*)
Al Ahad (weekly)	Khalid Abdel Kader (*Prop. and Ed.*)

UNITED ARAB REPUBLIC

Name of Party	Proprietor, Editor, etc.
Al Hilal (monthly)	Al Hilal Publishing House (*Props.*) Taher El Tanahi (*Ed.*)

NON-ARABIC

Le Journal d'Egypte (morning) In French	Edgard Gallad (*Prop. and Ed.*)
La Bourse Egyptienne (morning) In French	Al Tahrir Publishing Co. (*Prop.*—owned by Al Gomhouria) Georges Zezos (*Act. Ed.*)
Le Progrès Egyptien (morning) In French	Al Tahrir Publishing Co. (*Prop.*—owned by Al Gomhouria) Maurice Yaccarini (*Ed.*)
The Egyptian Gazette (morning) In English	Al Tahrir Publishing Co. (*Prop.*—owned by Al Gomhouria) Dr. Amin Aboul Enein (*Ed.*)
Images (weekly) In French	Al Hilal Publishing House (*Props.*) Jean Moscatelli (*Ed.*)
Radio-Monde Spectacles (weekly) In French	Elias Attia (*Prop. and Ed.*)
La Revue du Caire (monthly) In French	Alexandre Papadopoulos (*Prop. and Ed.*)
Le Journal d'Alexandrie (morning) In French (Alexandria)	Al Tahrir Publishing Co. (*Prop.*—owned by Al Gomhouria) Charles Arcache (*Ed.*)
La Réforme (morning) In French (Alexandria)	Comte de Saab (*Prop.*) Charles Boudagoff (*Ed.*)
Tachydromos (morning) In Greek (Alexandria)	B. Tinios (*Prop.*) George A. Tinios (*Ed.*)
Parikos (morning) In Greek	Potiris Nicolas and N. G. Aratakis (*Props.*) Costas Alatsis (*Ed.*)
Phos (morning) In Greek	A. Canakis and A. Bonaros (*Props.*) M. Papadatos
Anatoli (morning) In Greek (Alexandria)	Z. Halkiadis (*Prop.*) P. Castrounis (*Ed.*)

SYRIAN PRESS

Unless otherwise noted, papers are published in Damascus.

Name of Paper	Circulation	Political Affiliation	Owner and Editor
Al Manar	3,000	Moslem Brethren.	Bashir al-Awf (*Prop.*)
Al Nasr	3,000	Pro-Soviet.	Wadih Sidawi (*Prop.*)
Al Nur*	5,000	Communist.	Abd al-Baki Jamali (*Ed.*)
Sawt al-Arab	3,000	Independent.	Abd zl-Qadir al-Qawwas (*Prop.*)
Al Tarbiah (Aleppo)	3,000	Pro-Soviet.	Abdul Salam Kanili (*Prop.*)
Barq al-Shimal (Aleppo)	3,000	Independent.	Nicola Jangi (*Prop.*)

* Suspended.

UNITED NATIONS

Seat: New York, United States of America
Founded October 24, 1945*

THE CHARTER

The organization and functions of the United Nations are governed by a Charter of nineteen chapters comprising a hundred and eleven articles which was drafted by the United Nations Conference on International Organization at San Francisco. Amendments to the Charter require the ratification of two-thirds of the members of the United Nations, including all the permanent members of the Security Council. The Charter lays down the conditions of admission, suspension, and expulsion of State Members; the composition, functions and powers of the General Assembly and the Security Council; a system for the pacific settlement of disputes; action with respect to threats to the peace, breaches of the peace, and acts of aggression; the place of regional arrangements within the Organization; provision for international economic and social cooperation; the composition, functions and powers of the Economic and Social Council; a declaration regarding non-self-governing territories; provision for an international trusteeship system and the composition, functions and powers of the Trusteeship Council; provision for an International Court of Justice; provision for an international Secretariat; provision for the registration and publication of international treaties; provision for transitional security arrangements.

THE GENERAL ASSEMBLY

President: (thirteenth session): CHARLES MALIK (Lebanon)

Each Member State has one vote in the General Assembly and may have up to five delegates. The General Assembly meets in regular annual sessions. It may also hold special sessions. It has power to "discuss any questions or any matters within the scope of the present Charter" and (except when, according to Article 12 of the Charter, "the Security Council is exercising in respect of any dispute or situation the functions assigned to it in the present Charter") "may make recommendations to the Members of the United Nations or to the Security Council or to both" (Article 10). The General Assembly under the Charter is specifically empowered to make recommendations on international peace and security, including disarmament and the regulation of armaments, but where action is necessary the question is referred to the Security Council. The Security Council is required to report to the General Assembly on the measures decided upon or taken. In November 1950, however, the Assembly decided that if the Security Council, because of lack of unanimity of the permanent members, fails to exercise its primary responsibility for the maintenance of international peace and security in any case where there appears to be a threat to the peace, breach of the peace, or act of aggression, the General Assembly shall consider the matter immediately with a view to making appropriate recommendations to Members for collective measures, including, in the case of a breach of the peace or act of aggression, the use of armed force when necessary, to maintain or restore international peace and security.

* On this date ratification of the United Nations Charter had been deposited by China, France, the USSR, the United Kingdom, and the United States, and by a majority of the other signatory states. The first meeting of the General Assembly was convened in London on January 10, 1946.

UNITED NATIONS

The Charter charges the General Assembly to promote international cooperation in the political, economic, social, cultural, educational, and health fields; to encourage the progressive development of international law and its codification; and to assist in the realization of human rights and fundamental freedoms for all without distinction as to race, sex, language or religion. The Economic and Social Council and the Trusteeship Council function under its authority.

Other important functions of the General Assembly include: the election of the non-permanent members of the Security Council; the election of the members of the Economic and Social Council; the election of the elective members of the Trusteeship Council; confirmation of appointment of the Secretary-General; on the Security Council's recommendation, the admission of new members to the United Nations, the suspension of the rights and privileges of membership, and the expulsion of members; certain functions with respect to the international trusteeship system, including the approval of trusteeship agreements for areas not designated strategic; consideration and approval of the budget of the Organization.

Decisions on important questions require a two-thirds majority of those present and voting. A simple majority is sufficient on other questions.

STATES MEMBERS OF THE UNITED NATIONS

Afghanistan	Dominican Republic	Italy	Poland
Albania	Ecuador	Japan	Portugal
Argentina	El Salvador	Jordan	Rumania
Australia	Ethiopia	Laos	Saudi Arabia
Austria	Federation of Malaya	Lebanon	Spain
Belgium	Finland	Liberia	Sudan
Bolivia	France	Libya	Sweden
Brazil	Ghana	Luxembourg	Thailand
Bulgaria	Greece	Mexico	Tunisia
Burma	Guatemala	Morocco	Turkey
Byelorussian SSR	Guinea	Nepal	Ukrainian SSR
Cambodia	Haiti	Netherlands	Union of South Africa
Canada	Honduras	New Zealand	USSR
Ceylon	Hungary	Nicaragua	United Arab Republic
Chile	Iceland	Norway	United Kingdom
China	India	Pakistan	United States
Colombia	Indonesia	Panama	Uruguay
Costa Rica	Iran	Paraguay	Venezuela
Cuba	Iraq	Peru	Yemen
Czechoslovakia	Ireland	Philippines	Yugoslavia
Denmark	Israel		

COMMITTEES OF THE GENERAL ASSEMBLY

Main Committees
    First (Political and Security, including the regulation of armaments)
    Special Political Committee (To share the work of the First Committee)
    Second (Economic and Financial)
    Third (Social, Humanitarian and Cultural)
    Fourth (Trusteeship, including Non-Self-Governing Territories)
    Fifth (Administrative and Budgetary)
    Sixth (Legal)

Procedural Committees

  General Committee—21 members
  Credentials Committee—9 members

Standing Committees

  Advisory Committee on Administrative and Budgetary Questions—9 members
  Committee on Contributions—10 members

THE SECURITY COUNCIL

The Security Council is composed of eleven members of the United Nations, of which five (China, France, the Union of Soviet Socialist Republics, the United Kingdom of Great Britain and Northern Ireland, and the United States of America) enjoy permanent terms, and six are elected by the General Assembly—three each year for two-year terms. In the election of non-permanent members special regard is paid, first, to their contribution to the maintenance of international peace and security and to the other purposes of the Organization; and also to equitable geographic distribution. The Security Council is so organized as to be able to function continuously, with each of its members represented at all times at the seat of the Organization.

Decisions of the Security Council require seven affirmative votes. The concurring votes of the five permanent members are necessary for decisions on all but procedural matters. The single exception to this is the requirement that, where pacific settlement of a dispute is being attempted, a party to the dispute shall abstain from voting.

The Security Council has "primary responsibility for the maintenance of international peace and security" (Article 24) and was made the principal agency for conciliation or inquiry (Chapter VI). It determines the existence of any threat to the peace, breach of the peace or act of aggression (Chapter VII), and decides what measures not involving the use of armed force should be employed to give effect to its decisions (Article 41). Should these be inadequate it may take military action to enforce its decisions (Article 42). The Members of the United Nations undertake to make available to the Security Council on its call armed forces, assistance, and facilities (Article 43). So that the United Nations may take urgent military measures the Members are expected to hold immediately available national air force contingents for combined international enforcement action (Article 45).

The Security Council encourages the pacific settlement of international disputes by regional agencies. But, with the exception of measures against any state which during the Second World War was an enemy of any of the Charter signatories, the consent of the Security Council is necessary for enforcement action under regional arrangements or by regional authorities. However, "nothing in the present Charter shall impair the inherent right of individual or collective self-defense if an armed attack occurs against a Member of the United Nations, until the Security Council has taken the measures necessary to maintain international peace and security." (Article 51).

The Security Council is responsible for all functions of the United Nations relating to strategic areas in the trust territories (Article 83).

UNITED NATIONS

MEMBERS OF THE SECURITY COUNCIL

The Presidency of the Council is rotated monthly by Member States in alphabetical order.

Permanent Members

| China | USSR | United Kingdom |
| France | | United States |

Until 1960

| Canada | Japan | Panama |

Until 1961

| Argentina | Italy | Tunisia |

MILITARY STAFF COMMITTEE

The Military Staff Committee consists of the Chiefs of Staff of the permanent members of the Security Council or their representatives. It advises and assists the Security Council on its military requirements for maintaining international peace and security, the employment and command of forces placed at its disposal, the regulation of armaments and possible disarmament.

DISARMAMENT COMMISSION

This Commission is composed of all members of the United Nations. It was established by General Assembly resolution 502 (VI) of January 11, 1952, to prepare proposals for the regulation, limitation and balanced reduction of all armed forces and armaments, for the elimination of all major weapons adaptable to mass destruction, and for effective international control of atomic energy. The Disarmament Commission which reports to the Security Council and to the General Assembly replaced the Atomic Energy Commission and the Commission for Conventional Armaments.

This Commission formerly had 25 members but was enlarged in 1958 for the year 1959 "on an *ad hoc* basis to include all the Members of the United Nations."

THE ECONOMIC AND SOCIAL COUNCIL

The Economic and Social Council consists of eighteen members of the United Nations elected by the General Assembly, with six members elected each year for a term of three years. Each State member has one vote and one representative. Decisions are by majority vote of those present and voting. The Council normally holds two sessions yearly and may hold special sessions.

Under the authority of the General Assembly, the Economic and Social Council is directed to work for higher standards of living and full employment; the solution of international economic, social, and health problems; international cultural and educational cooperation; and universal respect for, and observance of, human rights and fundamental freedoms. The Economic and Social Council is empowered to study and report on these subjects and to make recommendations on any of them to the General Assembly and the Members of the United Nations. It has established commissions to aid it in its work. The Economic and Social Council may furnish information to the Security Council and assists the Security Council upon its request.

UNITED NATIONS

MEMBERS OF THE ECONOMIC AND SOCIAL COUNCIL
President: George F. Davidson (Canada)

Until 1960

Finland	Pakistan	USSR
Mexico	Poland	United Kingdom

Until 1961

Chile	Costa Rica	Netherlands
China	France	Sudan

Until 1962

Afghanistan	New Zealand	United States
Bulgaria	Spain	Venezuela

COMMISSIONS OF THE ECONOMIC AND SOCIAL COUNCIL

Transport and Communications
Statistical
Population
Social
Human Rights
Status of Women
Narcotic Drugs
International Commodity Trade
Economic Commission for Europe
Economic Commission for Asia and the Far East
Economic Commission for Latin America
Economic Commission for Africa

Four standing committees and six special bodies, including the United Nations Children's Fund (UNICEF), also report to the Economic and Social Council.

Various specialized intergovernmental agencies dealing with peaceful uses of atomic energy, economic, social or related matters have been brought into relationship with the United Nations under agreements approved by the General Assembly of the United Nations and the appropriate organ of the specialized agency concerned. The Economic and Social Council as a rule may coordinate the activities of these agencies by consulting with them and making recommendations to them. As of December, 1958, agreements defining the relationship between the United Nations and the following inter-governmental agencies were in force:

International Labour Organization
Food and Agricultural Organization of the United Nations
United Nations Educational, Scientific and Cultural Organization
International Civil Aviation Organization
International Bank for Reconstruction and Development
International Monetary Fund
World Health Organization
Universal Postal Union
International Telecommunication Union
World Meteorological Organization
International Finance Corporation
International Atomic Energy Agency

THE TRUSTEESHIP COUNCIL

President: EMILIO ARENALES CATALAN (Guatemala)

The Trusteeship Council functions under the authority of the General Assembly. On it are represented all States Members of the United Nations administering trust territories, permanent members of the Security Council not administering trust territories, and as many other members elected by the General Assembly for three-year terms as may be necessary to ensure that the membership is equally divided between those members which administer trust territories and those which do not. Each member of the Trusteeship Council has one vote. Decisions are made by majority vote of those present and voting. The Council usually holds two regular sessions yearly and may hold special sessions.

The Trusteeship Council considers reports submitted by an Administering Authority, accepts petitions and examines them in consultation with the Administering Authority, and provides for periodic visits to the trust territories. It has formulated a questionnaire on the political, economic, social and educational advancement of each trust territory, on the basis of which each Administering Authority makes an annual report to the General Assembly or, in the case of "strategic areas" under trusteeship, to the Security Council.

On December 13, 1946, the General Assembly approved draft trusteeship agreements for eight territories formerly held under mandate: New Guinea (Australia); Ruanda-Urundi (Belgium); Cameroons (United Kingdom); Tanganyika (United Kingdom); Togoland (United Kingdom); Cameroons (France); Togoland (France); Western Samoa (New Zealand).

On April 2, 1947, the Security Council approved the text of a Trusteeship Agreement for the former Japanese mandated islands (Marshall, Mariana and Caroline Islands) which had been submitted by the United States Government. The Trust Territory of the Pacific Islands was designated as a "strategic area."

On November 1, 1947, the General Assembly approved a Trusteeship Agreement for the former mandate of Nauru (administered by Australia on behalf of Australia, New Zealand and the United Kingdom).

On December 2, 1950, the General Assembly approved a Trusteeship Agreement for the former Italian Colony, Somaliland, to be administered by Italy for a period of ten years, at the end of which the territory is to become a sovereign independent state.

The former Trust Territory of Togoland under British administration was joined with the Gold Coast when the latter became the independent Sovereign State of Ghana on March 6, 1957.

MEMBERS OF THE TRUSTEESHIP COUNCIL

Australia[1]
Belgium[1]
Burma[3]
China[2]
France[1]
Haiti[4]
India[4]
Italy[1]
New Zealand[1]
Paraguay[3]
USSR[2]
United Arab Republic[3]
United Kingdom[1]
United States[1]

[1] Administering authorities.
[2] Permanent Members of Security Council not administering Trust Territories.
[3] Elected for term ending December 31, 1961.
[4] Elected for term ending December 31, 1959.

UNITED NATIONS

THE INTERNATIONAL COURT OF JUSTICE
Seat: The Hague, The Netherlands

The International Court of Justice is the principal judicial organ of the United Nations. It is governed by a Statute which is based upon the Statute of the Permanent Court of International Justice and forms an integral part of the United Nations Charter.

The fifteen judges of the Court are elected by the General Assembly and by the Security Council for nine-year terms. States which are not members of the United Nations may, by special arrangements, become parties to the Statute and participate in the election of judges.

Only states may be parties in cases before the Court. If a party to a case disregards a judgement, the other party may have recourse to the Security Council which may make recommendations or decide upon measures to give effect to the judgments.

The General Assembly and the Security Council may request the Court for advisory opinions on any legal question. Other organs of the United Nations and specialized agencies, if authorized to do so by the General Assembly, may request advisory opinions of the Court on legal questions arising within the scope of their activities.

The present Registrar of the Court is Julio Lopez Olivan.

THE JUDGES OF THE INTERNATIONAL COURT OF JUSTICE
President: Helge Klaestad (Norway)

Until February 5, 1961

Muhammad Zafrullah Khan	(Pakistan)
Green H. Hackworth	(United States)
Helge Klaestad	(Norway)
Feodor I. Kojevnikov	(USSR)
E. C. Armand Ugon	(Uruguay)

Until February 5, 1964

Roberto Córdova	(Mexico)
Jules Basdenant	(France)
J. Gustavo Guerrero*	(El Salvador)
Hersch Lauterpacht	(United Kingdom)
Lucio M. Moreno Quintana	(Argentina)

Until February 6, 1967

Abdel Hamid Badawi	(Egypt)
V. K. Wellington Koo	(China)
Sir Percy Spender	(Australia)
Jean Spiropoulos	(Greece)
Bohdan Winiarski	(Poland)

*Deceased October 25, 1958.

THE SECRETARIAT
Secretary General: Dag Hammarskjold (Sweden)

PRINCIPAL OFFICERS

Ahmed Bokhari (Pakistan)†	Under-Secretary for Public Information
Ralph J. Bunche (USA)	Under-Secretary for Special Political Affairs

Andrew W. Cordier (USA)	Executive Assistant to the Secretary-General
Anatoly Dobrynin (USSR)	Under-Secretary for the Department of Political and Security Council Affairs
Victor Hoo (China)	Under-Secretary for Conference Services
Hugh L. Keenleyside (Canada)	Director-General, Technical Assistance Administration
John McDiarmid (USA)	Acting Director of Personnel
Chakravarthi V. Narasimhan (India)	Under-Secretary for Special Political Affairs
David Owen (United Kingdom)	Executive Chairman, Technical Assistance Board
Maurice Pate (USA)	Executive Director, United Nations Children's Fund
Dragoslav Protitch (Yugoslavia)	Under-Secretary for the Department of Trusteeship and Information from Non-Self-Governing Territories
Philippe de Seynes (France)	Under-Secretary for Economic and Social Affairs
Constantin Stavropoulos (Greece)	Legal Counsel
Bruce Turner (New Zealand)	Controller
David B. Vaughan (USA)	Director of General Services
P. P. Spinelli (Italy)	Director of the United Nations European Office (Geneva)

† Deceased December 5, 1958.

BUDGET

The budget of the United Nations for 1959 was adopted at $60,802,120 and the working capital fund was established at $23,500,000.

OFFICES

The permanent headquarters of the United Nations are in New York.

The European office of the United Nations is in Geneva. As of December, 1958, United Nations Information Centers and offices had been established in Accra, Athens, Bangkok, Belgrade, Bogota, Buenos Aires, Cairo, Copenhagen, Djakarta, Geneva, Karachi, London, Manila, Mexico City, Monrovia, Moscow, New Delhi, Paris, Prague, Rio de Janeiro, Rome, Santiago, Sydney, Tehran, Tokyo, The Hague and Washington.

INTERGOVERNMENTAL AGENCIES RELATED TO THE UNITED NATIONS

International Labour Organization
    Founded: April 11, 1919
    Seat: Geneva, Switzerland
    Director-General: DAVID A. MORSE (United States)

Food and Agriculture Organization of the United Nations
    Founded: October 16, 1945
    Seat: Rome, Italy
    Director-General: BINAY RANJAN SEN (India)

United Nations Educational, Scientific and Cultural Organization
    Founded: November 4, 1946
    Seat: Paris, France
    Director-General: DR. VITTORINO VERONESI (Italy)

International Civil Aviation Organization
  Founded: April 4, 1947
  Seat: Montreal, Canada
  President of the Council: WALTER BINAGHI (Argentina)
  Secretary-General: E. C. R. LJUNGBERG (Sweden)
International Bank for Reconstruction and Development
  Founded: December 27, 1945
  Seat: Washington, D.C.
  President: EUGENE R. BLACK (United States)
International Monetary Fund
  Founded: December 27, 1945
  Seat: Washington, D.C.
  Managing Director: PER JACOBSSON (Sweden)
World Health Organization
  Founded: April 7, 1948
  Seat: Geneva, Switzerland
  Director-General: DR. MARCOLINO GOMES CANDAU (Brazil)
Universal Postal Union
  Founded: July 1, 1875
  Seat: Berne, Switzerland
  Director of the International Bureau: FRITZ HESS (Switzerland)
International Telecommunication Union
  Founded: as International Telegraph Union, in 1865
  Seat: Geneva, Switzerland
  Acting Secretary-General: DR. GERALD GROSS (United States)
World Meteorological Organization
  Founded: March 23, 1950
  Seat: Geneva, Switzerland
  Secretary-General: D. A. DAVIES (United Kingdom)
International Finance Corporation
  Founded: July 20, 1956
  Seat: Washington, D.C.
  President: ROBERT L. GARNER (United States)
International Atomic Energy Agency
  Founded: July 29, 1957
  Seat: Vienna, Austria
  Director-General: W. STERLING COLE (United States)
Inter-Governmental Maritime Consultative Organization
  A Convention of the Inter-Governmental Maritime Consultative Organization was drawn up by the United Nations Maritime Conference and opened for signature on March 6, 1948. The Convention came into effect on March 17, 1958. IMCO will formally come into existence early in 1960.
International Trade Organization—General Agreement on Tariffs and Trade
  The International Trade Organization charter was drawn up at the United Nations Conference on Trade and Employment which opened at Havana, Cuba, on November 21, 1947. Although establishment of ITO has been postponed, one of its objectives has been embodied in an international commercial treaty known as the General Agreement on Tariffs and Trade (GATT).

UNITED STATES

Capital: Washington
Area: Continental United States 3,026,789 square miles;
including outlying possessions 3,623,995 square miles
Population: Continental United States 174,000,000 (1958 estimate)

President
DWIGHT D. EISENHOWER (Republican)
Assumed office on January 20, 1953
Elected November 4, 1952; re-elected on November 6, 1956,
for term ending in January 1961

Cabinet
Republican
Assumed office in January 1953

PARLIAMENT
(Congress)

UPPER CHAMBER
(Senate)

Election of November 4, 1958 (six-year term; renewed by thirds every two years)

President: RICHARD M. NIXON (Republican)

Parties	Representation
Democratic	64
Republican	34
Total	98

LOWER CHAMBER
(House of Representatives)

Election of November 4, 1958 (for two years)

Speaker: SAM RAYBURN (Democrat)

Parties	Representation
Democratic	283
Republican	153
Total	436

PARTY PROGRAMS AND LEADERS

There are no fundamental differences between the major political parties of the United States—the Republican and the Democratic—corresponding to the parliamentary bloc system of Continental Europe or to the clear distinction between the Labor and the Tory parties in England. Even in the case of the principal issue of the tariff, the economic changes which have occurred in recent years, such as the growing industrialization of the Southern states, have caused modifications in the programs of the parties, bringing their views on this major question more and more into accord. Formerly the Republicans, centering in the North and industrial East, advocated a high or protective schedule, while the Democrats of the agricultural South stood for a tariff for revenue only. A careful examination of the programs of the Republican and Democratic parties, which follow, will reveal few important differences. There are liberal and conservative Republicans, liberal and conservative Democrats. Obviously, a popular program in either case must be a compromise between these extremes.

The fundamental difference between the parties of Europe and the United States grows out of the federal character of the American Union. Thus, while every nation-wide party is compelled to maintain a national organization, which becomes especially active during the quadrennial presidential campaigns, it must also have an organization in every state in order to carry on campaigns for state offices, and also to assist the national organization in presidential years. Each state organization is autonomous and at liberty to adopt any platform of principles which it chooses, and between the state organizations there is frequently a diversity of interest or at least a diversity in the selection of paramount issues.

In occasional instances blocs representing sectional, or economic, or personal interests are formed within the major parties. Sometimes these result in open secession, when independent candidates are supported. But these splits have been of brief duration, and compromises or termination of the cause that led to them have effected the return of minorities to the major party, in which they sometimes continue to operate as blocs.

The Progressives, who for long paid nominal allegiance to the Republican party, became an independent group in 1934, and an independent national party in 1938. This party did badly in several elections, and returned to the Republican Party in 1946.

In the 1944 elections Mr. Roosevelt was supported by the American Labor Party and the Liberal Party (formed from the right wing of the American Labor Party). Both parties were formed in New York state. They also participated in the 1946, 1948, and 1952 elections, usually supporting Democratic candidates. The American Labor Party was dissolved in 1946, but the Liberal Party supported the Democrats in 1956 and 1958.

In addition to the two principal parties, several minor parties present candidates at national elections. These, with their candidates in 1956, included: Socialist Party—Darlington Hoopes; Socialist Labor Party—Eric Haas; Poor Man's Party—Henry B. Krajewski; Greenback Party—Fred C. Proehl; Prohibition Party—Dr. Enoch A. Holtwick. Their total vote was very small.

The Communist Party disbanded in 1944 but maintained itself as the Communist Political Association. In 1945 it once again became an active political party. In 1948 the Communists supported Henry A. Wallace for President. The leaders of the party were convicted under the Smith Act of advocating the overthrow of the Government by force, and were sentenced to prison. In 1954 Congress passed a law making the Communist Party illegal. In June, 1958, the following officers were elected by the National Committee of the party: Eugene Dennis (National Secretary), Robert Thompson (Executive Secretary), James Jackson (Secretary for Negro and Southern Affairs), Arnold Johnson (Legislative Secretary), Elizabeth Gurley Flynn (National Field Organizer). The National Executive Committee now includes: Benjamin Davis, Eugene Dennis, Mrs. Elizabeth Flynn, Arnold Jackson, A. Krchmarek, Claude Lightfoot, Micky Lima, Hyman Lumer, George Meyers, Burt Nelson, Jack Stachel, Robert Thompson, and Carl Winter.

The programs, or platforms, of the parties are adopted at the quadrennial conventions, when the presidential candidates are chosen. It should be pointed out that the parties do not necessarily carry out the pledges in their platforms, even though they succeed in electing a majority in both houses of Congress. The platforms often serve to get candidates elected rather than specifically to guide them after they attain office. The programs, as adopted in 1956, and leaders of the two principal parties are as follows:

REPUBLICAN PARTY: Traditionally the high-tariff party, strong in the Northern and Central States. In *foreign policy:* its basic objectives are peace and freedom. Advocated: vigorous support of the United Nations and collective security as deterrent to war; help to friendly nations to maintain such local armed forces and economic strength as to provide a bulwark against communist aggression and subversion; continued efforts with friends and allies to assist underdeveloped areas of the free world in their efforts to attain greater freedom, independence and self-determination and to raise their living standards; a policy of impartial friendship for peoples of the Arab states and Israel to promote a peaceful settlement of conflicts in the Near East, including the problem of the Palestine-Arab refugees, maintenance of the integrity of an independent Jewish state and support of Israel against armed aggression; reunification of Germany in freedom, and liberation of satellite states; continuation of opposition to seating of Communist China in the United Nations and of efforts to free remaining Americans held prisoner by Communist China; encouragement of productivity and profitable international trade by reducing barriers to flow of capital and trade on a gradual, selective and reciprocal basis with safeguards for domestic enterprises, agriculture and labor against unfair import competition; barring of any trade with the Communist world that would threaten the security of the United States or its allies; reaffirmation of the principle of freedom for all people and eventual end of colonialism; progressive elimination of barriers that interfere with the free flow of news, information and ideas; exchange of persons between the free peoples and the captive peoples of the world, and continuance and development of exchange of persons programs between the free nations; continuance of bipartisan development of foreign policies; continued cooperation with sister states of the Americas for the strengthening of security and economic and social ties.

In *domestic policy* advocated: a dynamic economy through further reductions in Government spending, continued balancing of the budget, a sound dollar, gradual reduction of the national debt; continuation of aid to small business; revision and improvement of the Taft-Hartley Act so as to protect more effectively the rights of labor unions, management, individual workers and the public; continued support for its newly created Department of Health, Education and Welfare, Federal assistance in building schools to relieve critical classroom shortage, increased Federal aid for medical care of the needy, encouragement of voluntary health insurance, extension of social security system; aid to agriculture by developing farm programs that are fair to all farmers and that provide full freedom instead of regimentation, flexible price supports for farm products, development of soil bank program to reduce surpluses of farm products and to improve soil, water, and timber resources; vigilance against corruption and waste, improvement of efficiency as proposed by Hoover Commission, guarding against unwarranted growth of centralized Federal power and dispensing with Federal activities competing with private enterprise; a non-political career civil service; immediate statehood for Alaska and for Hawaii; self-government, national suffrage and representation in Congress for residents of the District of Columbia; a constitutional amendment to provide equal rights for women; accepts decision of U. S. Supreme Court that racial discrimination in publicly-supported schools be eliminated and concurs in the conclusion of the Court that school desegregation should be accomplished with "all deliberate speed" locally through district courts. Advocates maintenance and improvement of military strength "which is the key factor in the preservation of world peace."

Leaders: Dwight D. Eisenhower (President of the Republic), Richard M. Nixon (Vice-President of the Republic, President of the Senate), Styles Bridges (Chairman of the Policy Committee of the Senate), Joseph W. Martin,

UNITED STATES

Jr. (Minority Leader in the House), H. Meade Alcorn, Jr. (Chairman of the Republican National Committee). There is a National Committee of 108 members and 48 chairmen of State Committees who may all be considered party leaders.

DEMOCRATIC PARTY: Traditionally the low-tariff party; strongest in the Southern States. In *foreign policy* advocated: support of the United Nations, opposition to admission of Communist China to the United Nations and continued support to Nationalist China; continued efforts to effect release of Americans detained by Communist China; enforced disarmament, meanwhile maintaining armed strength to deter war; betterment of living conditions of members of armed forces; scholarships and loan assistance for training of youth in scientific and technical fields; strong civil defense; collective defense arrangements, such as NATO; support for underdeveloped countries and a reappraisal of the foreign aid program; invocation of United Nations to pressure Soviet Russia to withdraw its troops from captive countries so as to permit free elections; expanding world trade; encouragement of European unity; peace with justice in the Middle East; assistance to Israel to build a sound and viable economy; assistance to Arab states to develop their economic resources and raise their living standards; aid for resettlement of Arab refugees; supplying of defensive weapons to Israel; assistance to free governments of Asia to improve their living standards; restoration of "good neighbor" policy in the Western Hemisphere; revision of immigration and nationality laws to eliminate provisions under which admission to the U. S. depends upon quotas based on national origin.

In *domestic policy* advocated: reassertion of principles of the Full Employment Act; a truly balanced budget, equitable tax revisions and money policies; reduction and elimination of poverty; full parity of income and living standards for agriculture; repeal of the Taft-Hartley Law and a new legislative approach toward labor-management problems; raising minimum wage to at least $1.25 per hour; aid to small business; development, protection, management and conservation of all natural resources; expanding nuclear development and atoms for peace program; administration of the Government on a sound, efficient and honest basis; effort for world-wide freedom in gathering and dissemination of news; a constitutional amendment to provide equal rights for women; immediate statehood for Alaska and Hawaii; home rule for District of Columbia; continued efforts to eliminate discrimination of all kinds; rejection of all proposals for use of force to interfere with desegregation in schools as determined by the courts; the following full prosperity objectives during the next four years: (a) $500,000,000,000 national economy, (b) increase of 20 percent or better in average standard of living, (c) an increase of annual income for American families with special emphasis on those with incomes below $2,000, (d) a determined drive toward parity of incomes and living standards for agriculture, (e) addition of all necessary classrooms for primary and secondary schools, construction of needed new homes, increase of benefits for old age assistance and old age survivors, insurance programs, expansion of hospital facilities and medical research, doubling of Government program for resource development and conservation, and national defense outlays based upon national needs—not permitting false economy "to jeopardize our very survival."

Leaders: Adlai E. Stevenson (Presidential Candidate in 1952 and 1956), Harry S. Truman (former President), Lyndon B. Johnson (Majority Leader in the Senate), Sam Rayburn (Speaker of the House), John W. McCormack (Majority Leader in the House), and Paul M. Butler (Chairman of the Democratic National Committee). The 108 members of the National Committee and 48 Chairmen of State Committees are all party leaders.

THE CABINET

The members of the Cabinet are: John Foster Dulles (Secretary of State), Robert B. Anderson (Secretary of the Treasury), Neil H. McElroy (Secretary of Defense), William P. Rogers (Attorney General), Arthur E. Summerfield (Postmaster-General), Fred A. Seaton (Secretary of the Interior), Ezra T. Benson (Secretary of Agriculture), Lewis L. Strauss (Secretary of Commerce), Arthur S. Fleming (Secretary of Health, Education and Welfare), and James P. Mitchell (Secretary of Labor). There are three Secretaries in the defense department without Cabinet rank: Wilber Marion Brucker (Army), Thomas S. Gates, Jr. (Navy), James H. Douglas (Air Force).

PRESS

(*m.* morning; *e.* evening)

Name of Paper	Circulation*	Political Affiliation	Proprietor, Editor, etc.
ALABAMA			
Post-Herald (*m.*) (Birmingham)	98,085	Independent.	John W. Frierson (*Pres.*) James E. Mills (*Ed.*)
Advertiser (*m.*) (Montgomery)	61,478	Democratic.	R. F. Hudson (*Pres.*) Grover C. Hall, Jr. (*Ed.*)
ALASKA			
Times (*e.*) (Anchorage, Alaska)	17,247	Independent.	Robert B. Atwood (*Ed.*)
News (*e.*) (Anchorage, Alaska)	11,847	Republican.	Norman C. Brown (*Ed.*)
News-Miner (*e.*) (Fairbanks, Alaska)	9,404	Independent Republican.	Clifford Cernik (*Ed.*)
Empire (*e.*) (Juneau, Alaska)	4,358	Independent.	William P. Allen (*Pub.*) Morgan Coe (*Gen. Mgr.*)
CALIFORNIA			
Examiner (*m.*) (Los Angeles)	354,865	Independent.	Hearst newspaper (See Note p. 215) Franklin S. Payne (*Pub.*)
Times (*m.*) (Los Angeles)	464,453	Republican.	Norman Chandler (*Pub.*) L. D. Hotchkiss (*Ed.*)
Chronicle (*m.*) (San Francisco)	194,400	Independent Republican.	Charles De Young Thieriot (*Pub.*)
Examiner (*m.*) (San Francisco)	254,279	Independent.	Hearst newspaper (See Note p. 215) Charles Mayer (*Pub.*)
COLORADO			
Post (*e.*) (Denver)	254,519	Independent.	Palmer Hoyt (*Pub.*) Robert W. Lucas (*Ed.*)
Rocky Mountain News (*m.*) (Denver)	157,848	Independent.	Jack Foster (*Pres. and Ed.*)
CONNECTICUT			
Courant (*m.*) (Hartford)	103,521	Republican; oldest daily in the United States; established in 1764.	John R. Reitemeyer (*Pub.*) Herbert Brucker (*Ed.*)
Times (*e.*) (Hartford)	118,644	Independent Democratic.	Ward E. Duffy (*Ed.*)

* Circulation is taken from *Editor & Publisher, International Year Book, 1958.*

UNITED STATES

Name of Paper	Circulation	Political Affiliation	Proprietor, Editor, etc.
DISTRICT OF COLUMBIA			
Post and Times-Herald (m.) (Washington)	390,649	Independent.	Eugene Meyer (Ch. of Bd.)
Star (e.) (Washington)	254,992	Independent.	B. M. McKelway (Ed.)
FLORIDA			
Florida Times-Union (m.) (Jacksonville)	151,883	Independent.	R. C. Millar (Pres.) C. J. King (Ed.)
GEORGIA			
Constitution (m.) (Atlanta)	196,693	Democratic.	Clark Howell (Pub.) Ralph McGill (Ed.)
ILLINOIS			
News (e.) (Chicago)	584,911	Independent.	John S. Knight (Pres. and Ed.)
Sun-Times (Chicago)	584,509	Independent.	Marshall Field, Jr. (Pub. and Ed.)
Tribune (Chicago) (m.)	951,297	Republican.	Chesser M. Campbell (Pub.) Leon Stolz (Ed.)
INDIANA			
News (e.) (Indianapolis)	168,347	Independent.	Eugene C. Pulliam (Pres.)
Star (m.) (Indianapolis)	316,206	Independent.	James A. Stuart (Ed.)
IOWA			
Register (m.) (Des Moines)	219,313	Independent Republican.	Gardner Cowles (Pres.) Kenneth MacDonald (Ed.)
KANSAS			
Capital (m.) (Topeka).	64,538	Republican.	Jim Reed (Ed.)
KENTUCKY			
Courier-Journal (m.) (Louisville)	214,533	Independent Democratic.	Barry Bingham (Pres.) Mark Ethridge (Pub.)
LOUISIANA			
Times-Picayune (m.) (New Orleans)	189,758	Independent Democratic.	John F. Tims (Pres.) George W. Healy, Jr. (Ed.)
MAINE			
News (m.) (Bangor).	70,979	Independent.	Mrs. Fred T. Jordan (Pres.) Richard K. Warren (Ed.)
MARYLAND			
Sun (m. and e.) (Baltimore)	196,725(m.) 214,938(e.)	Independent Democratic.	William F. Schmick, Sr. (Pres.) Phillip M. Wagner (Ed.)
MASSACHUSETTS			
Christian Science Monitor (e.) (Boston	158,729	Independent; published by Christian Science Publishing Society, but not a religious organ; has wide general circulation.	Erwin D. Canham (Ed.)
Globe (m. and e.) (Boston)	225,162(m.) 149,070(e.)	Independent.	Wm. D. Taylor (Pres.) Laurence L. Winship (Ed.)
Herald (m.) (Boston)	204,395	Republican.	R. B. Choate (Pub. and Ed.)
MICHIGAN			
Free Press (m.) (Detroit)	471,203	Independent.	John S. Knight (Pub. and Ed.)
News (e.) (Detroit)	468,167	Independent.	Warren S. Booth (Pres.) Harry V. Wade (Ed.)
Times (e.) (Detroit)	397,832	Independent.	Hearst Newspaper (See Note p. 215) Phil de Beaubien (Pub.)
MINNESOTA			
Star (e.) (Minneapolis)	285,227	Independent.	John Cowles (Pres. and Pub.) William P. Steven (Exec. Ed.)
Pioneer Press-Dispatch (m.) (St. Paul)	92,708	Independent.	Bernard H. Ridder (Pres.) Herbert Lewis (Ed.)

Name of Paper	Circulation	Political Affiliation	Proprietor, Editor, etc.
MISSOURI			
Globe-Democrat (m.) (St. Louis)	338,884	Independent.	Richard H. Amberg (Pub.) Louis LaCoss (Ed.)
Post Dispatch (e.) (St. Louis)	403,068	Independent Democratic.	Joseph Pulitzer, Jr. (Pub. and Ed.)
NEBRASKA			
World Herald (m. and e.) (Omaha)	127,397 (m.) 120,081 (e.)	Independent.	Harry Doorly (Ch. of Bd.) W. E. Christenson (Ed.)
NEW JERSEY			
News (e.) (Newark)	281,356	Independent.	Edward W. Scudder, Jr. (Pres.) Lloyd M. Felmly (Ed.)
NEW YORK			
Herald Tribune (m.) (New York City)	326,478	Republican.	Howard D. Brundage (Pres.) George A. Cornish (Exec. Ed.)
Journal of Commerce (m.) (New York City)	37,581	Commercial.	Bernard J. Ridder (Ch. of Bd.) H. E. Luedicke (Ed.)
Times (m.) (New York City)	570,717	Independent Democratic.	Arthur H. Sulzberger (Pub.) Charles Merz (Ed.)
Wall Street Journal (m.) (New York City)	481,275	Financial.	W. H. Grimes (Ed.)
World-Telegram and The Sun (e.) (New York City)	454,137	Independent.	Scripps-Howard newspaper (See Note p. 215) Roy W. Howard (Pres. and Ed.)
NORTH CAROLINA			
Observer (m.) (Charlotte)	151,649	Independent Democratic.	James L. Knight (Pub.) C. A. McKnight (Ed.)
News & Observer (m.) (Raleigh)	123,658	Democratic.	Jonathan Daniels (Ed.)
OHIO			
Enquirer (m.) (Cincinnati)	205,461	Independent.	Roger H. Ferger (Pub. and Ed.)
Plain Dealer (m.) (Cleveland)	304,005	Independent Democratic.	Sterling E. Graham (Pres.) Wright Bryan (Ed.)
Press (e.) (Cleveland)	313,749	Independent.	Scripps-Howard newspaper (See Note p. 215) L. B. Seltzer (Ed.)
OKLAHOMA			
Oklahoman (m.) (Oklahoma City)	147,786	Independent Democratic.	E. K. Gaylord (Pres. and Ed.)
World (m.) (Tulsa)	95,591	Independent.	H. G. Henthorne (Ed.)
OREGON			
Oregonian (m.) (Portland)	229,636	Independent Republican.	M. J. Frey (Pres.) Herbert Lundy (Ed.)
PENNSYLVANIA			
Bulletin (e.) (Philadelphia)	707,406	Independent.	Robert McLean (Pres.) Melville F. Ferguson (Ed.)
Inquirer (m.) (Philadelphia)	619,054	Independent.	Walter H. Annenberg (Pub. and Ed.)
Press (e.) (Pittsburgh)	297,902	Independent.	W. W. Forster (Ed.)
RHODE ISLAND			
Bulletin (e.) (Providence)	146,231	Independent.	John C. A. Watkins (Pub.) Sevellon Brown, III (Ed.)
TENNESSEE			
Commercial Appeal (m.) (Memphis)	201,143	Independent.	Enoch Brown (Pres.) Frank R. Ahlgren (Ed.)
TEXAS			
News (m.) (Dallas)	203,011	Independent Democratic.	E. M. Dealey (Pub.)

UNITED STATES

Name of Paper	Circulation	Political Affiliation	Proprietor, Editor, etc.
UTAH			
Tribune (m.) (Salt Lake City)	98,017	Independent.	J. F. Fitzpatrick (*Pub.*)
VIRGINIA			
News Leader (e.) (Richmond)	107,671	Independent Democratic.	D. Tennant Bryan (*Pub.*) J. J. Kilpatrick (*Ed.*)
WASHINGTON			
Post Intelligencer (m.) (Seattle)	193,329	Independent.	Hearst newspaper (See note below) Charles B. Lindeman (*Pub.*)
Times (e.) (Seattle)	213,423	Independent.	Elmer E. Todd (*Ch. of Bd.*)
WISCONSIN			
Journal (e.) (Milwaukee)	352,566	Independent.	J. D. Ferguson (*Pres. and Ed.*)

OUTLYING TERRITORY

Advertiser (m.) (Honolulu, T.H.)	47,039	Independent.	L. P. Thurston (*Pres.*) Raymond Coll (*Ed.*)
Star-Bulletin (e.) (Honolulu, T.H.)	97,309	Independent Republican.	Mrs. Elizabeth Farrington (*Pres.*) Riley H. Allen (*Ed.*)
El Imparcial (San Juan, Puerto Rico)	63,175	Independent; in Spanish.	Antonio Ayuso Valdivieso (*Pub.*)
El Mundo (San Juan, Puerto Rico)	57,304	Independent; leading paper in Puerto Rico; in Spanish.	Pablo Vargas Badillo (*Dir.*)

NEWSPAPER GROUPS

One of the noteworthy developments of the press of the United States is the increase of newspaper groups. There are now approximately fifty such groups and their combined circulation is nearly 40 per cent of the total for the daily papers of the country. Most of these groups are sectional. Only the following two may be said to have national scope:

Name of Group	Political Affiliation	Proprietor, Editor, etc.
Hearst newspapers	Independent; composed of 17 papers in 11 cities.	Hearst Consolidated Publications (*Prop.*) J. D. Gortatowsky (*Chairman of Board*)
Scripps-Howard newspapers	Independent; composed of 20 papers in 18 cities.	Charles E. Scripps (*Chairman of Board*)

A number of important papers which maintain large staffs of foreign correspondents operate syndicated news services which are used extensively by other papers. The larger services of this kind include those of the New York *Times*, the Chicago *Daily News*, and the Chicago *Tribune*.

NEWS AGENCIES

Associated Press	News cooperative of more than 3,000 newspapers and radio and television stations in the United States and a like number abroad; independent.	Frank J. Starzel (*Pres.*) Alan J. Gould (*Exec. Ed.*)
United Press International	News agency serving more than 1,400 newspapers in the United States and many other countries; politically independent.	Frank H. Bartholomew (*Pres.*) Kingsley Smith (*Vice Pres.*)

UNITED STATES

FOREIGN LANGUAGE PRESS IN THE UNITED STATES

The following are the more important non-English language newspapers in the U.S. In each case the newspaper chosen is the one with the greatest circulation of all papers in the given language. Circulation figures are based on *Editor & Publisher, International Year Book, 1958*.

Name of Paper	Circulation	Language	Proprietor, Editor, etc.
Chinese Journal (*m.*) (New York City)	17,650	Chinese	Yu Ching-chen (*Ed.*)
Denni Hlasatel (*m.*) (Chicago, Ill.)	61,232	Czechoslovak	Edward Rezabek (*Ed.*)
Tyomies (*m.*) (Superior, Wis.)	3,426	Finnish	George M. Wastila (*Ed.*)
L'Independent (*e.*) (Fall River, Mass.)	4,960	French	Philippe A. Lajoie (*Ed.*)
Staats-Zeitung und Herold (*m.*) (New York City)	21,813	German	Erwin Single (*Ed.*)
Atlantis (*e.*) (New York City)	18,579	Greek	V. Constantinidis (*Ed.*)
Amerikai Magyar Nepszava (*m.*) (New York City)	19,225	Hungarian	Zolton Gombos (*Ed.*)
Il Progresso Italiano (*m.*) (New York City)	59,450	Italian	Fortune Pope (*Ed.*)
Draugas (*m.*) (Chicago, Ill.)	49,870	Lithuanian	Leonard Simutis (*Ed.*)
Polish Daily Zgoda (*m.*) (Chicago, Ill.)	34,360	Polish	Karol Piatkiewicz (*Ed.*)
Rafu Shimpo (*e.*) (Los Angeles, Cal.)	10,500	Japanese	Teiho Hashida (*Ed.*)
Diario de Noticias (*e.*) (New Bedford, Mass.)	8,970	Portuguese	Antonio F. Cacella (*Ed.*)
Novoye Russkoye Slovo (*m.*) (New York City)	22,420	Russian	Mark Weinbaum (*Ed.*)
El Diario de Nueva York (*m.*) (New York City)	39,444	Spanish	Stanley Ross (*Ed.*)
Jewish Daily Forward (*m.*) (New York City)	61,941	Yiddish	Harry Rogoff (*Ed.*)

PERIODICALS

(*w.* weekly; *s.m.* semi-monthly; *m.* monthly; *q.* quarterly)

Name of Journal	Character	Proprietor, Editor, etc.
American Economic Review (*q.*) (Menasha, Wis.)	Economic.	Bernard F. Haley (*Mg. Ed.*)
American Historical Review (*q.*) (New York City)	Historical.	Boyd C. Shafer (*Mg. Ed.*)
American Journal of International Law (*q.*) (Washington, D. C.)	Political and legal.	Herbert W. Briggs (*Ed.*)
American Political Science Review (*q.*) (Columbus, Ohio)	Political.	Harvey C. Mansfield (*Mg. Ed.*)
Annals of the American Academy of Political and Social Science (bi-monthly) (Philadelphia, Pa.)	Political and Social.	Thorsten Sellin (*Ed.*)
The Atlantic (*m.*) (Boston, Mass.)	Literary, political and economic.	Edward A. Weeks (*Ed.*)
Barron's (*w.*) (Boston, Mass.)	Financial.	Robert M. Bleiberg (*Ed.*)
Business Week (*w.*) (New York City)	Economic and financial.	Elliott V. Bell (*Pub. and Ed.*)
Commonweal (*w.*) (New York City)	Catholic; literary and political.	Edward S. Skillin (*Ed.*)
Current History (*m.*) (Philadelphia, Pa.)	Political and current events.	Carol L. Thompson (*Ed.*)
Department of State Bulletin (*w.*) (Washington, D. C.)	Official, political, economic and international affairs.	Department of State (*Pub.*)
Federal Reserve Bulletin (*m.*) (Washington, D. C.)	Financial and economic.	Federal Reserve Board (*Pub.*)
Foreign Affairs (*q.*) (New York City)	Political, economic, financial; leading review devoted to international relations.	Hamilton Fish Armstrong (*Ed.*)

UNITED STATES

Name of Journal	Character	Proprietor, Editor, etc.
Foreign Commerce Weekly (Washington, D. C.)	Official; survey of foreign trade.	Department of Commerce (*Pub.*)
Fortune (*m.*) (New York City)	Political, economic and social.	Henry R. Luce (*Ed. in Chief*) Hedley Donovan (*Mg. Ed.*)
Geographical Review (*q.*) (New York City)	Geographical.	Wilma Belden Fairchild (*Ed.*)
Harper's Magazine (*m.*) (New York City)	Literary, political and economic.	John Fischer (*Ed.*)
International Organization (*q.*) (Boston)	United Nations and international organization.	Alfred O. Hero (*Mg. Ed.*)
Journal of Asian Studies (*q.*) (Ann Arbor, Mich.)	Far Eastern political and historical.	Donald H. Shively (*Ed.*)
Journal of Central European Affairs (*q.*) (Boulder, Colo.)	Central Europe; political and historical.	S. Harrison Thomson (*Mg. Ed.*)
Journal of Modern History (*q.*) (Chicago, Ill.)	Historical.	Charles Loch Mowat (*Ed.*)
Journal of Political Economy (bi-monthly) (Chicago, Ill.)	Economic and political.	Albert Rees (*Ed.*)
Life (*w.*) (New York City)	Pictorial, political, social and economic.	Henry R. Luce (*Ed. in Chief*) Edward K. Thompson (*Mg. Ed.*)
Middle East Journal (*q.*) (Washington, D. C.)	Middle East; political.	William Sands (*Ed.*)
Nation (*w.*) (New York City)	Political, social, and current events; left tendency.	Carey McWilliams (*Ed.*)
Nation's Business (*m.*) (Washington, D. C.)	Organ of U. S. Chamber of Commerce.	Alden H. Sypher (*Ed.*)
New Republic (*w.*) (Washington, D. C.)	Political, social, and current events; left tendency.	Gilbert A. Harrison (*Ed. and Pub.*)
Newsweek (*w.*) (New York City)	Weekly news organ.	Malcolm Muir (*Ed. in Chief*)
Pacific Affairs (*q.*) (New York City)	Far Eastern political, social and economic questions.	William L. Holland (*Ed.*)
Political Science Quarterly (New York City)	Political and economic.	Thomas T. Peardon (*Mg. Ed.*)
Public Opinion Quarterly (Princeton, N. J.)	Public opinion issues.	Frederick F. Stephan (*Ed.*)
Quarterly Journal of Economics (Cambridge, Mass.)	Economic.	Arthur Smithies (*Ed.*)
Reporter (*s.m.*) (New York City)	Political and current events.	Max Ascoli (*Pub. and Ed.*)
Saturday Evening Post (*w.*) (Philadelphia, Pa.)	Political, social and current events.	Curtis Publishing Co. (*Prop.*) Ben Hibbs (*Ed.*)
Social Research (*q.*) (New York City)	Political and sociological.	Dr. Alvin Johnson (*Ed.*)
Survey of Current Business (*m.*) (Washington, D. C.)	Official; statistical exhibit of current economic developments in the U. S.	Department of Commerce (*Pub.*)
Time (*w.*) (New York City)	Weekly news organ.	Henry R. Luce (*Ed. in Chief*) Roy Alexander (*Mg. Ed.*)
United Nations Review (*m.*) (New York City)	United Nations activities.	United Nations (*Pub.*)
U. S. News & World Report (*w.*) (Washington, D. C.)	Record of government activity and international events.	David Lawrence (*Ed.*)
Virginia Quarterly Review (Charlottesville, Va.)	Political, literary and economic.	Charlotte Kohler (*Ed.*)
Vital Speeches (*s.m.*) (New York City)	Political and current events.	Thomas F. Daly, Jr. (*Pres.*)
World Politics (*q.*) (Princeton, N. J.)	International affairs.	Bernard C. Cohen (*Mg. Ed.*)
Yale Review (*q.*) (New Haven, Conn.)	Political, literary and economic.	J. E. Palmer (*Ed.*)

URUGUAY

Capital: Montevideo
Area: 72,153 square miles
Population: 2,650,000 (1955 estimate)

National Council
Composed of nine members, six elected by Colorado Party and three by Blanco Party; took office March 1, 1955, for term ending March 1, 1959

President of the National Council
CARLOS L. FISCHER
Term March 1, 1958, to March 1, 1959

Cabinet
Faction of Colorado Party known as List 15

PARLIAMENT

SENATE
Election of November 1958
President: LEDO ARROYO TORRES

Parties	Representation
Blanco (Herrera and Crespo)	16
Colorado (Batllista)	13
Socialist	1
Catholic	1
Total	31

CHAMBER OF DEPUTIES
Election of November 1958
President: JUAN RODRIGUEZ CORREA

Parties	Representation
Blanco (Herrera and Crespo)	50
Colorado (Batllista)	39
Catholic	3
Socialist	3
Communist	2
Reformist Democratic Union	2
Total	99

RECENT POLITICAL EVENTS

Recent constitutional changes date from a plebiscite in 1951 when the people of Uruguay adopted constitutional amendments which made certain basic changes in their form of government. The presidential form was superseded by a nine-man National Council of Government, six of the majority party and three of the minority.

Each of the nine-man executive council has equal power, with the Presidency of the National Council passing on an annual basis to the first four members of the majority party on the ballot. The President of the National Council serves as President of Uruguay for protocol purposes and as chairman of the Council meeting.

PARTY PROGRAMS AND LEADERS

The Colorado (liberal) and Blanco (conservative) Parties date from the civil war in 1835, their names being taken from the colors of the emblems which the two warring factions then adopted. As the struggle between them for the control of the government has continued for more than a century, adherence to one or the other group has become, in general, a question rather of traditional loyalty than of political program.

Under the Uruguayan political system, factions (using *sublemas*) are recognized within the parties (using *lemas*) for the purpose of running candidates for the presidency and the higher elective offices. The right of any group to use the *lema* or *sublema* is a legal one which must be granted by the electoral court. In national elections the total of the votes cast for each *sublema* is credited to the *sublema* candidate having the greatest number of votes within the *lema* itself. In effect, this procedure combines a primary with a general national election. As an example of this, in the general election of 1954 the Colorados ran three candidates representing factions (*sublemas*) of the Party (*lema*). Luis Batlle Berres' vote was highest, so he was awarded the total Colorado vote and was elected over the Blanco candidate.

COLORADO PARTY: The Colorado Party controlled the executive power for over ninety years until 1958. While under the dominance of the Batllista group, its program was very progressive, advocating: advanced labor laws; extension of physical education and public playgrounds; old-age and unemployment pensions; government ownership and operation of public utilities and of other enterprises serving the public; continued separation of Church and State; and close cooperation in inter-American affairs. The dominant forces in the Colorado Party is the Batllista faction. It scored a victory in the 1954 elections, assuring Señor Batlle Berres' faction the control of the National Council. The Batllistas are divided into two factions (*sublemas*): List 14 and List 15.

Leaders: List 15—Luis Batlle Berres, Dr. Alberto Zubiría, Arturo Lezama, Carlos Fischer, Justino Zavala Muniz, Zoilo Chelle (Members, National Council of Government), Ledo Arroyo Torres (President of Senate), Dr. Amilcar Vasconcellos (Minister of Finance), Zelmar Michelini (Deputy). List 14—César Batlle Pacheco (Deputy), Senators Luis Alberto Brause and Antonio Gustavo Fusco. Independent Colorado Party—Senator Eduardo Blanco Acevedo.

BLANCO PARTY: The old Blanco Party, which won the election of 1958, now known as the National Party, split in two *sublemas* in 1954, one led by Dr. Luis Alberto de Herrera and the other by Daniel Fernandez Crespo. In general they both opposed the Colorado Administration in any legislation of importance, more particularly over such issues as: constitutional reform, increased inter-American ties and Uruguayan participation in hemisphere defense.However, in 1951 the Party helped vote into existence the present National Council system of government through reform of the 1942 Constitution. Later, however, the Herreristas reverted to their earlier opposition to the Council type of administration. The Party membership comprises most of the large landowners and their adherents and finds its strength principally in the interior towns and agricultural districts in contra-distinction to the Colorado Party, which has made its appeal to the urban classes. Blanco policy is conservative almost to the point of reaction.

An independent wing of the Blanco Party joined forces with the Movimiento Popular Nacional under Fernandez Crespo and the Reconstrucción Blanco group under Eduardo Rodriguez Larreta to form a new group called the Union Democrática which contested the leadership of Party in the 1958 elections.

URUGUAY

Leaders: Herreristas—Luis Alberto de Herrera, Benito Nardone, and Ramón Viña (Members, National Council of Government), Senators Martin R. Echegoyen and Eduardo V. Haedo. Union Democrática—Daniel Fernandez Crespo and Senator Salvador M. Ferrer Serra (Crespistas); Senator Eduardo Rodriguez Larreta and Washington Beltrán (Reconstruction Blancos); Javier Barrios Amorin, Adolfo Tejera, Juan Andrés Ramírez and Pantaleon L. Astiazaran (Independent Blancos).

THE CABINET

The Members of the Cabinet are: Prof. Oscar Secco Ellauri (Foreign Affairs); Dr. Glauco Segovia (Interior); Dr. Amílcar Vasconcellos (Finance); Dr. Raúl Gaudín (Defense); Florentino Guimaraens (Public Works); Dr. Washington Isola (Health); Joaquín Aparicio (Livestock & Agriculture); Dr. Hector A. Grauert (Industries & Labor); Clemente I. Ruggia (Public Education and Welfare).

PRESS

Unless otherwise noted, papers are published in the capital city.

Name of Paper	Circulation	Political Affiliation	Proprietor, Editor, etc.
Acción	20,000	Colorado-Batllista.	Luis Batlle Berres (*Dir.*)
El Bien Público	5,000	Catholic.	César Luis Aguiar (*Ed.*)
El Debate	8,000	Blanco.	Washington Guadalupe (*Dir.*)
El Día	60,000	Colorado-Batllista.	Rafael Batlle Pacheco (*Dir.*)
El Diario (Evening)	135,000	Colorado-Riverista.	Pablo Pesce Barceló (*Dir.*)
El Popular	6,000	Communist.	Enrique Rodríguez (*Dir.*)
La Mañana	35,000	Colorado-Riverista.	Carlos Manini Ríos (*Dir.*)
El Plata (evening)	100,000	Independent Blanco.	Juan Andrés Ramírez (*Dir.*)
El País	100,000	Independent Blanco.	Eduardo Rodríguez Larreta (*Dir.*)
La Tribuna Popular	30,000	Independent.	Carlos Quijano (*Dir.*)
Marcha (weekly)	15,000	Independent.	Julio Castro (*Dir.*)
Mundo Uruguayo (weekly)	18,000	Political and current events.	Pablo Bodo (*Dir.*)
El Sol (weekly)	4,000	Socialist.	Emilio Frugoni (*Dir.*)
El Diario Español	5,000	Nonpolitical.	Manuel Magariños (*Dir.*)

PRESS ASSOCIATION

Círculo de la Prensa	Independent.	Manuel Magariños (*Pres.*)
Asociación Gráfica	Independent.	Luis Franzini (*Pres.*)
Asociación de la Prensa Uruguaya	Independent.	Romeo Fiore (*Pres.*)

VATICAN CITY

Area: 108.8 acres
Population: 1,000 (1958 estimate)

Ruler

THE SUPREME PONTIFF, JOHN XXIII
Born November 25, 1881; elected Pope October 28, 1958
Crowned November 4, 1958

Department of State

Cardinal Domenico Tardini (Secretary of State)
Msgr. Angelo Dell'Acqua (Substitute Secretary, OrdinaryAffairs)
Msgr. Carlo Grano (Substitute Secretary, Ordinary Affairs)

THE COLLEGE OF CARDINALS

The Cardinals constitute the Senate of the Pope and are his chief advisors. Upon his death, they elect his successor for life. The Cardinals themselves are created by the Pope. The College now consists of 74 members. Their nationalities are: Italian 29, French 8, American 4, Spanish 4, Brazilian 3, Portuguese 2, Argentine 2, Canadian 2, German 3, Australian 2, Belgian, Chinese, Cuban, Hungarian, Ecuadorean, Colombian, Irish, Yugoslavian, Polish, Indian, Syrian, Mexican, English and Uruguayan 1 each.

THE CURIA ROMANA

The Curia Romana, which carries on the central administration of the Roman Catholic Church, consists of 12 congregations, 3 tribunals and 4 offices.

FOREIGN REPRESENTATION

The Holy See has accredited diplomatic representatives in 42 countries. It receives the representatives of 46 countries in the Vatican City. It also has unofficial relations by means of Apostolic Delegates with a number of other countries.

GOVERNMENT

The immediate government of the State of the Vatican City, established by the Lateran Treaty of February 11, 1939, is in the hands of a Governor. He is assisted by a Counselor General and by a number of offices. The legal system is based on canon law with three courts to administer it, and pontifical constitutions and rules. There are no political parties and no parliament. There is a complete coinage system, postal system, railroad station and radio station.

PRESS

Name of Paper	Nature	Proprietor, Editor, etc.
Osservatore Romano (daily)	Semi-official.	Conte G. Della Torre (*Ed.*)
Osservatore della Domenica (weekly)	Non-official.	Conte G. Della Torre (*Ed.*)
Bollettino Ufficiale della Santa Sede (Acta Apostolicae Sedis) (monthly)	Official.	Msgr. Fillippo Giobbe (*Dir.*)
Annuario Pontificio (annual)	Official.	Office of the Secretary of State
Ecclesia (monthly)	Non-official.	Independent editorial direction

VENEZUELA

Capital: Caracas
Area: 352,051 square miles
Population: 6,200,000 (1958 estimate)

Junta of Government
Dr. Edgard Sanabria (President), Col. Carlos Luis Araque, Col. Pedro José Quevedo, Dr. Arturo Sosa, Captain Miguel Rodriguez-Olivares, Dr. Ignacio Iribarren-Borges (Secretary)
Created on overthrow of Pérez Jiménez régime on January 23, 1958

Cabinet
Reorganized November, 1958

PARLIAMENT
(Congreso Nacional)

Members of the bicameral National Congress were designated by the Constituent Assembly for the initial constitutional period. Upper house consists of 42 Senators; lower house, 127 Deputies. Congress meets in its regular 100-day session on April 19th of each year; may be called into special session at other times.

RECENT POLITICAL EVENTS

An attempted Air Force revolt on New Year's Day 1958 was followed by a civilian general strike on January 21 led by a clandestine "Junta Patriotica." Subsequent decision of military leaders resulted in the overthrow of the Pérez Jiménez régime on January 23. The Junta was created by its own decree as a provisional government. It pledged itself to return the country to constitutional government and to this end decreed a new election law and established a Supreme Electoral Council. Elections for a President, a Congress of 42 senators and 127 deputies, State Assemblies, and Municipal Councils were held on December 7, 1958.

The country is still operating under the Constitution of 1953 with the exception of minor changes decreed by the Government Junta. New legislation is established by decree of the Junta.

Rear Admiral Wolfgang Larrazabal, who presided over the Junta of Government organized after the overthrow of former Pres. Pérez Jiménez, resigned on November 14, 1958, to be able to run for President in the general elections held December 7, 1958, after being nominated by the Unión Republicana Democrática (URD) party.

Rómulo Betancourt, leader and candidate of Acción Democrática (AD), was the winning candidate. It is expected that Betancourt will be inaugurated January 23, 1959, as the new President, for a five-year term. His Cabinet will be announced when Betancourt is sworn in.

VENEZUELA

PARTIES AND PARTY PROGRAMS

There are now four principal political parties in operation and several minor parties. Following the overthrow of the Pérez Jiménez régime, leaders of Acción Democrática (AD), the URD (Unión Republicana Democrática), COPEI (Social Christian Party), and the Communists returned to Venezuela. The following were the candidates for President at the December 7, 1958, elections: Rómulo Betancourt (AD), Rear Admiral Wolfgang Larrazabal (URD), Dr. Rafael Caldera (COPEI). All parties are pledged to generally similar reforms in educational policy, social legislation, agrarian reform, and a greater share in the country's petroleum income.

THE CABINET

The members of the Cabinet are: Dr. Augusto Márquez Cañizales (Interior), Dr. René de Sola (Foreign Affairs), Dr. José Antonio Mayobre (Treasury), Brig. Gen. Josué Lopez Henriquez (Defense), Juan Ernesto Branger (Development), Dr. Luis Báez Díaz (Public Works), Dr. Rafael Pizani (Education), Dr. Espíritu Santo Mendoza (Health and Social Welfare), Dr. Hector Hernández Carabaño (Agriculture), Dr. Raúl Valera (Labor), Dr. Oscar Machado Zuloaga (Communications), Dr. Andrés Aguilar Mawdsley (Justice), Dr. Julio Diez (Mines and Hydrocarbons), Lt. Col. Jesús Manuel Gámez Arellano (Governor of the Federal District).

PRESS

Unless otherwise noted, papers are published in the capital city.

Name of Paper	Circulation	Proprietor, Editor or Director
La Esfera	50,000	Miguel Angel Capriles (*Prop.*)
El Mundo (afternoon)	33,000	Miguel Angel Capriles (*Prop.*)
El Nacional	100,000	Miguel Otero Silva (*Ed.*)
La Religión	38,000	Monsignor Jesús Hernández Chapellín (*Ed.*)
Últimas Noticias	100,000	Miguel Angel Capriles (*Prop.*)
El Universal	45,000	Dr. Luis Teófilo Nuñez (*Ed.*)
The Daily Journal (in English)	9,000	Howard Brisco (*Ed.*)
Diario del Occidente (Maracaibo)	20,000	Rodolfo Auvert (*Ed.*)
Panorama (Maracaibo)	47,000	Carlos Ramírez McGregor (*Ed.*)
El Carabobeño (Valencia)	10,000	Eladio Alemán Sucre (*Ed.*)
Tribuna Popular (Communist weekly)		Gustavo Machado (*Ed.*)

YUGOSLAVIA

Capital: Beograd (Belgrade)
Area: 98,674 square miles
Population: 18,041,000 (1957 estimate)

President of the Republic
MARSHAL JOSIP BROZ (Tito)
Assumed power on defeat and withdrawal of German troops from Yugoslavia in 1944; re-elected President on January 29, 1954, and April 19, 1958

FEDERAL EXECUTIVE COUNCIL
Elected April 19, 1958

President
JOSIP BROZ (Tito)

Vice-Presidents
EDVARD KARDELJ
ALEKSANDAR RANKOVIC
MIJALKO TODOROVIC
RODOLJUB COLAKOVIC

Secretary
VELJKO ZEKOVIC

Members as Presidents of Republican Executive Councils
LJUPCO ARSOV—Macedonia
FILIP BAJKOVIC—Montenegro
JAKOV BLAZEVIC—Croatia
OSMAN KARABEGOVIC—Bosnia-Hercegovina
BORIS KRAJGER—Slovenia
MILOS MINIC—Serbia

Other Members
Ljubo Babic, Dr. Marijan Brecelj, Hasan Brkic, Krste Crvenkovski, Peko Dapcevic, Stevan Doronjski, Ivan Gosnjak, Avdo Humo, Slavko Komar, Ivan Krajacic, Sergej Krajger, Moma Markovic, Nikola Mincev, Slobodan Penezic, Krsto Popivoda, Koca Popovic, Milentije Popovic, Vlado Popovic, Dobrivoje Radoslavjevic, Svettislav Stefanovic, Velimir Stojnic, Lidija Sentjurc.

YUGOSLAVIA

PRESIDENTS OF REPUBLICAN PEOPLE'S ASSEMBLIES
Jovan Vesilinov—Serbia
Vladimir Bakaric—Croatia
Miha Marinko—Slovenia
Djuro Pucar—Bosnia and Hercegovina
Lazar Kolisevski—Macedonia
Blazo Jovanovic—Montenegro

PARLIAMENT
(Savezna Narodna Skupstina)
President: Petar Stambolic

COUNCIL OF PRODUCERS	FEDERAL COUNCIL
Elected March 26, 1958.	*Elected March 23, 1958.*
Chairman: Pasko Romac	*Chairman:* Dr. Mladen Ivekovic
Number of members 216	Number of members 371

POLITICAL EVENTS SINCE 1944

During the war there were two main resistance groups in Yugoslavia: the Partisans led by Josip Broz Tito, the leader of the then illegal pre-war Communist Party; and the Chetniks, led by Draza Mihailovic, a Royal Yugoslav Army Officer and King Peter's representative in Yugoslavia until 1944. Both groups not only engaged the German and Italian occupying armies, but also fought against each other. Although the Western allies originally supported Mihailovic's forces, their assistance was shifted to Tito towards the end of the war.

Great Britain and the United States informed Tito on December 22, 1945, that they recognized the Yugoslav Government, notwithstanding its failure to hold free elections, thereby also recognizing the liquidation of the monarchy.

In the post-war period, the Yugoslav Communist Party, which had provided the core of the Partisan leadership during the resistance, consolidated its authority and concentrated on the reconstruction of the country.

THE NEW YUGOSLAV CONSTITUTIONAL SYSTEM

The new Yugoslav Constitution, as revised in January 1953, provides that the executive authority is concentrated in a Federal Executive Council (FEC). The Federal Assembly elects the officers and other members of the FEC. The President of the FEC, who also serves as President of the Republic, represents the country in international affairs, appoints and recalls diplomatic envoys, acts as commander-in-chief of the armed forces, and may stay the execution of any FEC order, provided he presents the issue immediately to the Federal Assembly.

The Federal People's Assembly, the supreme legislative body, is composed of two houses: the Federal Council and the Council of Producers. There are 282 deputies elected directly by voters to the Federal Council, apportioned on the basis of one deputy to every 60,000 inhabitants. These deputies are nominated in voters' meetings or by petition in individual constituencies. Legislative bodies in the republican and other subordinate government units also elect deputies to the Federal Councils. Deputies to the Councils of Producers are elected by councils of producers in districts and towns on the basis of one deputy to every 70,000 members of the "producer" population.

YUGOSLAVIA

POLITICAL ORGANIZATIONS

Under the existing one-party system, the League of Communists is the sole independent political organization in Yugoslavia. It is supported by the Socialist Alliance. The members of its executive committee (formerly Politbureau) are: Josip Broz Tito, Edvard Kardelj, Aleksandar Rankovic, Jovan Veselinov, Ivan Gosnjak, Svetozar Vukmanovic-Tempo, Djuro Pucar, Lazar Kolisevski, Franc Leskosek, Vladimir Bakaric, Miha Marinko, Blazo Jovanovic, Petar Stambolic and Veljko Vlahovic. Marshal Tito is Secretary-General.

The Socialist Alliance, the leading mass organization in the country, has numerous functions, including leadership in electoral campaigns. Most of the top leaders of the Socialist Alliance are also the top leaders of the League of Communists. The Socialist Alliance has been given the responsibility for maintaining contacts with political organizations abroad.

Two other important Yugoslav organizations are the Yugoslav Federation of Trade Unions led by Suetozar Vukmanovic and the People's Youth led by Mika Tripalo. Vukmanovic is a member of the Communist League's Executive Committee.

THE CABINET

Under the new Constitution of January 13, 1953, the Cabinet has been superseded by State Secretariats for the execution of administrative duties. State Secretaries are responsible to the Federal Executive Council. The Secretaries are as follows: Koca Popovic, Foreign Affairs; General of the Army Ivan Gosnjak, Defense; Svetislav Stefanovic, Interior; Nikola Mincev, Finance; Dr. Marijan Brecelj, Commodity Trade; Ljubo Babic, President of Committee for Foreign Trade.

PRESS

Unless otherwise noted, papers are published in the capital city.

Name of Paper	Character	Director, Editor, etc.
Borba	Socialist Alliance.	Ivo Sarajcic (*Dir.*)
Politika	Daily.	Danilo Puric (*Ed.*)
Kommunist	League of Communists.	Cvijetin Mijatovic (*Dir.*)
Narodna Armija	Army.	Stevo Maodus (*Ed.*)
Rad	Trade Unions, Yugoslavia.	Fogel Danilo (*Ed.*)
Vecernje Novosti	Evening subsidiary of *Borba*.	Vanja Kraljevic (*Ed.*)
Ekonomska Politika (weekly)	Economic.	Jasa Davico (*Ed.*)
Mladost (weekly)	People's Youth.	Aleksandar Petkovic (*Ed.*)
Nin	Weekly.	Djordje Radenkovic (*Ed.*)
Duga (weekly)	Illustrated.	Vladimir Paskaljevic (*Ed.*)
Front	Illustrated Army review.	Vojislav Maricic (*Ed.*)
Dnevnik (Novi Sad)	Socialist Alliance, Vojvodina.	Slobodan Posarac (*Dir.*)
Narodni List (Zagreb)	Socialist Alliance, Zagreb.	Milan Nozinic (*Dir.*)
Vjesnik (Zagreb)	Socialist Alliance, Croatia.	Djuro Kladarin (*Dir.*)
Slovenski Porocevalec. (Ljubljana)	Socialist Alliance, Slovenia.	Rudi Janhuba (*Dir.*)
Novi List (Rijeka)	Daily.	Milan Slani (*Dir.*)
La Voce Del Popolo (Rijeka)	Daily, in Italian.	Luciano Michelazzi (*Dir.*)
Oslobodjenje (Sarajevo)	Socialist Alliance, Bosnia-Hercegovina.	Vilko Vinterhalter (*Dir.*)
Slobodna Dalmacija (Split)	Socialist Alliance, Split.	Sibe Kvesic (*Ed.*)
Nova Makedonija (Skoplje)	Socialist Alliance, Macedonia.	Trpe Jakovlevski (*Dir.*)
Pobjeda (Titograd)	Socialist Alliance, Montenegro.	Ante Slovinic (*Dir.*)

NEWS AGENCIES

Tanjug	Official.	Jovan Marinovic (*Dir.*)
Press-servis	Enterprise of Federation of Yugoslav Journalists.	Boza Radenkovic (*Dir.*)

OTHER COUNTRIES

ALBANIA
Capital: Tirana
Area: 10,629 square miles
Population: 1,400,000 (1957 estimate)

Form of Government
Communist Republic

Premier
MAJ. GEN. MEHMET SHEHU

CAMBODIA
Capital: Phnom Penh
Area: 67,000 square miles (estimated)
Population: 5,000,000 (estimated)

Form of Government
Constitutional Monarchy

Rulers
KING NORODOM SURAMARIT AND
QUEEN SISOWATH KOSSAMAK
Ascended the throne March 2, 1955

Premier
PRINCE NORODOM SIHANOUK
Took office July 10, 1958

ETHIOPIA
Capital: Addis Ababa
Area: 400,000 square miles (estimated)
Population: 19,260,000 (1955 estimate)

Form of Government
Constitutional Monarchy

Ruler
EMPEROR HAILE SELASSIE I

Deputy Prime Minister
TSEHAFE TEZAZ AKLILOU HABTE WOLD
In 1952 Eritrea was federated with Ethiopia

GHANA
Capital: Accra
Area: 92,000 square miles
Population: 5,000,000 (1958 estimate)

Form of Government
Parliamentary
(Member of British Commonwealth)

Sovereign
QUEEN ELIZABETH II

Governor General
WILLIAM FRANCIS HARE, EARL OF LISTOWEL
Appointed June 24, 1957

Prime Minister
DR. KWAME NKRUMAH

OTHER COUNTRIES

GUINEA
Capital: Konakry
Area: 95,218 square miles
Population: 2,600,000

Guinea declared her independence from France on October 2, 1958

Form of Government
Republic

President
SEKOU TOURÉ

KOREA
Capital: Seoul
Population: 30,000,000 (1951 estimate)

Form of Government
Republic

President
DR. SYNGMAN RHEE

Foreign Minister
C. W. CHO

LAOS
Administrative Capital: Vientiane
Royal Capital: Luang Prabang
Area: 89,166 square miles (estimated)
Population: 2,500,000 (estimated)

Form of Government
Constitutional Monarchy

Ruler
KING SISAVANG VONG
Born on July 14, 1885; succeeded April 28, 1904

Premier
PHOUI SANANIKONE

LIECHTENSTEIN (PRINCIPALITY OF)
Capital: Vaduz
Area: 61 square miles
Population: 15,700 (1958 estimate)

Form of Government
Constitutional Monarchy

Ruler
PRINCE FRANCIS JOSEPH II
Born in 1906; succeeded July 25, 1938

Chief of Government
ALEXANDER FRICK (Conservative)
Appointed September 3, 1945

OTHER COUNTRIES

FEDERATION OF MALAYA
Capital: Kuala Lumpur
Area: 50,680 square miles
Population: 6,278,763 (1957 census)

Form of Government
Constitutional Monarchy
(Member of British Commonwealth)

Supreme Head
(Elected every five years from among rulers of Malay States by the rulers themselves)
Tunku Abdul Rahman ibni Al-marhum Tuanku Muhammad

Prime Minister
Tunku Abdul Rahman Putra Al-haj

MONACO
Capital: Monte Carlo
Area: .59 square miles
Population: 20,422 (1956 census)

Form of Government
Monarchy

Ruler
Prince Rainier III
Born in 1923; succeeded in 1949

MONGOLIAN PEOPLE'S REPUBLIC
Capital: Ulan Bator
Area: 625,783 square miles
Population: 2,077,669 (1936 estimate)

Form of Government
Communist Republic

Premier
Tse Den Bal

MOROCCO
Capital: Rabat
Area: 200,000 square miles
Population: 9,825,000 (1958 estimate)

Form of Government
Monarchy

Ruler
King Mohammed V

Premier
Abdullah Ibrahim

OTHER COUNTRIES

MUSCAT AND OMAN
Capital: Muscat
Area: 82,000 square miles (estimated)
Population: 550,000 (1951 estimate)

Form of Government
Sultanate

Ruler
SULTAN SAYYID SA'ID IBN TAYMUR
Born in 1910; succeeded in 1932

NEPAL
Capital: Kathmandu
Area: 54,000 square miles
Population: 9 to 10 million (estimated)

Form of Government
Monarchy

Ruler
KING MAHENDRA BIR BIKRAM SHAH DEVA
Born in 1920; succeeded March 14, 1955

Premier
GENERAL SUBARNA SHAMSHER

SA'UDI ARABIA
Capital: Riyadh
Area: 927,000 square miles (estimated)
Population: 8,000,000 (estimated)

Form of Government
Monarchy

Ruler
KING SA'UD IBN ABDUL-AZIZ AL SA'UD
Born in 1902; proclaimed King November 9, 1953

Premier
CROWN PRINCE FAISAL IBN ABDUL-AZIZ AL SA'UD

SUDAN
Capital: Khartoum
Area: 967,500 square miles
Population: 10,255,912 (1957 estimate)

Form of Government
Military Dictatorship
Established November 17, 1958

Premier
LT. GEN. IBRAHIM ABBOUD

OTHER COUNTRIES

TUNISIA
Capital: Tunis
Area: 48,195 square miles
Population: 3,783,000 (1958 census)

Form of Government
Republic

President
HABIB BOURGUIBA

VIET NAM
(After the Geneva agreement of July 1954)
Capital: Saigon
Area: South of 17th parallel 65,000 square miles (estimated)
Population: South of 17th parallel 12,000,000 (1957 estimate)

Form of Government
Republic

President
NGO DINH DIEM
Replaced Chief of State Bao Dai on October 26, 1955, under a provisional Constitutional Act following a national referendum which he won. Became President on adoption of Constitution by the National Assembly and its promulgation on October 26, 1956.

YEMEN
Capital: Sana
Area: 75,000 square miles (estimated)
Population: 5,000,000 (1954 estimate)

Form of Government
Monarchy

Ruler
IMAM AHMAD